CASSAVETES DIRECTS

KAMERA BOOKS

KAMERA BOOKS

WWW.KAMERABOOKS.CO.UK

MICHAEL VENTURA

CASSAVETES DIRECTS

ON THE SET OF *LOVE STREAMS*

Kamera
BOOKS

First published in 2007 by Kamera Books
P.O.Box 394, Harpenden, Herts, AL5 1XJ
www.kamerabooks.co.uk

Series Editor: Hannah Patterson

A CIP catalogue record for this book is available from the British Library.

ISBN 10: 1-84243-227-3 (hardcover)
ISBN 13: 978-1-84243-227-3 (hardcover)

ISBN 10: 1-84243-228-1 (trade paperback)
ISBN 13: 978-1-84243-228-0 (trade paperback)

2 4 6 8 10 9 7 5 3 1

Typeset by Avocet Typeset, Chilton, Aylesbury, Bucks
Printed by J.H.Haynes & Co Ltd., Sparkford

For
John Ertha

...who, when I was a boy, was the first in my experience to embody the passion, courage, mind, and rascality that could be: a man.

You know I think that movies are a conspiracy – they are actually a conspiracy, because they set you up, Florence, they set you up from the time you're a little kid. They set you up to believe in everything. They set you up to believe in ideals, and strength, and good guys, and romance, and, of course, love – love, Florence. So – you believe it, right? You go off and start looking. It doesn't happen. You keep looking. You get a job, like us, and you spend a lot of time fixing up things, your apartment and jazz, and you learn how to be feminine… There's no Charles Boyer in my life, Florence, you know? I never even met a Charles Boyer! I never met Clark Gable, I never met Humphrey Bogart, I never met any of them. You know who I mean. I mean, they don't exist, Florence, that's the truth. But the movies set you up, you know? They set you up. And no matter how bright you are, you believe it. And, Florence, you know that we're bright? Florence, we're geniuses compared to some of them! I mean, we go the movies and…

– Gena Rowlands as Minnie, in John Cassavetes' *Minnie and Moskowitz,*

Art is a put-up-or-shut-up proposition. – Michael Berger

The only thing that remains constant is the love of what you're doing.
– John Cassavetes

Introduction:

The Art of the Unpredictable

"I think he's a genius. I always have." So said Steven Spielberg when I asked him about John Cassavetes.

The year was 1982. In two weeks Spielberg would premier *E.T.* Our interview had turned to the question of influences. Spielberg named Frank Capra, Michael Curtiz, and David Lean, influences whom anyone schooled in cinema would assume. But Spielberg's best films feature performances of tense immediacy, a realistic roughness-around-the-edges not associated with classic Hollywood. I was fishing when I asked about John Cassavetes, but Spielberg lit up at the name and told the kind of story many tell about John, a story of generous and unpredictable engagement.

"Cassavetes is one of the first people I met in Hollywood, one of the first people who ever talked to me and gave me the time of day. He met me when I was sneaking around Universal Studios watching other people shoot TV shows. He was doing an episode of Chrysler Theater, that Robert Ellis Miller was directing, and he pulled me aside and said, 'What do you want to do?' And I said, 'I want to be a director.' He said, 'Okay, after every take you tell me what I'm doing wrong, and you give me direction.' So here I am, 18 years old, and there's a professional company at Universal Studios doing this TV episode, and after every take John walks past the other actors, walks past the director, he walks right up to me and says, 'What did you think? How can I improve it? What am I doing wrong?' And I would say, 'Gah, it's too embarrassing right *here,* Mr. Cassavetes! Mr. Cassavetes, don't ask me in *front* of everybody, can't we go around the corner and talk?'

"And he made me a production assistant on *Faces* for a couple of weeks, and I hung around and watched him shoot that movie, and John was much more interested in the story and the actors than he was in the camera. He loved his cast. He treated his cast like they had been part of his family for many years. And so I really got off on the right foot, learning how to deal with actors as I watched Cassavetes with his repertory company."

I said, "It's funny about Cassavetes. When I first met him, you know – he's short, but you're never aware of it, because of the way he holds his head, like he's looking *down* at you, like a tall guy. He tilts his head down, and his eyes burn up at you."

Spielberg laughed at my imitation. "You *got* that, you got that. It's funny you mention that, because I've always thought that one of the best ways of being a director was, as John did, scrounge around for the cast, promise them anything but give them quality, and look with great poignancy and attitude at your cast and crew up through your eyebrows, with your nose facing the ground. That's something I learned from John."

As I write now, in 2006, 17 years after his death, Cassavetes is a hero of cinema, lionized as the "founder" of the independent film movement in America. There's an Independent Spirit Award named after him, given annually for the best film made with a budget of under $500,000. He's even been featured on a postage stamp. But when Spielberg told me that story in 1982, mainstream critics in print and academia were dismissive toward Cassavetes. If occasionally they liked his work they praised the performances more than the film, as though the picture was effective in spite of John. He'd had a hit in 1980 with *Gloria,* a studio-produced picture he later claimed to dislike. But his previous independent film, *Opening Night* (1978), now considered a masterpiece, received bad press and closed quickly. *The Killing of a Chinese Bookie* (1976), disliked by audiences as well as critics, played briefly, and only in New York and Los Angeles. Nor did his last film, *Love Streams* (1984), find many friends in America. Cassavetes rarely admitted bitterness or disappointment, but in the early days of home-video I ventured to him that at least now his films could be issued on tape. He glared, shook his head *no*: "If they didn't come to see us in theaters, fuck 'em."

That was then. Now Cassavetes is revered. His family has released on DVD the five films he produced, which include his finest save for *Husbands* and *Love Streams*. His pictures disquiet audiences as much as ever, but many recognize that Cassavetes' techniques have become central to the vocabulary of contemporary cinema.

John Cassavetes released his first film, *Shadows,* in 1959. In films prior to that year, nothing resembles the camerawork and scenic pacing of *Shadows.* Its last frames announced, "The Film You Have Just Seen Was An Improvisation." American critics missed the point, assuming that improvisation was a loose, anything-goes process. But for Cassavetes the word *improvisation* meant what it means in jazz: a carefully structured but freely performed whole. Misunderstanding this, American critics did not credit John with *intent*. But Cassavetes' next major work, *Faces* (1968), was scripted (his screenplay even won an Academy Award® nomination). *Faces* made clear that John's camerawork, dialogue, and performances were precisely what he intended.

His intentions were as unique as the techniques he created for their expression. Ingmar Bergman's people may or may not make peace with God, or the Void, or whatever; Fellini's may or may not make peace with themselves; and the characters of John Ford, Howard Hawks, and Steven Spielberg relate to themselves as part of a story that is larger than themselves. But Cassavetes' people must make, or fail to make, peace with each other. There is no "larger story." There are only common people facing each other in rooms as common as any. He tolerated no other terms. Two people, able or unable to look into each other's eyes – that was his ultimate test for all codes, manners, morals, politics, psychologies, and beliefs. To give that test its due, he reshaped the vocabulary of film.

John Cassavetes' work is the art of the unpredictable, because he felt that in life one never knows what will happen next. His is the art of the edgy and unresolved; in daily life he saw no resolutions or solutions and no certainty that would not be tested by tomorrow's uncertainty. He invented a cinematic form in which this vision could be both expressed and *embodied*. Cassavetes' is an art of crowded close-ups and irregular pacing. His is a dialogue of sentence-fragments, commonplaces, outbursts, reveries, and overlapped lines, punctuated with silences – moments when one character looks at another in a naked plea for acceptance, without understanding as a condition. In cinematography, John Cassavetes does away with the *certainty* of the camera's point of view – and, with that, he destroys the viewer's certainty. Other directors had given us, through their cameras, a defined space in which to view a story; but with Cassavetes the camera's point-of-view is that of an anxious child or stranger, uncertain of precisely where to be or of what it's seeing, the frame often undefined and always shifting. His eye doesn't pretend to see all, but sees only a fragment perceived in a particular moment. This creates a connective uneasiness with the viewer, who becomes as uncertain as the characters on screen. Thus the inviolate boundary usually conferred by the screen is pierced, creating an effect as immediate as theater. Cassavetes establishes a deliberate bond between viewer and character, as though they are in the same room. Everybody's uncertain. As in the "scenes" of life, no one knows what's coming next and you never know when a Cassavetes scene will end. It may cut off abruptly or drag on beyond endurance – as do the scenes of our private hours.

That Cassavetes' innovations have proved pivotal to the evolution of cinema is not difficult to demonstrate. Watch a few double-features and you'll see for yourself.

Watch Stanley Kubrick's pre-*Shadows* films (*The Killing, Paths of Glory*), then watch the camera-work and performances of his post-*Shadows* masterpiece, *Dr. Strangelove* (1964). Kubrick was the first major American director to incorporate Cassavetes' innovations into his own style.

Watch *Shadows* and Martin Scorsese's *Mean Streets* (1973). Scorsese has written that *Shadows* was "the film that had the biggest impact on me," but you don't need to know that. All you need do is watch. The speech rhythms, antics, pacing and even some shots of *Shadows* are emulated in *Mean Streets*. *Mean Streets* is great in its own right, and Scorsese's themes are quite different from Cassavetes', but it's clear that Scorsese's absorption of Cassavetes' cinema is intentional and complete – so much so that sometimes *Mean Streets* seems a kind of re-make, *Shadows*-plus-violence.

Watch *Shadows* or *Faces* and Robert Altman's *M.A.S.H.* (1970) or *Nashville* (1975), remembering that those Altman films are the template for many contemporary comedies. Altman's objective was satire, in which Cassavetes had no interest. But Altman sought an anti-Hollywood style of comedy, and he found his means in his own version of the open-ended pacing and edgy yet fluid camerawork pioneered by Cassavetes.

Double-feature *A Woman Under the Influence* (1974) and the director's cut of Spielberg's *Close Encounters of the Third Kind* (1977). The marital scenes between Richard Dreyfuss and Teri Garr in *Close Encounters* mirror the immediacy and audacity of Peter Falk's and Gena Rowlands' in *Woman*. Before *Close Encounters*, there'd been no such scenes in a major studio production.

Watch Cassavetes' *Minnie and Moskowitz* (1971) and Woody Allen's *Annie Hall* (1977). Allen shares few, if any, intentions with Cassavetes. But, like Spielberg, Woody Allen domesticated Cassavetes' innovations, melding Cassavetes' scenic immediacy with a Hawks-like omniscient camera.

Through Scorsese, Altman, Spielberg, Allen, and others, John Cassavetes taught filmmakers new dimensions of what a motion picture could communicate. His influence is everywhere now, from Quentin Tarantino's violent wet dreams to Fernando Meirelles' elegant *The Constant Gardener.* Television, too, has absorbed and adapted Cassavetes. Watch how TV used to be shot in programs like *Star Trek, Kojak,* and *Columbo;* then watch, to name only two, ABC's *Lost* or the Sci-Fi Channel's *Battlestar Galactica,* with their erratically mobile and intimate camerawork. The difference: techniques John pioneered in *Shadows* and *Faces,* taken for granted now even on prime-time TV.

The proof is on the screen.

It all started with one man working on his own, on his own terms, unabashed and unafraid. Referring to the public's relation to his art he told me, "They're going to be ready for us maybe five minutes a day." John Cassavetes staked his life on that slim possibility, and indelibly enlarged the possibilities of the motion picture. Watch these double-features and see for yourself how Cassavetes' cinematography, dialogue, and scenic pacing are as influential as those of any director you can name. In cinema, John is of the pantheon.

What Pablo Picasso said of himself could also be said of John Cassavetes.

"You do it first, then others come and do it pretty."

The proof is on the screen.

JOHN CASSAVETES DIRECTS *LOVE STREAMS*

THURSDAY, MARCH 17, 1983 – *Trying to get it*

It's after 10 at night, the phone rings, I pick up, and the caller announces, "Michael! This is John!" Then he launches into a monologue I can barely follow, while I'm trying to figure who "John" might be. I don't know any Johns very well. It takes a few moments to realize that this is Cassavetes speaking. Surprised – no, stunned – I wish I'd listened harder to his initial barrage of sentences. The man is very enthusiastic about *something.* I'm trying to get my bearings while he's praising me for an interview we'd done six months before, the last time we'd spoken. During the interview he'd stopped suddenly and said, "This isn't going well," and I said, "Trust me, I see your words as printed sentences as you're saying them, and this is going very well." Now it seems he agrees, and that I know my business is something he respects. Of course this pleases me very much, but still his rap tonight doesn't compute – my impression of the man is that it's not like him to make conversation, and, at the moment, that's what he's doing. The thought occurs: maybe he's drunk. In his circles, as in mine, people often are.

Now he's saying that he's gotten a deal to direct *Love Streams.* Do I remember the play?

Yes, but more vaguely than I admit. A year, no, it was two years ago, John produced a trilogy of plays written by himself and Ted

Allan. *Love Streams* was Allan's, and what, if I am honest, do I retain of it? An airy Jon Voight never quite connecting with the material, while Gena Rowlands played with that same material as a child plays in fresh-fallen snow, totally involved, utterly captivating. What I remembered most painfully, however, was how after the play John took about 20 of us to Ma Maison, where I drank too much and made an ass of myself, *really* made an ass of myself, conversing with two famous women. I wasn't used to dining with stars and I proved it.

But the play… there was this dog… strangest dog I've ever seen, because it wasn't really a dog, it was a man. That is, the dog was played by a man. The man – Neil Bell – wore no doggy make-up, wore nothing on his well-molded body but shorts. He had reddish hair and beard, and serious, penetrating, dog-like eyes. But why did we believe he was a dog? It wasn't only because his physical imitation was perfect – he growled, leapt, flinched and panted so very like a dog. It was that Neil Bell found that place where dogs and people understand one another; rather than just imitating a canine, Bell *played* that area of understanding. In what was otherwise a relentlessly realistic play, we accepted his dog-ness without question. I can't quote a line of the play, but I will always remember that dog-man leaping over furniture, growling, backing Jon Voight up against a wall.

And, now that I think of it, I remember very well another play of the trilogy (though not its title), written by Cassavetes, where Peter Falk is being questioned on the witness stand about killing his wife. The lawyer asks, "Did you love your wife?" Falk looks at the lawyer, looks away, thinks, looks at him again, says: "On which day?"

Meanwhile, on the phone, Cassavetes is saying of *Love Streams*, "Every bit of it there's no melodrama, it's just misplaced sincerity all the way through."

He is in the midst of his thought while I'm faking my half of the call, trying to catch up. He describes what he thinks will be the last shot of the film: a dog barking in the rain. "So it's the dog's picture! He has the last word!"

Now Cassavetes comes round to why he's called. He's always

thought it would be interesting to have a book written on the day-to-day making of a film. To his knowledge, it's never been done. He wants not a book about filmmaking but about "the play between the people who make the film and the ideas within the film."

"It would be a daring book, a tough book," he says. Would I be interested in writing it?

Quickly I say yes. And stammer about how honored I feel to be invited, a subject in which John is not much interested.

He talks on while I'm kind of weirded out, as we used to say. Cassavetes is an inclusive man, he'll talk and listen to anybody high or low; but he's also a deeply private man. It doesn't seem like Cassavetes to want somebody staring at him, taking down his every word, making a book of the quicksilver ups and downs of his days. Yet he wants this book very much, he's talking now about its possibilities as enthusiastically as he's talked about his film, while I'm wondering if it's possible to catch what some people call "the creative process." Even if you watch its actions, can it truly be seen? Also… I suspect John Cassavetes is not the easiest man to be around on a daily basis.

I make the mistake of saying the word "genius." That is, calling him one. His response is sharp: "There are no geniuses. It's just a lot of fucking hard work and *trying to get it.*"

We get off the phone and I want to pour a drink, but – doctor's orders – I'm not drinking this year, nor smoking either, alas. My ticker's been on the fritz. It would have been good to toast the honor I've been bestowed – before telling my wife (we've been married five months this day) that all our plans from now through August are cancelled.

Now-through-August is pre-production and shooting of *Love Streams.*

She takes the news gracefully, and has the generosity to be excited for me. She knows John and I go back a long way, longer than John knows.

In 1956, when I was an 11-year-old street-kid in a Brooklyn

slum, I'd play hooky from school and use my 25-cents-for-lunch to go to a movie, any movie, whatever was playing. For me, as a kid, movies didn't have titles, they weren't directed, and I cared for no actors whose names weren't John Wayne, Tony Curtis, or Marilyn Monroe. Rather, to me movies were another order of existence, a fascinating form of life that ran parallel to the cockroach realities of my streets. I'd see any picture, often sitting through a double-feature twice, to experience this strange enhanced cinematic "other world" – very other, but somehow more real than ours. One day in 1956 I forgot very quickly (and didn't re-discover until decades later) the title of the picture I was seeing, *Edge of the City*. What struck me (and that is not a cliché, I was *struck*) was a black man such as I had never been exposed to (for I knew not one), a man of complexity, humor, strength, and grace – my street-prejudices would never be the same, I was so impressed with this man. It wasn't until years later that I'd fasten to him the name Sidney Poitier. The white man he befriended struck me just as hard, for he was the first I'd seen on screen who was like *us* – a person who embodied the street as I knew it. Edgy, contradictory, tense with violence and a desperate grace. You wanted to like him, but there was something about him you didn't trust. You wanted to dislike him, but there was something about him you couldn't help liking. Years later I would see that John Cassavetes never played to be liked or disliked, but played for both at once. As a kid, all I saw was someone I recognized. A real street-guy, not (as with James Dean and Marlon Brando) an artist's concoction. At that age I couldn't articulate my impression, and I forgot or never registered John's name, but he revealed to me this: what I knew to be genuine could find its place on the screen.

Years later, still innocent of the mechanics of cinema, I got off work as a typist in Manhattan and wandered into a theater called the Little Carnegie, around the corner (or was it down the block?) from Carnegie Hall, to see a movie, any movie. The movie was *Faces*. I was 22 or 23. I left that movie frightened, wishing I'd never seen it, but wanting to see it again. Its people behaved as irrationally, as compulsively, as the people of my life – as I did myself. *Faces* was a confirmation I did not desire: that craziness was normal, and that normal was insane. In a word, it helped me face growing up.

I was working a typing job in Boston in 1970 when *Husbands* was released there. In the course of 10 days I saw *Husbands* five times. After the first time I rounded up anyone I could find to go with me, and our friendships deepened or ended on whether or not, and to what degree, they *got* that film. For here were men like my father, like my uncles, heroic precisely to the degree that they were not heroes, trying and failing every day to live a normal life. They would always fail and, in some screwed up way, they would always try. And this film made that beautiful. Who else had ever honestly conferred the quality of beauty upon such men?

As for *A Woman Under the Influence,* by then I was writing for the *Austin Sun,* my first writing gig. *Woman* played Austin in the spring of 1975. Watching *Woman* I saw not only my own childhood but the family-life of all my relatives. My cousin Rocco visited me and his first act upon seeing me was to lift me off my feet (Rocco is strong), saying, "Did you see *that movie!?*" I knew he was speaking of *Woman.* "Isn't that the way it *was*?! I kept sayin', 'Ok, now he's gonna lie,' but he *never lied.*"

Then… 1979, Los Angeles. Ginger Varney and I helmed the film section of *LA Weekly.* In those days before videos, Los Angeles boasted more "revival" theaters than any city in the world. A dozen at least. On Melrose Avenue, a block or so from Paramount Studios, on the south side of the street, there was a revival house that I believe was called The Continental, where one night they featured a rare screening of *A Woman Under the Influence.* Ginger and I plugged it in our paper, thinking we'd draw crowds. There was almost no one. Then, just before the film screened, John Cassavetes entered with a gaggle of friends. His friends were dismayed – they'd expected a full house, a kind of party. Cassavetes tried to appear undismayed, but his eyes were crazy. The picture began. The film broke. Was mended. Continued. Broke. Several times. It was excruciating. And every time it broke Cassavetes cackled. When it was all thankfully over,

I went to him and asked to shake his hand. Names weren't exchanged. His eyes asked, "Friend or phony?" Mine tried to convey, "Friend." He shook my hand. I never expected to see him again.

John and I finally met professionally in 1981, through my function as a journalist. There was a screening of *Woman* at USC. I was asked to moderate a discussion with John and Gena after the film. I arrived early, saw him across the lobby, walked toward him, and while I was still several yards away he said, "Ventura, right? I know by the walk."

I never quite got that one.

Now this night, March 17, 1983... John calls *me*. He doesn't know he's calling the kid who saw him in '56, or all those other versions of me, to whom he's meant so much.

I tell my wife, "I've gotta be careful not to hero-worship this fucker."

"Well he *is* a hero."

"He is."

"Then recognize that. Just don't worship him."

THURSDAY, MARCH 24 – *No more room on the napkin*

We're to meet at John's production office and discuss the book. This morning over tea (no more coffee, doctor's orders), I re-read my interview of the summer before.

Cassavetes: "I'm a totally intuitive person. I mean, I think about things that human beings would do, but I am just guessing – so I don't really have a preconceived vision of a way a performer should perform, or of 'the character.' I don't believe in 'the character.' Once the actor's playing that part, *that's* the person. And it's up to that person to go in and do anything he can. If it takes the script this way and that, I let it do it. But that's because I really am more an actor than a director. And I appreciate that there might be secrets in people. And that that might be more interesting than a 'plot.'"

As I read I hear his voice. The page does no justice to the way he says *appreciate*. Spoken, he said: "And I apPREciate that there might be *secrets* in people – and that – that might be more interesting than a '*plot*.'" His eyebrows shot up on *secrets* and slammed down on *plot*.

"I like actors, and I depend on them a lot. I depend on them to think. And to be honest. And to say, 'That never would happen to me, I don't believe it.' And to try to decipher what is defense and what is a real irregularity in someone's behavioral pattern. And then I try to find some kind of positive way to make a world exist like a family – make a family, not of us, behind the camera, not of the actors but of the characters."

"A shared world?" I'd asked.

"That they can patrol certain streets, patrol their house, and – that's what I feel people do, they know their way home. And when they cease to know the way home, things go wrong."

"How do you mean, know the way home?"

"You somehow, drunk or sober or any other way, you always find your way back to where you live. And then you get detoured. And when you can't find your way home, that's when I consider it's worth it to make a film. 'Cause *that's* interesting."

I notice this morning what I didn't during the interview. In those last sentences, Cassavetes shifted from talking about characters to talking in a kind of first-person "you," then shifted from "you" to "I." Had *he* lost his way home, and could nothing but making another film get him home again?

It's not the kind of question I ask people because I feel it's none of my business. Still, it feels like a question that won't go away. And it occurs to me, uncomfortably, that what is and isn't my business could become a sticky issue during the course of this book.

The offices of Cannon Films are in a building near Sunset and Vine. Seventy years ago on that corner, where a bank now stands, there was a big old barn. Cecil B. DeMille set up production offices in that barn when he directed *The Squaw Man,* the first feature-length movie shot in Hollywood. D.W. Griffith, Mary Pickford, and Mack Sennett were in town by then, so were Fatty Arbuckle and Mabel Normand, making one- and two-reelers. Chaplin and Douglas Fairbanks would arrive soon. The hills were green and flowered, there were many farms, and they say you could smell the sea all the way into the city. Now, what with the smog, you have to stand on the beach to smell the sea. But would-be filmmakers still flock here for the same reasons that brought DeMille 75 years ago and Cassavetes 25 years ago.

Movies can be made anywhere, but you still can't be part of the filmmaking community anywhere else.

So an Israeli director-producer named Menahem Golan and his cousin, producer Yorum Globus, successful filmmakers in their native land, moved here, bought a soft-porn outfit called Cannon Films, and financed a string of low-budget thrillers and comedies. They've captivated local media attention because their style goes back to the days of DeMille and Sennett – making deals on the impulse of a moment, writing binding contracts on a napkin in a bar. Which, according to John, is what he and Golan did. (The final negotiations, I'm sure, were as complex as always.)

John would tell me later, "He wanted to give me points in the picture but I said, 'Why? I'll never see them anyway.' I shouldn't have said it, I hurt his feelings. He said, 'I don't steal.' I said, 'If I don't have points I don't get mad about the points – anyway, there's no more room on the napkin!'"

So the *Love Streams* production offices are at Cannon. The company occupies two floors at 6464 Sunset Boulevard. On the 11th floor, in almost every room there's a typewriter. On the 10th floor, a Steenbeck (the editing console that's replaced the classic Movieolas). I am to meet Cassavetes to discuss this book.

Pre-production offices are surly by nature, and their surliness comes in two flavors. An uptight director will have an office of people working at tremendous speed who are, at one and the same time, artificially formal and artificially jovial. Suspicion lurks in every glance, and nobody makes the most minor decision without consulting somebody else. Everybody tries to cover their ass. And this usually shows up on screen.

In the pre-production offices of a vital director, a natural leader who relishes every decision he makes, the same phones constantly ring and everyone's job consists of the same relentless series of interruptions. But the surliness is the kind you find in a neighborhood bar. Rough humor, sudden verbal explosions of abuse mixed with laughter, no-nonsense shouting, bleak depressions, and occasional cries of triumph. Under it all, the constant hum of work, each person accumulating the hundreds of bits and pieces that will soon be a motion picture. In Cassavetes' office, there is an additional source of noise: friends dropping in. The fat-ish, gangster-ish guy John partied with in Boston sometime last year – or was it 10 years ago? – who's so happy Cassavetes is making another film that he had to visit and wish him well. Or someone vaguely recognizable to a watcher of Cassavetes' films – John Finnegan, as I find out later, a gangster in *Gloria,* a cabbie in *The Killing of a Chinese Bookie,* a stagehand in *Opening Night,* and one of Peter Falk's work-gang in *A Woman Under the Influence.* He's signing on again for two or three days of a bit part. Not for fame or fortune – there will be neither – but for the hell of it, for Cassavetes. This crew has a kind of mantra that I'm in the process of buying into: *Anything for John.*

Whatever else he is, John Cassavetes is a man, an artist, a leader, to whom people give everything they can. You might expect such devotion of fellow-artists, actors, would-be film-makers, but you don't expect it of secretaries, production go-fers, gaffers, techs, Teamsters. Composer and sound-mixer Bo Harwood would later give me a reason that felt true. They do it so that someday they can say, as Bo explained, "I rode with Billy the Kid."

It is always a surprise to see Cassavetes, because he is never quite the way you left him, especially these days – at 53, the intensity of his life is catching up with him.

To be honest: Half the time he looks awful. As though the skin of his face has lost all life of its own and only his eyes are keeping him alive. No one has eyes like him. Everything fierce, everything street-wise, every mockery and irony, everything that makes men laugh or long for tenderness, every anger, everything that cannot lie and everything that wants to, everything angelic or demonic in his soul – at one time or another in the course of a day, his eyes give it all away. Like any man he tries to protect himself, but his eyes don't participate in that. Yet, for all their frankness, you sense in John's eyes the presence of a terrible secret. Terrible, I mean, to him. I doubt anyone, except perhaps Gena, knows what that secret may be. He himself may not know. Whatever it is, you sense that it's driving him and that, through his eyes, it's looking at you. Some find him difficult to talk to, because even the gentlest of his looks can be uncomfortably direct. When Cassavetes looks at you, he looks at *you* – not your function, not your salary, not your contract, not your credits, and certainly not your pose. You. And he's interested. In the midst of his most hectic days he'll take the time to talk a little with – anybody. If he wasn't sincerely interested, it would be difficult for the timid to bear those eyes at all. In fact, considering how volatile he can be, if John didn't have a profound respect for human beings just because they're human beings, he might be, well, hard to take. His enormous charm isn't quite enough to overcome the impression that he's kind of scary – not in a sinister way, but in the sense that even at his most relaxed you feel he might at any moment quite literally blow up. I don't mean blow up emotionally. I mean blow like he does at the end of *The Fury*, when his whole body explodes and his head flies through the air. I am not being hyperbolic. There's that much concentrated energy in the man. And it all streams out of his eyes.

Those eyes don't change. The eyes of 26-year-old John Cassavetes in *Edge of the City* and his eyes today have the same force, frankness, and strange secrecy. But the rest of him changes drastically – partly because so many images of Cassavetes live in one's mind. The skinny maddened street-kid of *Crime in the Streets*… the handsome, svelt piano-playing detective of *Johnny Staccato*… the ugly wiry cackling soldier of *The Dirty Dozen*, sporting the first punk haircut… the unctuous sinister husband of *Rosemary's Baby*… puffy, happy, good-hearted Gus of *Husbands*… the doomed low-life hustler of *Mikey and Nicky*… the merciless conniver of that ludicrous picture, *The Fury*, which at least gave us the strangely believable image of John exploding… the intellectual, mystic, spookily frail Prospero of *Tempest*… too many Johns to keep track of. But all have the same eyes. All of which is to venture the hypothesis that John Cassavetes is not a man who can be known. I'd better just try to *see* him, clear, and hope for the best.

So today, walking into the neighborhood-bar-like atmosphere of *Love Stream's* production offices at Cannon, I have no notion of what to expect. I'm waved in, introduced around, quickly and casually, to Cassavetes' rough-and-ready staff – my first blurred impression is of an office staffed by male and female old-school Manhattan cabdrivers. Which is homey for me, since my father was such a cabdriver. Cassavetes offers me a vodka, a Coke, a coffee, in the same breath that he's saying two or three other things, and asks Helen Caldwell to get them – a lovely woman in her 20s with very wide-lensed glasses. She raises an eyebrow. He raises a more formidable eyebrow: "Didn't I get you *your* coffee this morning? I did, right?"

"As a matter of fact, you did."

Helen Caldwell rises from her chair to get me a Coke. (Doctor's orders, I shouldn't be drinking Coke any more than I should be drinking coffee. But it was tough enough to turn down the vodka. Especially when he's drinking vodka. Early in the afternoon.)

Physically, he's changed again. The face more drawn, the skin more wan, and he's gained weight in the oddest way. His face, arms, legs, and butt are skinny, but his stomach – his stomach has ballooned. He looks three months' pregnant. His belly is huge and tight as a drum, as though his shirt has been buttoned with difficulty over a basketball.

Cassavetes is a man of immense ego but little vanity. He either won't or can't get that stomach down, but he does nothing (like wear looser shirts) to hide it. He intends to play the belly as part of his *Love Streams* costume. The film's Robert Harmon will be weighed down with Cassavetes' belly, and on Robert Harmon it will be an emblem of the dead weight of his life. Cassavetes is about to enact a scathing portrayal of the weaknesses and needs of men, a portrait of desperation and longing, culminating in a most unlikely vision of redemption. But for dying his gray hair dark brown, he will use what is most ravaged in his appearance to convey the reality of Robert Harmon.

*

Cassavetes and I sit in his office speaking of the possibilities of this book. But Cassavetes rarely speaks of one thing at a time, or even on one level at a time. The silly and serious, the sacred and profane, the intimate and impersonal, interweave from sentence to sentence. What holds his conversation together isn't any sense of narrative but his intense presence, the style of the man.

He is speaking of the book: "Everybody just refers to their own experiences and they call that truth."

Then of the character he will play in *Love Streams*: "I think that a man is composed of two things: confusion and pride."

Then of the film: "They're going to be ready for us maybe five minutes a day."

I'd like to stop and unpack those sentences with him. In the first is his declaration that all art, all vision, is relative. In the second he is either stripping men of any possible nobility or emphasizing how impossible and beautiful it is when such creatures rise to anything noble. In the third he's sized up his chance with his audience and dismissed that chance – a chance upon which he is willing to stake his entire effort.

Or so you may be thinking, but he's left you to think what you want and has gone on to the necessity of trying to persuade his producers that the picture needs a first-class caterer. A film crew, like an army, marches on its stomach. "All these things that they call luxuries are really the cheapest things," he says, "compared to what it costs for one day's fuck-up if people don't feel that they're *making a movie*."

The production designer, Phedon Papamichael, arrives with pieces of cloth and artificial flowers. He is Cassavetes' cousin, Greek by birth and rearing, and he's worked with Cassavetes since *Faces*, as well as doing art direction and production design for directors like Jules Dassin and Michael Cacoyannis. Phedon is a few years older than Cassavetes, tells even more stories, and smokes just as much. (Have I neglected to mention that John's offices are always thick with smoke? Temporarily a non-smoker, I'm a rarity here.) A difference between Phedon and John is that

Phedon tends to light each cigarette precisely, as though to prove a point, whereas John can light a match and not notice it's burning down to his fingers while he talks on. Phedon always knows where his cigarettes are and carries elegant lighters, while John's constant "Does anyone have a cigarette?" is a joke on his sets, he rarely has a match, and he's capable of leaving his innumerable packs of Marlboros anywhere and everywhere. (Well into the *Love Streams* shoot a pack he left on the dashboard of my car will remain there in anticipation of the next time I give John a lift.)

When they want to be, Papamichael and Cassavetes are two of the most stubborn men in town, which is perhaps why they have so much patience with each other. They need it. Phedon's scraps of cloth and artificial flowers are cause for an argument that would leave most people not speaking for days, if ever again. They hiss, yell, and curse. Phedon passionately argues for *this* cloth and *this* flower, but John wants this *other* cloth and *other* flower, and maybe not even them, maybe none of it's right, goddamn all such scraps and plastics to hell. Phedon storms out of the office, Phedon storms back, they argue more until suddenly John says quietly:

"You may be right." Phedon stares in surprise. John smiles grimly, "After all my bullshit, you may be right."

And the matter is settled. For today.

I will learn that this scene is typical of a Cassavetes production. He expects you to fight him for what you want, really *fight*. As often as not, he'll wind up agreeing with you – and, in his way, he'll apologize for "all my bullshit."

After this argument there is, to the surprise of this observer, no residue of tension whatever. Phedon asks after the health of John's mother. She is in the hospital and seems to be doing well. Cassavetes speaks whimsically of how, the other day, a nurse came in while he was visiting and said to his mother, "Oh, is this your husband?" He mimes how his mother was embarrassed and flattered, and how she looked shyly away from the nurse toward him.

Then suddenly, somehow, they're arguing about Socrates. (I will learn they often argue about Socrates.) The argument begins so suddenly that I don't catch its trigger, but I sense it's been going on for the better part of 20 years. Then Socrates evaporates as quickly as he materialized, and just as suddenly these two are speaking of love. Sooner or later, if you speak with Cassavetes, you'll speak of love. Something in the ringing phones, or the poster of *A Woman Under the Influence* above Helen Caldwell's desk, or the argument about Socrates, which (now I get it) sprang out of a reference to Aristophanes, which in turn was a reference to the comedic elements of *Love Streams* – something, in short, hard to put your finger on, but present in the room, now has John thinking:

"That was the biggest discovery I ever made – that love stops. Just like a clock. Or a watch. Or anything. Then you wind it up and it goes again. 'Cause if it stops forever, then you die."

What kind of love, love for whom, and who stopped loving whom, who stopped loving what? – are questions that are none of my business.

"Love," says Phedon, as though about to say something further, but John interrupts with:

"I know what love is."

"You don't," Phedon says quietly.

"You know I know."

"And, if you know?"

"Love – is the ability of not knowing."

That sentence will buzz in my head for a long time. For a while I'll conclude it means: love is having faith.

No. Faith is a kind of knowing.

Now I think John means: Unless you realize that there exist aspects, depths, topologies of your beloved that you'll never know, touch, or even guess at – unless you realize this, you're not really loving, you're merely filling in the blanks with what you imagine and prefer. *Not* to do so takes what John calls "ability" – learned capacities cultivated with difficulty over time. Yes, it takes a cultivated strength, and a humble admission, to learn *not to know*, and yet to love.

Not a half hour after I leave his office Cassavetes receives word that his mother has had a massive heart attack.

Several days later...

John's mother, Katherine Cassavetes, dies.

While waiting beside her deathbed, he thinks to tell Helen Caldwell to call me and assure me that the picture and the book are still on, still being attended to.

It's not unusual in this business to wait days or weeks for a call from a director, or from anyone else. As a journalist, I've been guilty of such delays with no more excuse than the confusion of being too busy. But at his mother's deathbed, John thinks to have Helen call me. Cassavetes hates politeness – he's always saying, "You *can't* be polite, it just gets used against you." Polite or not, he is considerate, in the big things. For all his volatility, that fundamental sense of consideration is a signature of the man.

APRIL-MAY – *Friends of Sam*

John wants me on the set when *Love Streams* starts shooting in May, since pre-production will consist mostly of countless repetitive hours not unlike John's "discussion" with Phedon about cloth and artificial flowers. The most crucial activity during this period is finishing the shooting script, an activity I'm not invited to witness and, as a writer, I well understand why.

Cassavetes worked with Ted Allan on the *Love Streams* screenplay off and on for years, but at this stage John's preferred method is to dictate, mostly late into the night. He does this with Helen Caldwell, who, I'm told, can take dictation at 250 words a minute.

"I'll tell you how he works," Helen relates on the set later. "On pre-production we'd work all day, and it was impossible to write the script during the day because there were so many people coming in and grabbing him. So we would stay up at night and write the script. We'd start writing it at seven or eight in the evening and work until three or four in the morning. The man has an incredible amount of energy. It's like he's *obsessed* with creativity. He'd sit down and dictate a scene, and I'd take it down in shorthand. While I was taking it down, there'd be things in there that I would think, 'I don't understand why he's doing this,' so when we'd get done with the scene I would ask him about it. And he'd explain to me his reasoning behind it, the impact, and he would take the time to *really* explain. A lot of writers don't do that [she's done this work before]. They'll just – this is their script, their idea, they don't want any questions, if you don't get it then tough.

"So – it's very presumptuous of me to say this, maybe – but I think my questions contributed, because they let him clarify what he was thinking. One night we were working together real late, and John all of a sudden says to me, 'You know, Helen, this is the most special part of the whole process. We share something that no one else on the whole picture can share, just you and me, and without us this picture wouldn't be here. There wouldn't be a crew, we wouldn't be hiring all these people, we wouldn't have all this pre-production. Without the script we have nothing.' He always gave me the feeling that I was really contributing, which is very satisfying to me in my work.

"Oh, I get pissed off at him. Sure. The first time I got *really* pissed off at him, we were working on pre-production and he was getting really uptight about some things. And so I kept catching his fly-off, and he would be short with me and everything. For about a week this was going on. I was really miserable about it, I would talk to my *mother* about it! Finally, one day, we were sitting in a meeting, and we'd just written a scene, and we were reading it back to Al [Ruban, long-time Cassavetes collaborator] and whoever, to get feedback, and something happened – I hadn't typed the scene exactly the way he'd imagined it. 'Cause sometimes, when you speak to him, he's the kind of person you can talk to for five minutes and afterwards you think, '*What* did he *say*?!" So, anyway, it hadn't come out the way he wanted it to, and he was disagreeing with me. And it was the first time I'd ever raised my voice to him. I *raised* my voice to him, I was really upset. But afterwards he comes up to me, after the meeting, he gives me this big hug, and he says, 'It's good to see you *yell* once in a while, it's good to know you're *human*.'"

This seems to me a lot of re-writing for what Ted Allan first conceived as a play. When I ask John, he says, "I'm really *motivated* by Ted's material. It really *begins* with Ted's material. Every day we [he and Helen] worked, Ted worked. And every time I couldn't discover what to do working alone, I could always discover it with Ted."

As a writer, this interests me – because, frankly, I don't believe it. Or I don't believe all of it. Cassavetes' pictures, after all, have been so individual. There doesn't seem room for two visions to meet in his densely textured films.

So I go to Ted Allan. In his late 60s, he now celebrates his birthday on the anniversary of his last major heart attack. By this count, he is five years old. For a five year old he's had quite a life. A Canadian, when just a boy in the 1930s he went to fight for the Spanish Republic against the fascist General Franco. Later he was blacklisted in the United States during the McCarthy era. He's written many plays, including one directed by Bertolt Brecht. He's had success in the theater in London and Paris, and volunteers that a major character in Doris Lessing's *The Golden Notebook* is based upon him – he says it resentfully, he doesn't like her portrait, but *he* volunteered the information. His screenplay *Lies My Father Told Me* received an Academy Award® nomination, and at this I light up and tell Ted that I often quote him. In that film, the little boy's grandfather is an immigrant Jewish junkman with an old horse and an older wagon. The boy rides with Grandpa on his rounds through Toronto's alleys, picking up useable stuff. The thoughtful boy asks, "Grandpa, do you believe in miracles?" "No – but I depend on them."

"Let me tell you a story which may or may not be useable for you," Ted says to me, "that will give you an indication of his relationship with me. I was living with a girl in London called Genevieve. We lived together for six or seven years. I adored her, even though we kept splitting up. And during one of the split-ups, John and I started to work on this *Love Streams* screenplay. And I was saying to John, 'God, I miss Gen. I love Gen. I really love her.' 'Yeah, okay,' John would say. And this went on for about six or seven months while we were working together. I kept missing Gen. Loving Gen. Missing Gen. And in the middle of writing a scene I said, 'Oh God, I love Gen. God, I miss her so much.' Finally, after six or seven months of this, he said, 'Okay, enough.' I said, 'Enough what? What do you mean?' He said, 'I've heard enough.' I said, 'What do you mean, you've heard enough?' He said, 'For six to seven months now, I've been hearing you tell me how much you love Gena, and – enough!' I said, 'What?' He said, 'Yeah, *what*! Enough.' He thought I was talking about GENA! Loving Gena, being in love with Gena, and missing Gena. He never once mentioned it to Gena. And he never once mentioned it to me, and accepted it *totally* – that if I was in love with Gena, all right, I was in love with Gena.

"Now, I find that incredible. So I said, 'Are you crazy? *Genevieve!*' I said. He said, 'Oh.' 'Do you think I've been talking about Gena?' He said, 'Yeah, I've been thinking that all this time. You keep telling me about Gena.' Now, I know if *I* were working with a guy who was telling me how much he missed my wife, I would say, 'Gee, what the hell goes on here?' after the first declaration. This man did not. Now, Ventura, what do you make of that story?"

"What do *you* make of it?!"

"What I make of it is this. That he trusts me. Trusts her, *totally.* He knew, as far as he was concerned, that despite the fact that I kept saying how much I was in love with his wife, how much I missed her, that never would I make a move. And he knew that never would she. That's what I make of the story. And that's why I tell the story, because it's a reflection about our relationship, and it's a reflection on their relationship. For the man to tolerate this guy for six months telling him how much he loved his wife, and during that time our relationship never changed! We were as close as ever, despite the fact that he 'knew' I was madly in love with his wife."

Ted can't go on talking for laughing. When he calms down he says, "I told Gena, and she screamed with laughter. I said, 'He thought I was talking about you.' She said, 'Oh, goody!' '*Goody,*' said Gena."

"How long had you known him then?"

"We met in Ireland about 25 years ago. He arrived in Dublin to play the lead in a movie I had written, the name of which I very understandably have forgotten. And I knew him as a television actor. Never had met him. He was a very handsome man. He was a very vibrant man. He was quick. And he criticized the script in quite detailed fashion, so that the director kept saying, 'Uh-huh, uh-huh,' but I, listening to him criticizing the script, got the very peculiar feeling that he had never read the script. But he had mentioned, as he walked into the room, he had whispered to me quickly, 'I'm a friend of Sam's,' meaning a friend of Sam Shaw. [Sam Shaw is a photographer, producer, Cassavetes' mentor and long-time collaborator. I've gotten the impression that being a friend of Sam Shaw was like an underground password among New York's artistic community 20-odd years ago.] And that was why I kept quiet. Otherwise I would have said, 'I don't know what you're talking about, I don't think you read this script.' The director just listened as if every word uttered by John was from God. And finally, when we were alone, I said, 'Did you read the script?' He started laughing, he said, 'No, I forgot it in a bar on my way to the airplane.' And then he said, 'Sam and I are very close friends.' And I said, 'Why did you do this?' And he said, 'I don't know.'

"Well, that's my first meeting with John. I've known him 25 years since that first meeting and he's one of my closest friends. And, while this collaboration is exciting for me, when people ask, 'How do you feel when he changes things?' – well, I feel marvelous when he changes things that I agree with. When he changes things I don't agree with, I don't feel marvelous. I feel awful. But this is the choice I made. I know how John works. Once I allow myself the luxury to work with John on a collaboration, I know that John is going to change. I accept that. Other directors I have worked with, I don't accept it. Neither do I accept them as fellow-writers. They're not. He is. I feel that he has become, in a way, my alter ego. He is really extending and exploring what I set out to do."

"Which of you wrote the line '*I'm almost not crazy?*' That's my favorite line."

"I would love to claim it as my line, but it isn't. It's John's line. But John will probably tell you that I probably told him at one time or another in the last 25 years that my sister said that. But I agree with you, it's a marvelous line – for almost all of us can use it. We're almost not crazy."

I say, "He claims to be virtually unconscious of all his effects, which I don't believe."

"Neither do I," Ted says very seriously. (I'm glad to have this confirmed from someone who knows Cassavetes well.) Now Ted brightens: "I think – I'm going to write a play about John!"

"Don't let him near it."

"No, he would change it *totally*. This is a play about John that I will direct. It's the only way I can get back at him! We started to do a screenplay of *this* movie – six years ago! Versions of it, we had about – I don't know. How many does he remember? 15? We've had an enormous amount of revisions. We had one version when we arrived in London from Munich, after we had worked together in Munich, and I said, 'Take it, I don't want to have anything to do with it. Just do it, John. But take my name off of it.' I hated it. Absolutely hated it. And he turned absolutely white. 'Are you crazy? I'm not going to do it unless it's something you approve of.' I said, 'I don't want to have anything to do with it.' So he just put it aside until he approached me one day and said, 'Let's work on it.' And then we worked on it again until we got a version that I was happy with. But I know he changes as he goes along. That's John! The whole subject has fired him. My point is, he's made it his own. There's no question about that. It's become his movie."

There's something else that perhaps Ted Allan can shed light on, if anyone can. I ask, "What about John's relationship to his audience? There *is* an audience out there, and he *does* relate to it, but he's very secretive about how. Half the time he pretends it doesn't exist."

"I must tell you," Ted says with an especial relish, "that I saw a version of *Opening Night* at a Westwood cinema house, packed. A preview. The audience went wild, as I did. They cheered and stamped and stood up, they loved the movie! And I said, 'John, this is *it*!' And he looked very, very, very pale, and very disturbed. And he said nothing. The next time I saw the movie, he had changed the last 30 minutes *totally.* He seemed not to be very happy that they'd accepted it that enthusiastically. Now, you could say he doesn't want to be successful in America; or, he got frightened by the enthusiasm of their response; *or* he decided that he didn't want them to like it the way they were liking it, because they were missing the point. I don't know. I kept saying, 'Why'd you do that?' 'Because it wasn't *right,*' he said. He satisfies *himself* first and foremost, and the audience is secondary.

"But – I wouldn't swear to anything I ever said about John. I wouldn't swear to anything *John* ever said about John!"

Love Streams' final shooting script is dated May 11, 1983. The title page reads "Screenplay by Ted Allan and John Cassavetes / Based on a Story by Ted Allan." On screen the first writing credit will be "by Ted Allan & John Cassavetes." When screenwriters' names are joined by "&" it means the writers worked together; when joined by "and" it means the second writer re-wrote the first. John obviously desired to give Ted full collaborative credit. Well… the script runs 134 pages. By the last day of shooting in August, 34 pages would be changed substantially and 55 more would be cut; combine those numbers and you see that during the shoot John revised almost exactly 2/3rds of the script. Excised pages would include the ending, the script's last 34 pages – the passage which most closely corresponded to Ted Allan's play. John would jettison Ted's ending – *totally,* as Ted might say – and compose another and very different ending. The John Cassavetes film *Love Streams* would bear virtually no resemblance to a play of that name by Ted Allan.

WEDNESDAY, MAY 25 – *I don't understand where all this light is coming from*

A production note, concerning both *Love Streams* and this book:

Most films are shot according to when it's most economical to shoot a given location. Thus an actor might play a scene from the beginning of his film in the morning, then a scene from his film's end in the afternoon – then the company moves on and that location is never used again. Obviously if you shoot scenes from the middle of your picture during the first week, and scenes from its climax during the second, you're locked in. Everything else you shoot must be consistent with what you've shot already.

John Cassavetes refuses those constrictions. Insofar as humanly possible, John shoots in sequence, from page one to the end. Thus his actors can build a role in front of the camera as they might build a performance on stage. But, say an actor performs a scene differently from how John imagined it (though the spoken lines are the same); if John likes what he sees he'll stick with that performance, even if he must re-write later scenes to accommodate it. As he says, he'll let a performance "take the script this way and that." Thus his films evolve out of the actors' performances, rather than from a pre-conceived idea. He *begins* with the idea, an idea he's worked on for a long time – the idea is the foundation; but he'll often re-write along the way as the performances enhance and even change the original idea. This is not "improvisation," this is like jazz: composition-in-the-moment. In *Love Streams* he will do this more than in any film but *Shadows* and *Husbands.* Nearly every word spoken in *Love Streams* will be scripted, but often the script was written in the wee hours of the morning that it was shot. Yet in its final edit *Love Streams* will be, of all Cassavetes' films, his most formally structured.

In *Love Streams* he departs from shooting-in-sequence slightly, a departure necessitated by the story. This film shifts between Robert Harmon's life (John's character) and Sarah Lawson's (Gena Rowlands). Their paths don't intersect until 57 minutes into the picture. During that time we're given no clue as to what, if anything, these two have to do with each other. Cassavetes will film Robert's incidents first, in sequence; then Sarah's, also in sequence. After they meet, he proceeds in sequence as much as is feasible.

His method allows me to give this book a particular shape, blending the story the film tells with a journal of its making. My account of each day will begin with a summary, in italics, of the script-pages John intends to shoot; then I'll relate what happened to those intentions; finally I'll note what, of the footage shot, was used in the final cut.

Love Streams *has been in production six days before I can get there. What's been shot are Robert Harmon's segments of the shooting script's first 22 pages. The script opens in a bar where elegant men in tuxedos buy drinks for elegant men in dresses. Exclusive and (according to some people) decadent, the club's mood is that of a polite prelude to a serious orgy. There is one man desperate beyond politeness: Robert Harmon [Cassavetes]. We discover in these scenes that he's a well-known writer who makes lots of money writing trash-laced bestsellers about people who live on the edge. A heterosexual unintimidated at being in a gay club, he's there to gather material for his next book. In his tux he looks like a ravaged, depressed, disgusted Mephistopheles. His expression makes clear that his disgust is directed at himself. His weariness is boredom with his own company. All he's interested in is the club's singer, Susan [Diahnne Abbott], who's singing "Kinky Reggae" with two young female back-up singers [one played by daughter Xan Cassavetes].*

The script shifts to Sarah, a scene not yet shot. From that scene we cut back to the bar, a month later. Robert Harmon is determined to bed Susan. He drinks and drinks (he's always drinking) and perseveres through a miserably awkward situation until Susan finally sits with him. She volunteers that she's seen him on TV but doesn't have time to read his books. He can be charming, but the more he drinks the more she's seen it all before. In the shooting script this is the first time we hear Robert's idea that "all beautiful women, they have a secret – and the interesting thing – is to get that secret out, you know, if they volunteer that secret, you know?" Susan greets this with a bored, "Yeah, I guess so." When she abruptly rises to leave he drunkenly runs after her, pushes himself into her car, insists on driving, and has a minor fender-bender with a parked car. She struggles to get him out of the driver's seat, wrestling him, hitting him, but he will not give up his grip on the wheel, and they drive on. Can a man behave more boorishly? They park in front of her house in Silver Lake, one of LA's cheaper neighborhoods. More struggle ensues. There's a concrete stairway up a slope to her home; when Robert reaches the top, running after the fleeing Susan, he's so drunk he falls backwards and bloodies his head. She looks at him with the resigned disgust that a beautiful woman soon learns to feel for many men. But she can't bring herself to leave him on the street in that condition, so she helps him up and takes him inside, where he passes out.

In the morning, at her place, Robert's been cleaned and bandaged by Susan's mother Margarita. [Margarita is played Margaret Abbott, Diahnne Abbott's mother; Susan's little boy is played by Diahnne's son, Raphael DeNiro. As much as possible, Cassavetes likes his films to be family affairs.] Robert is effusively thankful. He flirts with the mother, she flirts with him, and we see when he says goodbye to Susan that, in spite of everything, Susan likes this guy.

Robert Harmon seems to have no filters on his behavior, he acts out every wisp of feeling as it passes, as though he's desperate to feel something, anything. When he's sober he's usually stiff; when he's drunk, or hung over, he exaggerates and acts out. But we're watching a man who seems to have nothing genuine left within.

All this work (edited, of course) will be used in the final cut of Love Streams, *though Cassavetes will choose to begin the film with scenes shot later.*

On the day I arrive they're to shoot Robert Harmon returning to his home in the Hollywood Hills, where he's hired a gaggle of young pretty women-on-the-edge to live in his house. He's observing and interviewing them for his next book.

Robert Harmon lives in Cassavetes' house. The Cassavetes family has moved out. Through July, this house will be *Love Streams'* central set.

John's home is something of a unifying metaphor for his work. Here is the kitchen where Lynn Carlin and John Marley fight in *Faces,* and at this breakfast-nook they go into giggle-fits about fellatio. In the dining room, *Opening Night's* Gena consults a crafty psychic played by the late Katherine Cassavetes, John's mother. Here too, in *Minnie and Moskowitz,* John comes home to tell his wife (Judith Roberts) of his affair with Gena (Minnie), and his wife runs into this bathroom to slit her wrists. In the bar, there hangs the same painting we saw in *Faces:* a young Cassavetes playing chess with a blond whose face is turned from us but who is obviously Gena. In the living room, where Seymour parties with the ladies of *Faces,* the furniture seems not to have changed or even been moved, except that there's a piano, and a large-screen TV (the first I've seen). The staircase to the second floor is the staircase in the last moments of *Faces.* Upstairs, John's and Gena's bedroom is where *Faces'* Lynn Carlin and Seymour Cassel make love, face death, and face each other. For *Love Streams,* all that's been done to make this home a set is to line the downstairs walls with photographs of young lovely women. Gena will tell me later, "Of all the things about making this movie, this is the strangest to me, that suddenly all the pictures are of people I don't know."

Not quite all. The photos that hang crowded on the walls of the hall and bar include some of the "permanent exhibit": John, Gena, and their children, parents, friends, from every era of their lives. Gena as a stunning young actress in the 50s, beside Gena in a housedress at breakfast not too long ago. John 20 years ago, smooth-faced, hugging his little son Nick. John getting punched in a Western. John's father, old and frail, looking wise, kindly, and a bit bewildered. And stills from all the films, from *Shadows* to *Gloria.* The lighting for most of *Love Streams* is so dark that these photos never register on film; when they might, the crew gets them out of the scene. John wants them up, he wants them looking over his shoulder as he creates *Love Streams.* He shoots in his home because it's a place where he knows what's true.

On this morning what's true is a thick air of tension. There are maybe 60 people milling about, in the dining room, bar, kitchen, living room, everywhere. The *Love Streams* crew, and a dozen or so pretty young women whom Robert Harmon is to interview. Nobody's working. Everybody's quiet. It costs a lot of money for nothing to happen on a film set. Something is very wrong.

And here comes John. He's wearing a tuxedo and he's a bloody mess.

Not real blood. Make-up. Robert Harmon took a bad fall the night before, bloodied his face and hands, the wounds are still fresh. John's skin glows younger than when I saw him last, and his hair is black – in March, his skin was colorless, his hair gray. The difference: make-up and dye, of course, but also action. John's in his element, in the action, and he feels better, at least this morning. Cassavetes is plainly angry and he's had no sleep; he's garbed in the costume of Robert Harmon after a night's debauch and a morning's hangover. Both characters shake my hand.

"Michael! I'm glad you're here. You should come to this meeting."

I follow him into the living room where on-lookers are shooed away and several troubled, quiet men sit and smoke. Young David Gurfinkle, the cinematographer, is slight, bearded, his face set in anger. His gaffer, Avram Liebman, sits beside him, his only ally, stocky, contained, stoic. Eddie Donno, Assistant Director, ever-present on the set, an incredibly energetic Italian-American who's John's traffic cop as well as stuntman, stunt coordinator, and actor. And Al Ruban, Executive Producer, silver-haired, self-contained, John's ally and collaborator since *Shadows*; among other things, Ruban was Cassavetes' cinematographer for the beautifully photographed *Opening Night*.

I sit down, I'm not introduced, I pull my ever-present notebook from my back pocket to take notes. Everybody but John shoots me a look – a stranger with a notebook is the last thing they want at this meeting. Which of course John knows; the more nervous everybody else is, in this situation, the better he likes it. They're talking cinematography. Gurfinkle is tight-lipped while Al Ruban, calmly and with his natural air of authority, articulates Gurfinkle's point of view to John, then explains John's point of view to Gurfinkle: Gurfinkle is working in such-and-such a way because of this-and-that, and it's a perfectly legitimate way to go about his business; John wants this-and-that because of such-and-such, and Gurfinkle needs to understand that this is not a normal production. You've got to feel for Gurfinkle. Until shooting began he was probably very excited at the prospect of working with that famous maverick, John Cassavetes.

Ruban's calm explanations are done and it's John's turn.

"The lighting is too heavy," he says to Gurfinkle, his voice tight, quiet, aggressive. "The crew is too small for this heavy stuff – it's takes a 70-man crew to do what you're doing – they'll be exhausted in six weeks and in 13 weeks they'll be dead."

Young Gurfinkle holds his temper. Perhaps that is his nature. Even if it isn't, there aren't many who'll go up against an angry Cassavetes.

Cassavetes moves the meeting into the hallway, which has already been lit for that day's shot. Crew-members skedaddle out of harm's way but try to stay in earshot.

"This is a *dark* hallway," says John, "I don't understand where all this light is coming from." Then, "If we don't come in here and pre-light and have a pattern, it's going to take forever to do this every day. It *has* to have a pattern."

It is a dark hallway and John wants a dark hallway, but "pre-light" and "pattern" are bullshit jargon. Quick jabs at a guy who can't fight back.

Cassavetes calls a wrap. No work today, no work until this problem is settled. The meeting breaks up.

John and I head for the kitchen to make some coffee.

In less than a minute Eddie Donno is standing in front of us. Eddie milks the moment, waiting a beat to say:

"He quit, you know."

Quit? David Gurfinkle was marched to the edge of a cliff and left with no dignified option but to jump. A slick way to fire a guy.

I'm new on the set but not new to the business. David Gurfinkle is producer Menahem Golan's man, the only Golan man on the crew with a significant job. John *can't* fire him outright; the guy's got to quit. And so he has. Now if Golan wants to know how the production is going, he'll have to come see for himself. For John's part: in a film in which he directs, acts, and rewrites as he goes, he hasn't time to teach a young stranger how to shoot a Cassavetes picture. From the beginning John's wanted Al Ruban to shoot his film. On a shot where the camera's in motion John can say (as he will), "Al, you do this any way you want, any speed that you want, you know?" – and John rightfully trusts Al to do it *a la* Cassavetes. But Ruban already has a 24-hour-a-day job: as Executive Producer, he makes almost as many decisions daily as John. Al didn't want both jobs, but who else is left? Where is another first-rate cinematographer who knows how to shoot Cassavetes' style and can start today? It's got to be Al. To save the picture, Al can't say no. (But Al tries. He says no at first. Al's "no" doesn't last the afternoon.)

This is John's 11th film, and all but one (*A Child Is Waiting*) have been completed his way. In this business that doesn't happen unless you're a savvy in-fighter and a first-rate puppeteer.

John and Al go off to what will certainly be an interesting emergency meeting with Golan at Cannon. Everybody's discussing the firing, or the quitting, comparing versions, taking sides, savoring and sharing overheard scraps. Helen Caldwell says to me:

"I wonder if he did that because you were here."

"I'm not that important," I answer, while I hope I'm covering my shock that the question would even occur to her. I *know* I wasn't part of John's equation, but it's interesting that she'd wonder. She's worked closely with Cassavetes for months, and she's learned that things can get so crazy Cassavetes might concoct all this drama to impress… a writer.

After the Cannon meeting – which, not surprisingly, goes John's way – he and Al return and shoot some establishing interiors with Robert Harmon's pretty young interviewees. Some of this footage will be in the final cut. "Al took a lot of chances," John tells me happily, "he backlit Leslie [Leslie Hope] – high contrasts!"

THURSDAY, MAY 26 – *We can't tell them the answer unless they ask the question*

Not one of the beautiful girls in Robert Harmon's house looks older than 20. They're hookers, b-girls, aspiring singers, models, actresses – droplets upon the wave after wave of young women who've journeyed to Hollywood every day for 70 years now. Harmon pays these gals just to hang out. They have the run of the house, eat and drink what and when they like, make messes, take showers, sunbathe, dance. He watches, listens, occasionally interviews one. Gets drunk with them. They're to be in his next book.

As the crew sets up the morning's shot in John's bar, everybody's milling around and Al Ruban calls loudly across the room to Eddie Donno, "Hey Eddie! How long have you been married?"

"11, 12 years."

"Is your wife still happy?"

"We don't want to start over. We have a mutual agreement, we don't want to start over."

A chuckle in recognition of marriage's dilemmas.

Nobody but me seems to think their exchange odd. To me, it sounds not like work-banter but like a private conversation in a bar. Then I see: we *are* in a bar. John's bar. (One of his first-floor rooms is a bar.) I can't shake the impression that this picture is being shot in the neighborhood bar that *is* the cinema of John Cassavetes – and now that I think of it, only John's thwarted studio picture, *A Child Is Waiting,* features no scenes in bars and bathrooms.

John walks in, ready to act, wearing the clothing and severe expression of Robert Harmon – wasted and depressed, a man at the end of his rope who doesn't seem really to like anything or anyone.

When an actor directs himself we enter a hall of mirrors, mirrors facing mirrors. One never gets the sense that Robert Harmon is John Cassavetes. Cassavetes can write a Robert Harmon; Robert Harmon could never reach deep enough to write a John Cassavetes. But on days when John directs himself one sometimes gets the sense that Robert Harmon is shooting this picture. Harmon is too difficult and desperate a character for John merely to step into at a moment's notice, especially when he's still getting used to this character, so John's attention is more inward than usual. In Harmon make-up and Harmon clothing, John carries the character with him all day. Sometimes a little more so, sometimes a little less so, but Harmon is always around. Sometimes, while John directs, you get the impression that Harmon and Cassavetes are two men trying to walk through the same door at the same time, bumping into each other, neither very happy about it.

They're to shoot a conversation between Robert Harmon and one of the girls, Joanie, played by Leslie Hope. Leslie is an 18-year-old Canadian with the creamiest, loveliest skin one is likely to see, and a face ripe for dreaming about. Her Joanie is a sometime-hooker with an expression already set in disillusioned boredom. Robert Harmon has gathered the girls together in his bar to tape interviews. Joanie's interview in the script runs five pages – a long conversation for Harmon. (He'll talk at length with only four other characters.) In anyone else's picture, such a conversation would mark Joanie as someone to watch, someone to care about. In John's films you never know. A signature of Cassavetes since *Husbands* is that, usually early on, a central character has a long-ish important scene with someone who then disappears from the picture. John's characters meet people, become involved, some come and go, some come and stay. In *Love Streams,* will Susan of the early scenes be pivotal? Will Joanie? No clue is given. Cassavetes quickly establishes that in his film, as in life, you have no way of knowing what will happen. The sense of not knowing is central to his vision; one way he embodies this in his film's form is never to signal the function of his supporting characters. While they're on-screen they have the film's full attention, as though they're co-stars; they may be there not for plot, as in most films, but to accent some aspect of life important to the story – an aspect of, as John will tell me, "some vague thing that life has."

John's bar is not a large room. Into this room squeeze the actresses, John, Al, Eddie, the cameraman, camera-assistant, sound-mixer, sound-boom guy, dialogue coach, script girl, location manager (!), and anyone else who can squeeze in without getting barked at by Eddie or Al. Me, I'm scrunched against a wall. And just outside the room, in the hall, there's almost everybody else. I won't repeat this description for every shot filmed in this house, but you may assume a similar crowd every time. Studio soundstages are enormous for a reason: it usually takes a lot of people to make a movie. Compared to a soundstage, we're shooting in a closet. We're all over each other. There's something about John Cassavetes, in life as on the screen, that's going to bump you up against other people and make you deal.

Leslie Hope and John take position, facing each other across the bar. She sits on a barstool, he stands. There are six takes. In between takes John doesn't break character; it's the ravaged, self-disgusted Robert Harmon who commands us. The first take is incomplete – he cuts because their energy is too flat. The second, they act all five pages of script precisely, but John thinks he stinks and doesn't want it printed. He cuts the third take because we can hear people talking in the backyard. Cuts the fourth – the film-magazine rattles. Cuts the fifth – a camera battery's gone dead. The battery is replaced. This takes longer than it should, which doesn't make Robert/John happy. The sixth take is complete. It's the only take he prints.

On the sixth take, he improvised – again, not as in "off the cuff" but as in the disciplined soloing of jazz:

Into the interview he inserts a version of the "beautiful woman/secrets" speech that we heard when he spoke with Susan, the singer, a speech *written* (though not exactly this way) elsewhere in the script.

"See – a beautiful woman – has to offer the man her secrets. I mean, that is so beautiful, I can't, I can't tell you. See, everyone in the world is – very screwed up. Now, I know that *you're* not screwed up – and I'm not. And I know the answer, and you know the answer, but – we can't *tell* them the answer unless they ask us the question. You see?"

Of course she doesn't see. Who would? But we, the viewers of the film, are made aware of something. Robert Harmon's interest in Susan and Joanie is superficial at best, but he *is* interested in something. Whatever it is, he wants it – badly. In his dead-end life it's the last and only thing he wants, though he can't articulate it even to himself. He calls it a "secret" and feels it is hidden in "a beautiful woman." He seems to think that if only he informs a beautiful woman that she possesses this secret, she'll know what he's talking about and she'll tell him.

Crazy? Maybe. No one would mistake Robert Harmon for an emotionally or mentally balanced person. But the repeated "beautiful woman/secret" speech indicates that underneath his compulsive acting-out something genuine and intense is going on. He doesn't know what it is, but he knows it's going on. He may be too wounded, and he may have ruined himself too deeply, ever to know what he's trying to find – but he feels that if he finds it, it might free him. That feeling is the last thing left of the man he maybe once was, or the man he wanted to be.

Later John will speak to me about "inner life." He'll say, "We're making a picture about inner life. And nobody really believes that it can be put on the screen! Including me! I don't believe it either – but – screw it!" And, "I know this guy doesn't know what he's doing – just like me… [Robert Harmon] has feelings but doesn't know how to express them." We watch Robert Harmon and we think, not always kindly, "What under Heaven and above

Hell is this guy up to, what's driving him?" The tormented quest of his inner life is given to us, as it were, in outline. We will never know him, but in the course of the film he will grow toward us as we will toward him, and we will come to feel his depth.

More precisely, we will come to feel *depth.* The fact of it. The ever-presence of it. Its inchoate power in our lives. "We're making a film about inner life."

The entire constellation of Romanticism that hovers around "every beautiful woman has a secret" has long haunted Cassavetes as an artist. (Is there a male artist whom it hasn't haunted?) In *Shadows,* Leila Goldoni's 18-year-old character believes in the secret as much as the men, and they're all young enough to *really* believe it, which imparts to *Shadows* its hopeful spark. In *Faces* men hound Gena Rowlands mercilessly for this "secret," though no one uses the word; she must fend off the illusions of every man who comes near. And Lynn Carlin and her girlfriends look for this very same Romantic secret from a young man, Seymour Cassel. *Faces* hinges on the moments when people collapse under the burden of their Romanticism and are forced to face each other.

The men of *Husbands* are haunted by the same notions, but frivolously, as a cover-up. What's really bugging them are the burden of their responsibilities, the limitations of their freedom, and the imminence of death. "Every beautiful woman has a secret" is the very soul of *Minnie and Moskowitz* and *A Woman Under the Influence,* though *Woman's* concerns range far wider. In each film, a goodhearted bewildered man (Seymour in *Minnie,* Peter Falk in *Woman*) tries to see into the soul of a woman (Gena in both). They fail. They end up with no choice but to accept her unconditionally. In *Woman,* Mabel doesn't seek to know Nick's nature – she's enthralled with her own. They love each other deeply, but both act as though he's just a piece of her puzzle.

In *The Killing of a Chinese Bookie* men are surrounded with beautiful nearly-naked women, but these guys have stopped looking, stopped questioning. It is the cruel world of men that

Cosmo (Ben Gazzarra) must attempt to survive. Men buy and sell secrets but don't know them. *Opening Night* strikes off into different territory: the inner life of a woman who is also a great actress. She quite consciously fears she has a secret, secret most of all from herself, and she puts herself through grueling confrontations to find it – almost as though she's wooing herself.

In *Gloria,* Cassavetes makes the beautiful woman's secret a game. It's a literal secret (a notebook), and gangsters are trying to kill her for it. Interesting symbolism: Gloria shoots men and protects a boy. The secret is dangerous to men and protective of boys. Men are trying to kill the bearer of the secret, and the secret will only nurture a boy who calls himself "the man"? Shrinks could wring quite a treatise out of that one.

Now in *Love Streams* the man is ravaged, desperate, hopeless, alone. He's still looking for that secret. He doesn't even know what it might be anymore, but he's looking.

So I'm wondering what Ted Allan meant when he told me, "John's life is like a Cassavetes movie."

The next scene is in the upstairs bathroom. Robert Harmon, grim, in a tux, strolls through the house just looking at the girls, making occasional small-talk, while the girls do this and that, whatever they like. He goes into the bathroom, where two naked young women frolic in the shower. He looks at them and leaves. Two set-ups: shoot the girls reacting to Harmon, and his reaction to them. It takes forever.

The lights are rigged in the bathroom, then John delays the proceedings by closing the door and moving his bowels.

It's his house, isn't it?

Even Al Ruban can't quite believe this.

"Did he go to the bathroom?!" he asks Eddie Donno.

"I told him," Eddie shrugs.

"We're not gonna be able to use that bathroom for an hour now!"

"I did what I could do," Eddie shrugs.

"Does he think his shits don't stink?"

Then one of the actresses doesn't want to be photographed in the nude. Can she wear a bathing suit? Fine. Should she duck down so it looks like she's naked. "No," says Cassavetes, "if you're in a bathing suit I want to see you in a bathing suit." To no one or everyone he adds, "I'm a kinky guy, I got one in a bathing suit and one not in a bathing suit."

Five takes from one angle, with three complete and printed. Another take, the same angle with a different lens. Three takes of a medium shot, Harmon watching them; two printed. Another from Harmon's point of view, one take, printed. Another, hand-held, the girls playing in the shower. Printed.

Two, three, four hours? One loses track.

"I don't wanna make a big thing outa this," John tells Al. "It's just a normal thing in this guy's life. We can't hold on it because this scene isn't going anywhere. If we hold on it, it's just titillation."

After one take John's shaking his head. "I hope *I* never get into that. Al, let's do it again, that took 18 years." To me, "I've had it with this scene. I can't stand to see all that shit." He means the nudity. Except for *The Killing of a Chinese Bookie,* there's no skin in his pictures. Interesting that this houseful of nubile gals is nowhere suggested in Ted Allan's play. These scenes of sexual boredom and confusion are wholly Cassavetes'.

Eleven long takes in all, and when they're finally done John is glum – unusual for him. He often says that he doesn't know what he's doing, but nobody who knows John or his work believes him. If he says it after this scene, we'll believe him.

He takes me aside, says, "I made a big mistake in not starting with Gena."

The next sequence is outdoors, on the hillside behind John's house. The heat is brutal. Everybody's short with each other.

"I don't know what they're doing," a woman says. She's answered by a woman in the wardrobe department: "I know what they're doing, they're doing what they're always doing, *they're changing their minds."*

They are. John decides the hillside doesn't look right. They pull up weeds and water plants. Though a crew of about 50 is at his disposal, John takes a hose and sprays the hillside himself – to give more color to the shot. They pick camera positions, change camera positions. Stage people. Change the staging. Shoot the girls sunbathing, dancing to radios, drinking. They shoot two more interviews. Hours and hours.

There's a screw-up, people who aren't supposed to be in a shot are in the shot, John loses it, screams, "Everybody get out of this shot, get your asses out of this shot! Anybody who's in this shot, you're all off the picture!"

One of the girls is Ted Allan's granddaughter. The written dialogue is only a page, but John plays with it, strings it out. Again he inserts, "It's always been my greatest hope to have a beautiful woman tell me her secrets. Willingly. That is so beautiful." This girl looks 14 years old, so the speech feels especially pathetic.

Six set-ups, 10 takes, and as it goes on the sequence seems more and more pointless. Murmurs of second-guessing. "What's he doing this for?" "Didn't we already do this scene inside?" Before one take a girl asks, "Should I be walking around?" Cassavetes says flatly, with no interest, "You can do anything you want."

But to the actress with whom he has dialogue, Bronwen Bober, he is all attention. Her delivery is a little stiff and John tells her gently, "When you say that don't *know* exactly what you're gonna say. Let it go."

An "assembly" is a draft of the edited film, before the picture "locks" – that is, before the final version, released in theaters, is decided upon. Sometimes, for preview purposes with test audiences, an assembly or draft will be printed and scored like a released movie, and there may even be credits. But not until the picture is locked is it, in effect, signed by the director and ready for release.

There will be many assemblies and private screenings of Love Streams. *I'll see most of them. During five months of editing, and several drafts of* Love Streams, *the Joanie interview will be absent. But finally, in the last locked version, Cassavetes will restructure the beginning of his picture, deciding to open not with the nightclub scenes but with fragmentary scenes of the girls in the house. The Joanie interview will be the beginning's centerpiece.*

In the final edit the shower scene will run for 12 seconds: two seconds on the girls, 10 on Harmon watching the girls – a powerful shot that establishes beyond doubt this man's utter disgust with himself and with life.

The hillside sequence will be discarded.

FRIDAY, MAY 27 – *People use that language when they're in trouble*

A light day scheduled: "pick-up shots," connective footage to string scenes together – the camera mounted on a car coming up the driveway, brief exchanges with the girls, Robert Harmon walking through his house. Also, a small scene with his secretary Charlene [Ted Allan's daughter Julie] and her little girl Renee [Renee LeFlore].

A new crisis threatens. Al Ruban tells John, "We just got word that the city is going to start building storm drains next door for the next eight weeks."

There's no way to use this location with sounds of construction pounding next door. If Cannon Films can't convince the city to delay construction, a new location must be found and this week's work re-shot. In the tone of a Mafia don John tells Al, "Take care of it." The subject never comes up again. Al takes care of it.

With today's easy schedule, many on the crew (wardrobe, make-up, set-dressers) haven't much to do. They lounge about the house, out of the heat. Already we take the house for granted, make coffee in the kitchen, freely use the glassware, some even raid the ice-box.

Cassavetes relaxes in his bar, conversing with a production assistant. On a film set the director is king, if not God Himself. Production assistants are serfs. In Hollywood, a feudal place, it's rare for a king even to notice a serf unless the serf screws up – in which case the serf is executed (fired). But John is deep in conversation with this guy. We'll call the guy Bill. Bill is tall, heavy-set, and blubbery, and Bill wears girl's elevator shoes in which he can barely walk. He hasn't washed his face in quite a while, nor brushed his teeth. As far as I can discover, nobody knows if he's even been hired. He just shows up. Most of us avoid him. Not John. Bill is telling John stories of his childhood. John listens intently. Bill's story is long and inconsistent, and now he interrupts himself to ask, "Is the cast party gonna be here?"

"I don't really give a shit," says John. "Every day's a party anyway, what do we need another party for, to be bored at?"

"I could get my guitar and perform for you guys."

"You could do that anyway. Play on the lunch break."

Bill's eyes brighten but he says nothing. John says, "Nothing worse than a party where nobody shows up – except a party where everybody shows up."

Bill never brings his guitar. Soon, he stops showing up.

Robert Harmon has a no-nonsense assistant named Charlene, played by Julie Allen. Charlene manages Harmon's business and household. She's pissed at all these voluptuous gals messing up her turf. Charlene has a daughter, Renee, maybe five or six years old. They have their own room in the house.

Cassavetes jokes rough with everyone, even kids. He scrunches his face at Renee LeFlore, becomes a little kid himself, says snottily, "I wouldn't be your friend for anything!" Renee takes him on, snappy, "So why did you pick me for the picture then!" He laughs and hugs her. She hugs him back. Today she's the only one with whom he's entirely at ease.

John decides there's not enough of Charlene in the script. He improvises with Julie Allen and Renee to work up a scene. He wants Charlene to be angry at Harmon – tell him off, show no fear of her employer. Feel free to yell at or care for him, whatever she thinks he deserves. They work up the business. Harmon will pick up Renee, walk through the house with her in his arms, show her the mess these Hollywood gals are making, Charlene will charge down the hall, accuse him of hiding behind her baby, tell him she's not a maid and he's a coward.

The action's decided, the cameras are set up. Six takes that don't suit Cassavetes. They keep working. In one sense, at least, John is old-school Hollywood: he believes in the adage, *The most important scene in the picture is the one you're shooting.*

He tells Julie Allan, "Just get the thought process going and you don't have to worry about the words." They rehearse a little.

"You're a coward," Charlene/Julie yells, "You're a fucking coward!"

"No, no, no, no, no," says John. "People use that language when they're in trouble. You're not in trouble, you're very definite about what you're saying. And you don't want to leave yourself in a screaming-mimi fit because you want to be calm when you say your last line to your daughter."

Improvisation, but not imprecise.

They rehearse again. Julie Allan finishes a line they've agreed upon, then lets it hang in the air with a slight pause. "Come on," John tells her, "don't wait for me, stop doing cues! You're getting real calm, real slick – you're not angry anymore. Get angry." Then: "Make-up? Where's make-up?"

The young make-up man, Mike Stein, is called in to powder their faces. John tells him, "I don't want to have to *ask* for make-up before every shot, Mike. I don't mean to chew you out, but I want make-up between the takes. Everybody's sweaty. I mean it."

Stein pads them down and fades. Eddie Donno steps near John, says quietly, "I've had this conversation 20 times with him about between shots – that's why I asked you the other day, 'Are you happy?'"

More rehearsal before the next take, more make-up. When next Michael Stein pads John's forehead John says, "I'm not mad at you, Mike – but that's your job. The way my job is to be in front of the camera making an idiot of myself. You gotta keep us dry, otherwise it looks like we've been working 10 years. And it'll look bad, and your name is on this."

Eddie wants to fire Stein now. John won't let him.

John and Julie rehearse once more. "You've gotta go harder," he tells her, "don't listen to what you're saying, just let it go."

She places herself down the hall. "A little further," John says, "there, sweet. Find your light, darling. That's good. Open yourself to the light."

He prints the next take. That's it for today.

Until the final draft of Love Streams *nothing shot today would be included, save for the car proceeding up the driveway. Then Cassavetes changes the beginning, starting his picture with today's scene, Charlene haranguing Harmon. So, in spite of all the hassle and aggravation, yesterday and today turn out to be quite productive after all. But we won't know this for months. The feeling on the set, expressed by John as well by many a minion, is frustration – we seem to be spinning our wheels.*

TUESDAY, MAY 31 – *The confusion of the action is the scene*

Over the holiday weekend John's written a new scene:

It's late that evening (the evening of the Joanie interview), in Robert Harmon's house. His fight with Charlene has blown over. Booze has made everybody comfortable. Charlene, little Renee, and all the girls, lounge with Harmon in his bedroom, and Renee lights a candle and asks each girl to sing. Most don't feel like it, but finally Joanie sings a little love song, then Charlene leaves with Renee to put the kid to bed. The party breaks up. Robert Harmon goes to sleep fully clothed with three girls. At four in the morning, Harmon awakes with a coughing fit. He gets up, goes downstairs, gets a glass of water, lights a cigarette, calls Susan, the singer. He wants a date with her. She hangs up on him.

"I gained six pounds over the weekend," John tells me. "I've gotta not drink on the weekends. Kidneys don't work."

That sounds serious to me (his stomach is notably larger), but John speaks of it with a boyish smile, as though it's only interesting because it's strange.

We're making coffee in his kitchen. Al Ruban walks in. "He stopped your check, John."

"*Who* did?"

"Eddie Donno. He said until you're a better actor you don't get it."

The long Memorial Day weekend has freshened everyone. Cassavetes has been re-writing. He wants a variation in Robert Harmon's attitude toward the girls.

"All my best ideas come from having no answer," John says to no one in particular. He'll say much the same sentence often. Just because the candlelight party scene is a little stupid and sentimental he thinks it might work.

Leslie Hope's Joanie will sing to Renee. But it won't be her voice. It'll be Bo Harwood's, the new soundman. Don't ask what happened to the old soundman. This is a Cassavetes set and I don't have eyes in the back of my head. I suspect it's another case of: out goes a Golan man, in comes a Cassavetes collaborator. Bo did music for *Minnie and Moskowitz,* sound and music for *A Woman Under the Influence* and *Opening Night.* I suspect John concocted the device of Bo singing Leslie's song to pull Bo into the midst of the action on his first day – ask him to do something nutty so he can get comfortable. (By the end of the shoot, Bo Harwood – with rings on his fingers, an earring in one ear – will marry Leslie Hope in Vegas, Phedon Papamichael his best man.)

John wrote the party scene to end with Harmon ordering everyone, "Go to bed." He cuts and re-takes without that line. "I'm not a fascist *yet.*"

They're shooting day-for-night, something Cassavetes doesn't like to do, but he wants this series of scenes over with. All morning the crew is up on scaffolds, draping black canvas on the south side of the house. Some rooms are pitch dark, some are washed in hard California sunlight.

In the bedroom, John speaks of why he's changed the tone of today's scenes – from the harshness we've seen to the drunken, easy familiarity of Harmon crawling into bed with three girls and passing out.

"It's streetlife, but not the way most people think of streetlife. They think it's black belts and sleaze and stuff, but that's not streetlife. Streetlife is searching. You search, you search – but there's never enough. And nobody wants to fuck when there's an *opportunity.*" A pause. "Could we get the three girls in here, Eddie, and I don't quite know what the scene is myself."

The girls come in, they all get in bed. "Now – I'm gonna start coughing. When I do, somebody go for the lamp, turn it on. I don't care how you get there, grope around, whatever you want. The confusion of the action *is* the scene. If it goes too fast, it's bullshit. The scene is to center on my illness, and that the bodies of the other people don't really matter to me. The only way you can see what you're going to be able to see is if it reveals *itself.* The problem is, if we rehearse this more than once it won't have the sloppiness it needs – *technically* it shouldn't be sloppy, but the subject should be sloppy."

They call for silence, the cameras roll. Three beautiful young women, a fully dressed ravaged man, sprawled drunk unconscious in bed. The man starts to cough. The cough gets louder, racks him, begins to frighten the rest of us – behind the camera we look to each other with expressions of, 'Is he alright?'

Later I'll wonder why we didn't ask this every day. John looks bad. Over the summer he'll look worse. But we rarely mention it, rarely really notice. Maybe it's because his intensity never lets up. Though he drinks a lot, and always has, he's never drunk – no sign of drunkenness, ever. Still, later I'll think it very strange that we have not registered what's plain to see. Soon John will learn he has advanced cirrhosis of the liver and may be dying.

The coughing is awful, jars Robert Harmon awake, a spasm rolls him off the bed onto the floor. One of the girls, half-asleep, fumbles to turn on the light. The other two are too drunk to notice, they stir, turn over. Harmon's cough subsides.

The take is exactly what John wants but it can't be used. The lamp the girl turns on is not the actual light; the actual light is operated by a technician whose timing was off. Also, John crawled out of frame before the camera could follow him. John says to the camera operator, "I'm the most important thing in this scene, I don't care about anything else, you've got to follow me."

Al Ruban says, "I want you to get in the scene and *stay* in the scene, like a *good* actor."

"What do you mean? I – whataya mean!" Mock anger. "I'm in every scene, in close-up."

Al pauses for effect, looks around, says, "Fuckin' guy, getting saved by kids."

"I'm running out of kids," John says under his breath.

Another take. Another. John sweeps the room with that Mephistophelean smile, puts on a phony English accent, "Do they think he knows what he's doing? No! They do not think he knows what he's doing!"

Larry Shaw, son of Sam Shaw, is the still photographer. He takes advantage of the pause to snap some pictures. Al tells him, "No belly-shots, please."

John flashes Al a look. Then he mutters, to no one in particular, "No idea, no idea about this scene. And I don't give a shit."

Directors don't do that. They don't admit, in front of their crew, that they're stuck, confused, lost. But what's fundamental to John's discipline is his commitment never to be phony. This commands respect, from the crew and everybody else.

Another take (that awful coughing), almost as good the first. He prints it, sits on the edge of the bed, shakes his head. "Ah, the hell with it. Next set-up."

Hours later, after many takes of what should be a simple phone call, we drive to "dailies" at a screening-room in Hollywood, as we will do almost daily, to watch the previous day's takes. "We" is usually John, Al Ruban, Helen Caldwell, Eddie Donno, Robert Fieldsteel (dialogue coach), Carole Smith (production office boss), me, sometimes others. George Villasenor, editor of *Love Streams,* awaits us. We're almost always late.

It's in Cassavetes' contract that Villasenor be editor. It's in Villasenor's contract that he shows edited footage to no one but Cassavetes. These are almost the only contractual guarantees Cassavetes demanded. He didn't even ask for final cut – the contractual right that no one re-edits *Love Streams* after he and George finish. "If they don't like the film," John tells me (*they* meaning the money-men), "they take it away from you anyway no matter what the contract says."

George Villasenor edited *Gloria.* His editing and Gena's performance are all Cassavetes claims to enjoy about that picture. Temperamentally, Villasenor is Cassavetes' opposite. Quiet where John is noisy, measured where John is excessive, and George loves smooth edits as much as John loves the rough-edged. But Cassavetes respects Villasenor's integrity tremendously. George always tells John exactly what he thinks, whether or not it's what John wants to hear. Cassavetes says he needs *Love Streams* to be a picture in which the smooth and the rough are balanced. He and Villasenor are the balance.

The dailies today seem interminable. But for some close-ups of John, and the Joanie interview, the scenes shot Thursday and Friday seem pointless. I sit next to John as the screening room fills with cigarette smoke – almost everybody smokes – and bottles of wine and beer are passed around. The takes go on and on. John says, "It's a lot of work to do very little. Jesus Christ, I better get with it – gettin' too fucking *light.*"

Nothing shot today will be used.

WEDNESDAY, JUNE 1 – *We find out what we can do, we take chances*

It's the morning after. Robert Harmon's unconscious, in bed (clothed) with two girls – one in a nightgown, the other in pajamas. A girl in a white pants-suit runs in looking for her shoes. We follow her downstairs, where she sees a car pull up in the driveway. She calls upstairs on the house intercom. The phone awakens a groggy girl beside Harmon. She wakes him to report a car has arrived, and there's a woman at the door with a boy who's holding a bouquet of flowers. Harmon (suddenly dressed freshly) goes to the door. The woman is his ex-wife Agnes (Michelle Conway). The boy is his son Albie (Jakob Shaw, grandson of Sam Shaw). Robert Harmon hasn't seen Albie since the day he was born.

Agnes wants four weeks back child support. Harmon writes the check without protest. But that's not what Agnes really wants. She wants to leave Albie with Harmon overnight. The reason is mysterious – in one line is suggested a seamy sort of life: "My husband and I have a chance to raise some money at someone's big house, and they don't want children." Hesitantly, Harmon accepts. Her tone is wheedling, his is brusque. He has no smile for his son. All the while the boy stares at him with pathetic eagerness and fear, holding flowers.

This simple action will be shot with 12 set-ups. (The rule of thumb on a studio picture is 1 hour per camera set-up. John shoots sometimes much faster than that, sometimes much slower.)

The day begins in the bedroom again, with Cassavetes and two young actresses, in costume, sprawled in bed. While the crew sets up, John and the girls lie there, cuddling, talking, even falling half-asleep. Another actress crawls in with them – she won't be in the scene, but she wants to cuddle too. The blonde holds John's hand. Eddie Donno is drawn to them, he stands near, a casual hand on the blonde's shoulder. Everyone's kind of dreamy. A most unlikely tableaux! John softly says, in the delivery of a 30s movie, "I could take you girls anywhere, we could go to foreign lands, we'll get to say to each other, 'Where were you, I couldn't sleep.'" Then he cackles, "I can't believe that we're all in clothes!"

Mike Stein comes in with make-up. John doesn't want to get out of bed.

"You wanna stay *there*?" Stein asks.

"I do, Michael."

So Stein joins the tableaux, climbing in bed amongst John and the actresses to apply their make-up.

Earlier John told me that he got the idea of Robert Harmon and the girls *clothed* in bed when the actress in the shower-scene wanted to wear her bathing suit: clothes-in-bed was precisely the right touch to reveal Harmon's sexual state, or lack of it, and protect these scenes from being vulgar. ("Vulgar" is his word).

The scene is shot efficiently, with exactly the "sloppy" quality John was looking for yesterday. The gal comes in looking for her shoes, John and the gals stir a bit in bed and slur a bit about being disturbed. The shoe-gal leaves. Then the intercom phone rings, one of the gals gropes for it, and, as he wanted yesterday, "the confusion of the action *is* the scene."

Still, John is concerned about the adrift, groping quality of these last few days. While the next shot sets up he tells me, "This picture, I don't know how, has gotten stuck in – I don't know – the beauty of ordinariness. Camera work. We've got to get *into* the picture now, or we're not going to have a movie." He turns to walk away, then turns back and says, to himself more than to me, "I don't have enough courage." (Some men get their courage by never thinking they have enough.) Then John says to me, "If I can't wake up my *own* self I can't expect to wake everybody else up."

What wakes up John Cassavetes the director – perhaps because it shocks Robert Harmon the character, and throws him off his game – is the arrival of little Albie, an eight-year-old seeing his father for the first time. The world of women is all too well known to Robert Harmon; the boy is the arrival of the unknown. Now Harmon must deal with male energy, for one thing, which it seems he's structured his life to avoid. The boy is what he made, and is a version of what he once was, and he won't be able to control or win over the boy with money or will power. For the first time in probably a long time, life is testing Robert Harmon. Can he face this?

The day's set-ups are intricate: angles, through the windows, of the girls noticing ex-wife Agnes' car drive up; Agnes and Albie getting out of the car, hesitating, afraid – again, seen through windows. Then Harmon, Agnes, and Albie at the front door. Close-ups of Agnes and of Harmon as they speak. The door is half-open, and there is a long shot on Albie from inside the house – a slow zoom, slowly ending in a close-up of the boy as he listens to his mother and father, never looking at his mother, staring at his father. In that shot we hear Agnes and Robert, but the half-closed door conceals them from our view. We're only on the boy.

No improvised dialogue today. The script is precise in its awkwardness. Harmon is cold to the point of cruelty. Agnes is anxious, needy, pretty in a haggard way, out of control in a tight way, sputtering with the energy of an intelligence gone unused and now unsalvageable.

There *is* one improvised line, but it won't be used in the film; as he will often do, Cassavetes speaks the line as a way to direct while in the midst of the scene. On a close-up, Michelle Conway is speaking Agnes' dialogue. The scene has been shot from several angles now and Agnes' lines are coming too glibly for John's ear. John, with no warning, his voice dripping with sarcasm, interrupts her to say, "You're such a beautiful kid, so sincere, money isn't important to *you*, right? What a cunt you are."

Michelle's expression is stripped raw, she hesitates, stumbles on with her lines – just what John wants. John told me the night before, "I don't direct. I set up situations, and either they work or they don't."

Concentrated, efficient shooting all day and everybody's into it. At dailies later, even Al Ruban is talky, enthusiastic – the only time he'll show those qualities in my presence. I respected him instantly, but we won't warm to each other and he'll refuse to be interviewed. (I'll often ask myself, "How come John Cassavetes doesn't intimidate me and Al Ruban does?") Ruban's brought his camera crew to tonight's dailies – to give them confidence, I believe. He praises their work. In particular, Ruban enjoys one shot from yesterday's effort: Robert Harmon walking out of the dark with his shirt half-buttoned, John's swollen belly catching the light. Al tells his team, "We find out what we can do, we take chances – that shot of him coming out of the dark, that was enough for me, that was beautiful."

After dailies, as we're walking to our cars, Ruban does me the rare honor of addressing me. He says of Cassavetes, "He's a man of great courage. He's not afraid to fall on his face."

"Gena asked Al yesterday," John says, "she asked him, 'What did you think of this stuff, are you excited?' He said, 'If I get happy, the penalties for being overly enthusiastic, the depression at the failure of it is so strong that I can't afford to commit myself.' I thought –" John laughs suddenly " – I thought it's wonderful to see this guy, who's most of the time quite stone-faced and strong, suffering so terribly on the work, you know? Because he's such a charming guy when he's not working. And quite charming when he is working, but totally non-committal. And very sensible."

Everything shot today will be used. Edited, of course, but – from the first draft to the final cut – these scenes will appear as conceived, without restructuring their original intent or placement. Interestingly, except for two close-ups of Harmon and one of Agnes that last for barely a second each on-screen, the doorway scene will consist entirely of the zoom onto Jakob Shaw's heartbreaking expression, seen from inside the house through the half-opened door – we will only hear Harmon and Agnes. Cassavetes' decides that in this scene the boy is most important.

THURSDAY, JUNE 2 – *Don't cry on my set*

"Wave goodbye to your mother" are the first words Robert Harmon has ever spoken to his son. Alone together, father and son don't know what to do or say. As they go into the house Harmon lightly, tentatively, pats Albie's hair – one pat. Harmon is stiff, his expression stern. Albie is plaintively and silently begging to be loved. When they enter the house, Albie compulsively hugs his father. Harmon doesn't hug him back, just pats the boy's shoulder – once – and says, "Okay" as though saying, "That's enough."

He introduces Albie to his assistant Charlene and her daughter Renee. Renee is jealous of the newcomer. The camera will be on Albie, clearly going through hell, biting his lip. Next Harmon introduces Albie to the bevy of gorgeous young women upstairs. The gals make a big fuss, pawing Albie, oooing and ahhhing. Albie bolts. Runs down the stairs, out of the house, down the winding driveway. Harmon just stands at the window, angry, watching his son run. The gals bound off to chase Albie, one telling Harmon that he's got to get the boy, "He's your son, for crissake." Suddenly Harmon runs downstairs, gets into his convertible, drives too fast down the driveway, narrowly missing some of the women. Harmon catches up to Albie down the street, forces him into the car, takes him back to the house. Albie is both crying and trying not to cry, and he keeps calling his father "Mr. Harmon."

"Don't call me 'Mr. Harmon'!" Robert commands fiercely. "That's insulting, and I know you know it."

"I hate you!"

"That's because I'm your father."

Last night John talked with me into the wee hours – while Gena was expressively annoyed at his drinking and cursing. He drank. I didn't. I'm exhausted. He's not. He can't afford to be, he's scheduled 20 set-ups today. And they'll get done.

Almost all will involve the boy.

Jakob Shaw has known John all his young life. Sam Shaw, John's mentor and collaborator, is Jakob's grandfather. Larry, the film's still photographer, is his father. Larry Shaw has groomed his son to be an athlete ever since the boy could walk, it seems, and on any pretext Larry and Sam speak proudly of how fast Jakob can run, how great he is at soccer, at wrestling, at anything sportive. Cassavetes and his friends are sports fanatics with a seemingly inexhaustible statistical knowledge of every man on every team of every sport – Jakob's athletics are *important* to the men in his life, so he is no stranger to high expectations and to staking his young honor on competition and endurance.

"Don't cry on my set," John tells him. John's eyes glint with humor, but it's a humor that means business.

"I'm not cryin'."

"*Don't*."

"I'm *not*."

Jakob knows this style of humor well. He doesn't smile on his comebacks, but looks Cassavetes straight in the eye with a familiarity laced, it seems to me, with suspicion.

"Okay," John says, "but if I come back here and you're crying, you're *out* of it, right away." This with a smile.

When John comes back he shifts tone, now he's like an uncle. "Do you know how to throw a punch?"

John holds up his hand and Jakob whacks a punch into his palm.

"Naw," John says. "When you throw a punch, you hold your fist *this* way –" he demonstrates the classic boxer's stance, fists turned slightly upward "– so that when you hit –" John punches in slow motion "–when you hit, it snaps." His fist turns down at the end of his punch. "More power that way. Otherwise, it's just arms."

No kid on a Cassavetes set is going to punch with "just arms."

Actually he's giving Jakob direction:

Don't cry. Punch hard.

Later today Robert Harmon will ask his son, "What are you crying about? I don't trust people who cry. I don't understand it, and I don't like it. People use crying as a weapon. If you feel bad, you don't say anything, you just take it." Now they're shooting Albie breaking away from the women, running down the hall, about to run downstairs and out the door. John wants Jakob to forget that he knows this house well – John wants him to be confused about where to turn. The first two takes (Jakob running so hard he's breathless) are "all straight lines," John says.

"Don't remember that you did it before," he tells Jakob. "Always do it for the first time. It's *good*, what you did – but don't remember where everything is. Be creative. Don't be afraid to fall apart."

Next take, Jakob gets part of this: the confusion of his moves is good. But "don't be afraid to fall apart" is tough for a kid. He is, of course, terrified of falling apart.

"Jake, yell *sonofabitch* before you run out the door."

Jakob is not used to saying, much less yelling, *sonofabitch* in front of his elders. The boy's yell on the next take is tentative, as though he can't quite believe he should *really* say that word.

"You really gotta be *mad* when you say sonofabitch, you *really* gotta be mad. Don't be afraid to scream, scream it OUT! Just DO it! You're *so* mad you could kill 'im."

So mad he could kill his *father?* (Jakob's father Larry is standing right there, calmly, silently.) Jakob is clearly uncomfortable but yells the curse loudly on the next take and runs like hell. He comes back breathing hard, asking Cassavetes straight out, "Was that good?"

"No," John tells him calmly. There's no blame in John's voice, but his impatience is growing and the kid can feel it just like everybody else. "It wasn't good because you didn't put anything into running away. I'll tell you –"

John's sentence hangs in the air. He takes a deep breath and his eyes flash. "I'm gonna tell you how to do this. If I catch ya, I'm gonna hit ya. If I catch ya, I'm gonna belt you so hard –" but he veers onto another idea without missing a beat. "No. Give *yourself* a belt in the face, so you know how it feels."

The kid hits himself, not very hard.

"This is not a game, so don't fool around. This is where we separate the men from the boys," the man tells the boy. "Give yourself a hit, then go." And right away: "Action, go, *go,* really hit yourself, hit yourself *hard.*"

Jakob hits himself so hard that the next day he'll have a black eye.

John prints that take.

Tomorrow Cassavetes will tell Jakob, "I've been up and down with you because I didn't know how far you'd let yourself go. *I* had to make that decision – I couldn't leave that decision up to you. Because people are going to be telling you, 'Oh, you're wonderful, your doing great, you're good' – and that's going to make you like *this.*" John takes a deep breath, puffing himself up. "Makes you crazy. I gave you a hard time and you stood up to it. Now I respect you as a person. Now we're two actors. When you have a problem you come to me, when I have a problem I'll come to you."

All scenes shot today will be in the finished picture.

FRIDAY, JUNE 3 – *It's harder to do slow*

A long day of pick-up shots, shooting entrances and exits, arrivals and departures – 23 set-ups! Also, Robert Harmon telling the girls they'll have to leave now, he and Albie need the house to themselves, then the party-like commotion of the girls getting paid and leaving.

Menahem Golan is holding back the checks for editor George Villasenor and his crew, miffed that George won't show him footage – though the contract stipulates that George is obliged to show footage to no one but John. Last night, after dailies, George told John, "I have to make a stand." If the checks aren't forthcoming he'll quit. Golan is playing John's game: if you can't fire a key player, goad him to exit.

"Don't quit on me, George," John said, severely, adding, "that's what they want. They're just trying to *get* to me."

John explained to George that if they don't pay him "they're in breach," they're reneging on the contract. George remained uncomfortable and unconvinced – he's not the kind of man who likes to play chicken. Then John guaranteed George's fee out of his own pocket.

"I don't want that," George said. But after a while he let himself be persuaded.

This morning I'm nearby when Al Ruban says to an assistant,

"Here, hold this, I shouldn't be holding this – it's the editor's checks. Give it to Carole [Smith, production office boss]."

I never learn whether those checks are signed by Cassavetes or Golan.

But John wins. George stays.

Movies often use cinematic shorthand for arrivals and departures. For instance, they cut from a character inside a cab to the same character inside a house, without showing him getting out of the cab, walking to the door and knocking – the transition is assumed. Audiences accept this. But in *Love Streams* nobody really *does* anything but arrive and leave; arriving and leaving is the basic *action* of this film. And they do so unpredictably – people keep showing up, like Robert Harmon's ex-wife and his son. There are many unexpected arrivals and leave-takings; and, with characters scattered all over the house, if you didn't shoot Robert Harmon walking through the halls, from one encounter to the next, the viewers would never know where they are. Transition cuts usual to most films would make *Love Streams* incomprehensible.

So John shoots every transition (any way in which his characters move from one situation to another) meticulously, almost ceremonially – carefully staged shots of people getting and out of cabs, walking up and down stairs, opening and closing doors, saying hello and goodbye. It must be "formal," John constantly says, otherwise there would be no sense of flow, no *stream*.

Important, tedious work, and, for all its necessity, not very interesting to shoot. It's easy for performers to lose their concentration. Harmon's ex-wife and Albie (Michelle Conway and Jakob) are getting out of the car and going to the front door. Midway to the door John yells, "Cut! You're racing, guys. You're racing. You gotta believe that if it's slow, it's slow. It's harder to do slow, I know."

After one take Bo Harwood announces that the sound was great.

"It's great for sound," John says to Al, "was it great for camera?"

"Not great. Pretty good."
"Pretty good, what's that? Can we use it?"
"Sure," Al says.
"So what's pretty good?"
"Pretty good is pretty good. If you want great, *you'll* have to shoot it."

Between set-ups I'm milling about with several others in John's office. Doe Avedon, the Cassavetes' secretary, holds up an invoice and announces: "Four thousand dollars, and John didn't remember signing for it!"

Today's work will be necessary to the final cut.

MONDAY, JUNE 6 – *About your life*

More pick-ups, transitions, and occasional re-takes. Some of today's work is experimental: ideas John had over the weekend, like inserting the "beautiful/secrets" speech as Harmon's secretary Charlene is about to drive away and leave him alone with Albie: "You know, there are secrets I always believe in. You know, I always believe that when people reveal these secrets they always become beautiful, and I always feel great." John is dropping this concept here and there, so when he edits he'll have many choices as to its place in the picture.

"You make a movie to tell what you know about life – about your life. But after waiting around for eight hours, for set-ups, for lights, all of it, when it comes time to shoot you're thinking, 'I don't wanna tell you about my life anymore! Why should I tell *you* about my life?!'"

John's speaking more to my wife than to me. It's her first time on the set and their first meeting, and it is in Cassavetes' code of courtesy that, when introduced to someone as important as a wife, he makes time. He even makes coffee. He sits and talks. Family is central to Cassavetes. I've been admitted to his film-making clan, so when I bring family not only are they made welcome, they're treated like they're *supposed to* be here.

There are three sets of three-generation families on *Love Streams.* Ted Allan is co-writer; his daughter Charlene plays the secretary; her daughter Bronwen plays one of the young women. Sam Shaw is an active consultant and works on publicity; his son Larry is the still photographer; Larry's son Jakob is Albie. Diahnne Abbott plays Susan, her mother Margaret plays Susan's mother, and her son is Susan's son. There were to have been four three-generation families in the picture – John's late mother was to play a cabdriver. His daughter Xan is a back-up singer at the club, and a sheet labeled "Cast List" and dated May 15 names daughter Zoe as Gena/Susan's daughter Debbie, a crucial role. More family and significant others abound: set designer Phedon Papamichaels is John's cousin; Phedon's girlfriend and Eddie Donno's wife will play hookers in Las Vegas; sons of Al Ruban and Seymour Cassel (playing Gena's husband) work on the crew; Gena's brother David Rowlands plays her psychiatrist. Cassavetes' films have featured his parents, Gena's mother and brother, the Cassavetes' children, and the family and friends of their friends. As he would say, "That's the way we make pictures." John never says, "That's the way *I* make pictures." Always "we."

As Phedon would tell me, in his Greek accent, "He gets everybody *involved* in the film and he gets everybody *love* making the film and makes everybody believe that it's *their* film, not John's." We. Even a guy with nothing to contribute but a notebook is already saying, "We shot this," "We did that."

This morning John is happy to have a new person, my wife, off whom to bounce ideas. He's spent the weekend making notes "to remind myself what the movie's *about.*" All his concentration is on Gena's first day of shooting, the day after tomorrow. He says he must keep the audience wondering, unsure if Gena's Sarah is Robert Harmon's first wife, old girlfriend, friend, or relative – so that viewers won't draw quick pat conclusions about Sarah and Robert.

Talking about the characters John never speaks of them by

name. Robert Harmon is "me" or "the guy." Sarah is "Gena."

"The guy is transferring his affections constantly, from this one to that other one, all the time, but when Gena comes she cuts through, right through all that. Where *she's* coming from is, the end of a marriage. Maybe her husband and her kid did love her, but they didn't want to live that way anymore, with fights and tension all the time. The memories were beautiful but it was over. They've been through times when someone knows you're vulnerable, knows it, but they keep sticking their finger in it, again and again. They can't stop. It becomes a habit. So relationships maybe end, but love doesn't end. But *he* thinks it does. But Gena knows that he's wrong, it *doesn't,* even when you want it to. It goes on. But the thing is, not to *say* that, in the script, but to *do* it. So that 10 scenes later *you* think, 'This guy's full of shit.'

"All he has, to hold him together, is style. Style is all a guy like this ends up depending on. But his style collapses in the presence of Gena. He's suffering mentally. He doesn't know it, even, but he's suffering mentally. Physically he doesn't even notice himself. Gets the shit kicked out of him, falls down stairs, could get laid five times over – doesn't notice. But Gena is suffering psychically – collapsing, having spells – because in her *mind,* her mentality, it's *decided.* She made a bargain, a marriage, and that's *it,* she doesn't want anything but."

Several people have been hanging just within earshot, waiting to interrupt when John takes a deep enough breath. They have questions, they need decisions on a thousand and one things, all the time. Cassavetes, like any director, is constantly shifting from the interior levels of his story to the exterior demands of what goes where and how much and when. Half the time his people leave these swift technical discussions exasperated because now that's it time to shoot a given shot Cassavetes is saying something different from what they'd discussed earlier. There is the usual altercation, the usual brand-new decision toward an unexpected approach to a scene that, just moments ago, seemed set and ready. As soon as his latest questioner is out of earshot, John says, "Only a schmuck comes on the set day after day, every day, and says it has to be *this* way, we have to follow *that* decision. The film goes its own way, makes its own demands, *and you go with it.* If you don't, you're dead. They say, 'You always change your mind.' Yes! I change my mind! I change."

It isn't until the day is over that my wife reminds me, "Didn't he tell us that this picture is about *his* life? You were taking notes, isn't that in your notes?" I look at the notes and there it is: "You make a movie to tell what you know about life – about your life." Obviously *Love Streams* can be no more than metaphorically about his life, since Robert Harmon and John Cassavetes lead, on the surface, very different lives. *How* it's about his life is... none of our business. But *he* said so. He said so while I sat there with a notebook writing it down, at his invitation.

No, I don't know just what to make of that. But there it is.

Most of today's shooting will be discarded or pared down to the most minimal possible use in the final cut.

TUESDAY, JUNE 7 – *A cinema of alcohol*

Thirteen set-ups in John's house while most of the crew converts a Burbank warehouse into a soundstage for Gena's first scenes tomorrow. Cassavetes shoots the following passage out-of-sequence: the beginning and end today, the middle [in brackets below] on June 14.

Robert and Albie in the morning in the empty house. Robert – formal in a gray sports coat and black shirt, smoking – stands looking at his sleeping son. Albie has slept in his clothes. He wakes, wants the bathroom, Harmon directs him to it. Albie asks to use his toothbrush, his father's answer is a curt "Use your finger." Robert says they'll have breakfast but they have to clean up the house first. "If I have breakfast without cleaning up, I vomit." [Smoking in his bar, Harmon pours himself a drink while the boy frantically runs around the house cleaning up the detritus left by the girls. Albie's very eager to please, calling in reports to his father that he's almost done. Then he sits across the bar from his father. Harmon offers him a choice between a Coke and a beer. Albie wants a beer. For the first time Harmon smiles a little at the boy, pouring him a beer. Harmon suggests a toast, but the boy scarfs down some beer without toasting. At this Harmon laughs softly, shaking his head slightly, his first sincere laugh in the film. They talk – much more difficult for Harmon than for Albie. Harmon urges eight-year-old Albie to finish his beer.] Then Albie's in the living room alone, singing nonsense syllables, trying to light a cigarette – clearly the kid is drunk.

Albie sees two cabs pull into the driveway, yells for his father, his father comes, Albie tells him of the cabs. Harmon, drunk, tells Albie to go outside and tell whoever it is to go away. The boy just stands there.

In 1959 Cassavetes starred in TV's *Johnny Staccato,* portraying a detective who plays jazz piano. In an episode he directed, a wasted blond chick (and "chick" is the word) tells Staccato, "Oh, don't worry, I'm a deceptive drunk. I don't slur, I don't weave, I don't stagger."

John drinks a lot but he neither slurs, nor weaves, nor staggers. His closest friends and drinking buddies swear they've never seen him drunk. They'll speak of, say, a two-hour conversation in which he downs an entire fifth of whiskey with no more effect than if he'd been drinking coffee. I haven't seen that, but I've seen enough to believe it.

Love Streams is John's 11th film. In all but two – *A Child Is Waiting* (1963), written by Abby Mann, and John's made-for-a-mass-audience *Gloria* (1980) – alcohol is central. Alcohol is almost a character in Casssavetes' cinema, an unnamed character who always shows up and makes things happen. In 1959's *Shadows,* crucial scenes pivot upon the characters' drunkenness. In 1961, *Too Late Blues'* central scene, the scene that changes every character in the film, could never have happened if they weren't all drunk. *Too Late Blues'* female lead, played by Stella Stevens, fits to a tee the cliché phrase "a hopeless alcoholic" – and, though nothing could be more clear, no character in the picture mentions it. In *Faces* (1968) and *Husbands* (1970), most of the characters are drinking and/or drunk most of the time. Gena Rowlands' establishing scene as Minnie (*Minnie and Moskowitz,* 1971) has her drinking during a conversation with an old woman; by the end of their talk she's so loaded she stumbles and almost falls down a flight stairs. Gena's Mabel in *A Woman Under the Influence* (1975) gets drunk enough to pick up a guy in a bar, take him home, and sleep with him in the bed she shares with her husband – an event that triggers her breakdown. As her husband Nick, Peter Falk lets his three small children drink beer on an outing so that when they get home they'll be tired enough to sleep. *The Killing of a Chinese Bookie* (1976) occurs mostly in bars, though if Ben Gazzarra's Cosmo is a drunk he's of the "deceptive" variety. And the climactic scene of *Opening Night* (1978) is Gena's actress taking the stage so drunk she can barely stand.

In *Love Streams* there's nothing at all deceptive about Robert Harmon's alcoholism – so much so, that all he can think to do with his eight-year-old is to drink with him.

Later I'll think it odd that in all our conversations about Harmon's character no one mentions he's an alcoholic; nor, during the shoot, do I myself notice this, even though I'm an alcoholic too and this summer I've only temporarily quit. But alcohol is such a given in Cassavetes' cinema, so ever-present (like the cigarettes), that it becomes almost invisible. It's as though the films themselves get drunk, but, like John, they yet remain fully alert. That's part of their magic, how they're always, again like John, a little crazy, a little dangerous, you never know what they'll do next, yet they grip and/or repel you like no other cinema.

I can't affix the jargon of dramatic criticism to the role of alcohol in John's films. Alcohol is far too penetrating a presence to be called a motif. (A Cassavetes motif would be: women who suddenly attempt suicide in bathrooms, as they do in *Too Late Blues, Faces, Minnie and Moskowitz,* and *A Woman Under the Influence.*) And the drinking is too unstated, its presence almost too unconscious, to be called a theme. Themes are, if not resolved, at least addressed.

Or perhaps one could make a case that, after all, the theme of alcohol is addressed in *Love Streams'* final shot:

Robert Harmon waving goodbye while gripping a goblet of whiskey.

Today's work will be in the final cut.

WEDNESDAY, JUNE 8 – *Gena's first day*

The two cabs whose arrival Albie announced to Robert Harmon carry Sarah Lawson [Gena Rowlands] and her many pieces of luggage. Now Cassavetes doubles back to the beginning of the film to shoot Gena's scenes in sequence until her character drives up that hill.

Today Cassavetes' shoots Gena's first scene. It's long – six pages of script. Sarah Lawson and her daughter Debbie [Risa Blewitt] enter a drab empty meeting-room. They're soon joined by Judge Dunbar [Joan Foley]. Sarah is tense, Debbie sullen. Sarah's lawyer [Al Ruban, an actor today] enters. Though his words of greeting to Sarah are perfectly normal, he speaks as though she's made of fine glass and will break if jarred. Sarah's husband Jack [Seymour Cassel] enters with his lawyer [Tom Badal]. The business of the meeting is the Lawsons' final divorce agreement. Jack wants their daughter to wait in the hall, Sarah doesn't; Jack, his face a study in resignation, accedes; Debbie stays. As soon as Judge Dunbar begins the meeting, Sarah changes the rules: she's taking Debbie out of town for an indefinite time, doesn't know when they'll be back. The judge is confused. Even Sarah's lawyer is surprised. The judge notes that Jack's visiting-rights are clear in the agreement; such a trip violates that agreement.

Sarah explains that she and her daughter often go to funerals and visit the sick, because "people like Debbie and me to be with them when they aren't feeling well, because we're cheerful." The judge doesn't understand. "Well, you see, Judge, when someone is temporarily insane, like Jack here – and he's a wonderful guy! – but you see, when someone is like that, they don't want to see the people they really love. Ok, then, I understand that. So when Jack finishes his sleeping around everywhere, and he wants to assume his responsibilities, he wants to be a real father to Debbie, he can see her. And if Debbie is a very old lady when he makes up his mind, that's when he'll see her. Ok?"

Her daughter is mortified, while Jack's expression is a study in guilt and grief. Jack explains to the judge that "my wife has been in institutions" since they got married, "and that's one of the reasons we're having difficulty with something we've already agreed to, she hasn't been cured."

"I have a problem," Sarah tells the judge, "I love my family. I love him and I love her, I love them, just them. And when I can't, eh, be cheerful – you know, when you get a headache, or you really feel bad – I go to the hospital, and I stay there until I feel that I can take care of things again… Until, until his little sex things are over, or whatever it is that causes me to get the headache – something like that."

These speeches read much more swiftly than they're spoken. Pauses, inflections, silences, looks between the characters, are the real content of the scene; the dialogue is merely their framework, and a vehicle for some information.

We're shooting in an industrial warehouse in a desolate neighborhood of Burbank. Phedon Papamichael and his crew have constructed the realistic interior of a faceless municipal building. They've painted the walls vaguely sickening shades of green and gray. The desks, filing cabinets, and such, seem decades old, coated with bureaucratic boredom. It looks like a place where no one wants to be. It looks just right.

Shooting at John's house everybody's bunched together and you see only those you're in the room with. In this warehouse you see everybody all at once, at their tasks or between tasks or goofing off or waiting to be told what to do, an international patchwork of Israeli gaffers and camera assistants, a Polish production assistant, a French photographer, a German production assistant, a Greek designer, a Mexican boom-man, Canadian sound-mixers and grips, New Yorkers (a nationality all their own), and various types and colors of Americans. Very like the mix you'll find crewing a circus.

Our ringmaster, for the first time, appears relaxed, even buoyant. It is the first shooting-day that John Cassavetes doesn't have to be Robert Harmon – doesn't need to wear, like a costume, Harmon's despair. In his at-home clothing of baggy pants and a knit sweater pulled tight over his alarming belly, he's holding forth to a few fascinated crew members, telling tales of Hollywood.

A Child Is Waiting, 20 years ago. A 33-year-old Casssavetes has been improbably hired by producer Stanley Kramer (director of *High Noon, Judgment at Nuremberg)* to direct Burt Lancaster and Judy Garland in a script by Abby Mann (writer of *Judgment at Nuremberg)* – all those traditionalists and rebellious Johnny Staccato (as I call him privately). The picture depicts the dilemmas of teaching mentally retarded children, and (in a brave move) all but the lead kid and one kid in a supporting role were actual retarded children. Garland looks like a misplaced showgirl, Lancaster a misplaced gunfighter, but nothing can diminish the beauty and poignancy of the children. John tells of Abby Mann patrolling the set, on the look out for improvisation – there must be no ad-libs, no changes to his precious script. Thumbing pages after a take Mann asks, "Did Burt improvise that line? Where's this scene? Where are we?" "Is *walking* improvising?" John retorts – then directs the actors to walk, just walk and walk, with cameras rolling, until Mann huffs off the set. John's verdict now: "He's not a bad guy, just square."

Which is one of the worst things Cassavetes can say about anyone.

Eddie Donno passes by, sniping, "There's one thing wrong with Al's sense of humor – he doesn't have one."

John goes on with his tale. Stanley Kramer and Abby Mann didn't let him near the editing room. When he saw their cut, they'd discarded many shots of the retarded kids. Lancaster and Garland seemed to be speechifying to themselves or to the audience, not in a classroom of unpredictable, beautiful, heartbreaking people. John went nuts. He charged the screen, tore holes in it, banged his head against the wall. "Nobody in the room said anything – but the next day I was out."

I'm thinking of what he said in our interview last summer:

"Well – I was young. And I felt that *everybody* had talent. And that for some reason they were being arbitrary and not employing that talent. 'Cause I thought, 'Well, these people are the giants of an industry, they must have a brain and a good heart and ability, how come they don't use it?' And Gena, she'd say, 'Look, a lot of people don't have the same drives, the same desires, the same gun that sparks them as you do. You're acting like these people understand you. Nobody understands you. *I* don't understand you! How the hell can anybody understand you?! You're nuts!'

"But I would think *she* was crazy! And I would go in and think, 'Naw, this sonofabitch understands what I'm talking about, he just, for some reason, doesn't want to do it. I don't know what the hell it is with this guy.' And I'd meet these people years later and we'd become friends and they'd say, 'I didn't know what the hell you were talking about.' Because I'd go like a maniac. Because I figure, if you work on a picture *that's your life.*"

Suddenly John isn't talking to us anymore. He's looking past us, his eyes are fixed and unblinking, his stare burns. His eyes possess, truly, the property of heat. He's staring at Gena.

She's just appeared, ready for her first take, about 15 yards away. Eyes fixed upon her, John absently tells a production assistant to get some accessory or other – a shopping bag, I think. Without another word to us, he walks swiftly to her.

John gives sharp, definite instructions, people move quickly, some shout "Rehearsal!" – while Gena stands dazed, as though hypnotized. She answers questions in an absent, disembodied voice, and usually her eyes focus far past the shoulder of the questioner. And nobody, but nobody, approaches Gena unless it's absolutely necessary. I've never seen anyone project such a powerful quality of private intensity; it surrounds her like a force-field in a sci-fi movie, a protective circle of energy, you can almost see it.

Her concentration is so total, she has a quality of incandescence.

After a few days Gena Rowlands will relax into the gentle, reserved, ironic and gracious person she usually is. There will be time to be "normal" after the tone of her performance is set, after her character has come to life. Standing here now, Gena carefully, delicately holds all the potentialities of Sarah Lawson; in these first few days she will *create* the character of Sarah in order to *play* that character for the rest of the picture. Now the actress Gena Rowlands is not wasting one instant of concentration on anything "normal."

The quality of her beauty has always been elusive – almost as though it hasn't much to do with her physicality or even with her classically lovely, highly intelligent visage. The gorgeous young stunner of *Faces;* confused Minnie of *Minnie and Moskowitz,* unsure whether or not life is passing her by; ragged Mabel of *A Woman Under the Influence,* pressured by fierce "influences" of all kinds; the elegant, brilliant theatrical star of *Opening Night;* the savvy, stylish gun-mol of *Gloria;* and Sarah Lawson now, middle-aged, not made up to be lovely but to reveal the strains of her experience (there are lines beneath her eyes that sometimes, in some lights, look like scars) – you could never mistake one of these characters for the other, but all radiate different frequencies of a pensive, almost preoccupied quality, something unspoken and never to be spoken ("every beautiful woman has a secret"). Whatever its elements, this quality shines a light upon any object of her attention, a revelatory light that changes our perspective of what we're seeing in unexpected ways – as thought *she's* lighting the scene. In person as well as on screen, we react to this quality much more than to her great beauty, and it complicates her beauty. Too complicated for Hollywood's usual scenarios (which is the only explanation for why Gena never became, in Hollywood's usual sense, a "big star"). John Cassavetes has devoted himself again and again, with a sense of mission, to revealing Gena Rowlands' unique quality on film in all its shades and variations – yet *she* never seems revealed, only this radiant force of hers, sometimes as disturbing as it is beautiful.

I see now that this disturbing beauty, or beautiful disturbance, is how Gena is very like her husband – as different as they may seem. Even when young and marquee handsome, John's was not a look most girls would moon over or most boys make a hero of. There was something disturbing about handsome young John, some wild depth, best approached warily. Both, in their way, are equally mysterious.

Even, perhaps especially, to each other. Later John will tell me, "Gena is so *absolutely* private that – I didn't know she played the piano for 10 years! I walk in one day, she's playing – I hear this, I thought it was a record, a fantastic concert. I walked in and I got terribly angry with her. 'What the hell are you doing?! You're playing the piano! You never told me you played the piano! This is such a double-cross, I don't understand what the hell is going on!' I walk out, I get angry, and she got angry back at me, see? And she wouldn't speak to me for two weeks over this thing. We never mentioned it again."

Gena will tell me, "You never know with John. You never know. John's very mysterious. And – and – keeps his, his – you just *really* never know."

And love, John has said, "is the ability of not knowing."

Seymour Cassel is also on set for the first time. He worked with John behind the camera on *Shadows* and was the very spirit of *Faces* in a performance nominated for an Academy Award®. In *Minnie and Moskowitz,* sporting long hair and a handlebar moustache, he wooed and married Gena. Today they're getting divorced. For *Love Streams* John told Seymour once again to grow Moskowitz's moustache.

Fast-talking Seymour constantly wisecracks, sometimes repeating a quip until he's sure everybody's heard. His beat-up face speaks of hard living; his eyes are direct, intelligent, sympathetic. Though his lines in *Love Streams* are few and fragmentary, the way he watches Gena is rich with nuance, indelible. He conveys the agony of a man who understands but who is incapable of implementing his understanding. The solemnity of his performance (is there another film in which Sey never smiles?) couldn't be less like his off-camera irrepressibleness. Seymour behaves like a man holding a lit match in each hand, squirming as they're about to burn his fingers, but he *must* say all that's on his mind quickly before he can say, "Ouch!" – and it would never occur to him to drop the match.

George Sims, a mainstay camera-operator on *Faces,* will man one of the two cameras in the scene we're to shoot – no doubt John asked him to participate on Gena's first day to make both she and Seymour more comfortable. Sey tells John he wants George to shoot his close-ups, "for luck."

The setting is a bare meeting room, furnished with two tables at right angles, chairs, a water cooler – together they occupy most of the available space. Into what's left John crams two 35-mm cameras (John on one, Sims on the other), two camera-assistants, script coordinator Helen Caldwell, dialogue coach Robert Fieldsteel, assistant director Eddie Donno, plus me and my notebook. With the actors, that makes eight people generating a lot of heat under hot lights on a hot day, while the air conditioning's turned off for the shot. The air just hangs there. It's like acting in a freight elevator.

"And to think we made this space for ourselves," quips Al Ruban.

There are four walls and they don't "fly," as they say in the theater, they're nailed firmly down. But if this wasn't the way Cassavetes wanted it, Phedon Papamichael wouldn't have built it. As John will say, "Who wants it to work smoothly? You *want* it to work rough." In this crucial scene he wants his actors to feel they're not on a set but in a room. And I suspect he wants an enclosure around Gena, so Sarah Lawson can feel trapped.

"I'm getting nervous," John tells me during while sound is testing the room. "When I'm an actor I have control. I can pick up a prop, move, whatever I want. But this… See…" His voice trails off. John distinguishes between directing and controlling. He wants his actors to surprise him, but, especially when directing Gena, it makes him anxious as hell. "I'm not interested in the *scene*. I'm just interested in what happens between people."

George Sims will shoot "the scene," master-shots, medium shots, close-ups. John will shoot "what happens between people," his camera roaming the room, searching out twitches, gestures, the husband staring at his lost wife, the girl pressing her cheek against her mother's shoulder (no one directed her to do that). Between takes John tells me, "It takes an awful lot of stuff [footage] to get an impressionistic shot. I'm going all over, trying to find what isn't there. The girl's eyebrow as she's leaning against her mother."

Just before the second take of Al Ruban's entrance, Robert Fieldsteel asks John, "Do you *want* Al to come in so early? Because they're still talking."

"Yeah, then it's reality, otherwise it's too theatrical."

John's actors are given great freedom of movement and gesture, but their choices are by no means random. Both Gena and Seymour perform speeches that are so realistic some will no doubt think they're improvised. They aren't (but for one Seymour ad-lib, which he then repeats exactly in other takes). In every take they give their lines the same emphasis, rhythmical values, timbres, pauses. On some takes the general energy works better than on others, but their precision is constant.

After changing one set-up John asks Seymour, "That's not the way you are the whole scene is it?"

"No," Sey tells him, "I do this, and then…" Quickly, like a tape on fast-forward, Seymour enacts all his various shifts of gesture and posture during an eight-minute take. Complete awareness. Later Gena does the same.

For the second time during a single take Gena's sound goes bad. Bo Harwood tells John, "I've gotta wire her again."

"Then let's break for lunch," John hisses, "'cause this is bullshit." He pauses, breathes. It's too early to break and he knows it. "Ok, if you gotta wire her again then *you* rewire her," not one of the assistants. Everyone hovers while Gena's rewired. At such times, and between set-ups, she is still, meets no one's eyes, quietly mouths her lines. When it's time for her shot they slap the slate right in front of her face, she winces, jolts, startled – as though, as far as she's concerned, the crew suddenly appeared out of nowhere.

In this small room John does 11 set-ups. Takes go on for eight or nine minutes. There are more technical distractions, infuriating. Masking tape peels off the lights, a guy's got to get a ladder and tape it up again. We wait. The room is so hot sweat's pouring down my legs inside my jeans. Eddie's goes to check out the delay and we hear him yell, "That's YOUR fucking job!" We're shooting again and film rattles in the camera magazines, John slams the magazine with his fist but doesn't call a cut, telling his actors, "Alright, kids, no fallin' apart now, I want to finish this scene." They roll, John surprises everyone with, "Cut! Just start again. Seymour, don't do *anything* unless you mean it." Rolling again, "Gena, look't the judge a minute, sweet." Still rolling, "Sey, move out of the way, just say your ad lib lines out loud now." When the take's done, "Marvelous, guys. Really wonderful."

When it's all over John grins at me. "Michael, Michael, Michael."

Though I've been in her line of sight most of the day, Gena now notices me as though I just walked in. "Michael! How are you?"

"Michael," Al calls, beckoning me to him. I go. "Michael, I want you to come in tomorrow a bit more depressed."

"I was *concentrating*."

He rolls his eyes.

Bo tells me he didn't mean to, but he insulted Gena with a comment about the sound screwing up because she wore silk and polyester that grate on the mike. He imitates her response: "Bo, we've worked together many, many years, and you know I never wear polyester."

At dailies, passing the booze around and lighting cigarettes, everybody feels great. We've watched a superb actress at her best. It's the real deal, and we all know it.

Well, everybody feels great except maybe Al. Not without humor, he scowls at John. "Fuckin' hustled into having to play a fucking scene where everybody turns their back on me."

Co-writer Ted Allan sits on John's left, I'm on John's right. John can't help second-guessing himself, maybe he should have tried for more humor today. Then, "Naw, it wouldn't work, it's too early in the movie." He loves the scene, but maybe he should shoot it again in the morning. Naw, he doesn't want to put Gena through that so soon. "Today I was so screwed up. But – I didn't know what was going on and I don't *want* to know, I don't want to know the answers." He laughs his wheezy laugh. "The editor's gonna kill me, we shot 12,000 feet of film today!"

As dailies roll Cassavetes tells Ted, "Are you pretending you know what this is about? Because if you *are*, I'm never going to speak to you again!"

"*I* don't know," Ted protests. "I'm the last person in the *world* to know."

After dailies I drive John home. He can't stop talking about the day. "I *love* making films. I love it. I love the process of it."

Today's work is key. These six pages of script and 12,000 feet of footage will make for an intense seven minutes of screen time – and two of those minutes are simply the business of everyone entering the room and settling down for the meeting, shot and acted so beautifully it's riveting.

THURSDAY, JUNE 9 – *If I die*

The same room, some weeks later. Things have changed. Debbie sits near her father. He's patting her hand. The lawyers and the judge are there. Sarah enters late, flustered, apologizing. She sits across the table from her husband. The meeting begins with Debbie announcing, "Mother, I wanna go with my father. I hate my life with you."

Sarah, slightly unsteady, stands, goes to her lawyer, asks for his chair, sits down as he moves to another chair. Sarah says some helpless words to her daughter, who stands and goes to her, stands behind her, says, "I wanna go with my father. I don't want to go with you anymore. I don't wanna be a slave."

Sarah gives a nervous laugh, stands. "I see. Nobody leaves this room – until we find out what it means. I can discuss it. I have lots of time."

The judge is confused. "What is it you want to discuss?"

"Love." Said as an exhausted brief syllable.

The judge tries to calm her down, but now there's something far-off in Sarah's expression, she walks toward the door, the judge protests, Sarah opens the door, walks down the hall as her lawyer hurries after.

In a large municipal office-room filled with desks and people at their bureaucratic chores, Sarah collapses. People rush to her, to revive her. Jack stands grimly, as though he's seen it all before. Debbie kneels and pats her hair.

Gena is still under glass, inaccessible behind the force of her concentration. She's preparing to say the word "love."

Someone once said of Billie Holiday that she never sang the word "love" casually – she'd bend it, twist it, breathe it, spit it, always extracting a different essence from that inadequate word. Gena's pronunciation of "love" today will remind me of that. Cassavetes' films revolve around souls who must, almost on pain of death, decipher for themselves that baffling word. This, he will tell me, is what *philosophy* is all about. I'm surprised he'd even use the word, and he explains why.

"*Philos,* in Greek, means 'friend' or 'love.' And any *ophy* is 'the study of.' So it's the study of love. And to have a philosophy is to know *how* to love. And to know where to put it. And to know the importance of friendships, and the importance of continuity. And all the other philosophies, negative philosophies, seem to be a more modern bastardization of what *philosophy* is.

"And I don't think a person can live without a philosophy. That is, where can you love? What's the important place where you can *put* that thing – 'cause you can't put it everywhere, you'd walk around, you gotta be a minister or a priest saying, 'Yes, my son,' or 'Yes, my daughter, bless you.' But people don't live that way. They live with anger and hostility and problems and lack of money – with tremendous disappointments in their life. So what they need is a philosophy, what I think everybody needs, in a way, is to say, *Where and how can I love, can I be in love so that I can live – so that I can live with some degree of peace?* You know?

"And I guess every picture we've ever done has been, in a way, to try to find some kind of philosophy for the characters in the film. And so that's why I have a need for the characters to really analyze love, discuss it, kill it, destroy it, hurt each other, do all that stuff – in that war, in that word-polemic and picture-polemic of what life is.

"And the rest of the stuff doesn't really interest me. It may interest other people, but I have a one-track mind. That's all I'm interested in, is *love.* And the lack of it. When it stops. And the pain that's caused by loss or things taken away from us that we really need. So *Love Streams* is just – another picture in search of that grail."

We're crammed into the room again. It's hotter than yesterday. Sarah Lawson will appear with her husband and daughter later in *Love Streams,* but only in dreams or fantasies or at different ends of a telephone. In those exchanges she will be an outcast, exiled from her family. Today is her last moment as wife and mother of a family together in one room, this room of divorce, where for eight takes we watch Sarah presented with her daughter's defection, and eight times – in the voice of an exhausted child, a voice of ancientness that children sometimes have – she says "love" as briefly and softly and with as much pain as it can be said.

The other actors respond to the word as though she's placed on the table some especially revolting object. They look here, there, everywhere but at each other, terribly uncomfortable. Only Seymour's Jack stares at Sarah, with no give in his stare.

Through it all, of course, is the business of direction. John telling Risa Blewitt (Debbie), "Don't look at the camera, please – look at your father, look at anybody, but don't look at the camera, it wastes the shot. Don't laugh, Ris." Sey was making faces at her. "Seymour, leave her alone. Ok, Gena." They roll, "Look at your wife, Seymour. Start again, Risa." Between takes Gena asks the script supervisor, "Helen, did I have my purse on my lap or on the desk?" When Gena/Sarah stands and walks out of the room, John's camera makes a wider movement than they'd rehearsed. Eddie Donno catches what's happening, gets the boom man out of the way, sweeps us all back with his arm and body, all of us silently cramming into one corner while Gena and Al, on camera, walk very near and past us.

While they're setting up the first shot in the outer office, where Gena collapses, I speak with Robert Fieldsteel. As dialogue coach, he works with John on line-memorizing. Fieldsteel tells me, "It's been pretty rare that something written gets changed. What usually happens is people filling in what isn't there." During line-sessions John will change the dialogue sometimes, "feeling for the moments," figuring how they'll be shot. "Re-writing happens then, instead of on-camera."

Nearby Helen Caldwell tells John a lady from ABC TV wants an interview. John instructs, "Call them back, tell them 'I can't get hold of him, he's shooting, he's not seeing anyone, you know how crazy he is.'"

Behind us Al Ruban thinks the next shot would be easier if the walls could 'fly' as they shoot, and confronts Phedon Papamichael: "*Will* that wall fly?"

"We have a way to get it out."

"*How* we gonna get it out?"

"We have a way to get it out."

"Tell me."

The wall doesn't fly. No way to "get it out" without dismantling it.

They work a long time on a tracking shot: the camera on a dolly keeping pace with Gena as she walks into the larger office and collapses. But the floor of this warehouse is too rough, the camera bounces – even the tiniest bounce registers on film. They polish the floor. Still too rough. The dolly-puller smooths the wheels with something oily. Still too rough. They try the tracking shot anyway. Several times. They instruct 'background' (the extras working at their desks), "Ok, Background, we have two cameras working [tracking and stationary], there's no place to hide, so have something to do at all times." The tracking shot never works. Too rough.

The first time Gena collapses she bravely falls onto the concrete floor. John winces. "We'll print that, it's very believable, but I'd like it to be so you know it's coming, so that it's not fainting." He doesn't want his wife to risk that again. Without needing rehearsal, in the next take Gena creates an extraordinary sequence in which we see Sarah slip into a kind of controlled catatonia, stopping, slumping, lying flat. Spooky, authentic. That's the take they'll use.

Now she's on the floor and must freeze in place while the next shot sets up. The 'background' who've run to help her must also freeze. For five minutes – fast for a new set-up, but a long time to freeze. Next take, John instructs an extra near Gena, "Take her hand," and tells Gena, "Keep your fingers stiff." She stiffens them. "Stiffer than that." Gena complies and says, "Like that?" "Stiffer than that."

Next take, Sey is slow to enter the action. "Come on, Seymour, shit, I said ACTION 10 minutes ago – ACTION is ACTION, come on, man."

Bo Harwood calls a cut. John wants to know why. "I'm trying to get some support for the wireless [mike], because the background sound is so loud, and when I brought it up I got a fizzle." A jet passes overhead – we're near Burbank Airport – and John says, "I know there's a plane in there but I think it sounds interesting." He prints the take.

There's a lot of this. Through all of it, Gena lies on the floor without moving a muscle. When it's over, she's not aware. John has to tell her, "You can get up, Gena."

During a pause, John whispers to me, "This is the part I hate."

Today there have been 10 set-ups, 28 takes.

At dailies, John shakes George Villasenor's hand. John often shakes the hand of someone he hasn't seen for maybe a day. It's a custom he makes a point of. Very Mediterranean, very Old World. In his life, as in his films, he carefully marks when someone enters his world and when someone exits.

We're watching the 12,000 feet of yesterday's work. Sitting next to John I'm aware of his utter fascination with each moment on screen – more intense than I've seen before, as though he never tires of watching Gena. He can see her deliver the same speech for hours of takes on the set, then watch those same takes during hours of dailies, and on the umpteenth take he'll be thrilled by some tiny thing she hadn't done before, some new wrinkling of her brow, and he laughs out loud, "Terrific! She's a terrific woman!"

Tonight I learn that he knows – knows how serious his condition is.

He smiles as the lights go up in the screening room and says quietly, to no one in particular, "This is a sweet film. If I die, this is a sweet last film."

Today's office scene will be crucial. The hours of work on Sarah's hall-walk and collapse will be 20 seconds of the final cut.

FRIDAY, JUNE 10 – *Love is a stream*

A hard sharp cut from Sarah's collapse to Sarah talking with her psychiatrist [played by Gena's brother, David Rowlands]. He tells her to go to Europe, get some "balance," get some sex.

Then we see her frantic in a Paris train station, with an insane amount of luggage, convincing a French porter to help her.

The warehouse again. John sees me come in and walks straight to me, gesturing to the new set, built during the night. "Now *this* scene – I'm really *interested* in this scene, 'cause we can *do* something now. The *bonds* are coming off. *Now* we can be there."

Pieces of yesterday's set are piled in a corner. Phedon's constructed a convincing new set of a psychiatrist's office. The first thing John does is place Gena behind the doctor's desk, in the doctor's chair. He sits the doctor, David, in the patient's chair, tells him to take his shoes off, rest his black-stockinged feet on the desk, saying, "In these offices the patient is always in the dark. That's why we switch places. Because psychologists are always mysterioso, and *he* doesn't know these people."

Quietly to Gena as they roll film, "Don't think anything. Just sit there, don't think anything."

They start the scene and soon John cuts. "Start all over again." Gena has a cigarette in her hand. "Throw the cigarette." She throws it. "I want to see nothing but jokes."

"*Jokes*?" she asks.

"Jokes."

Nobody knows what he's talking about. This scene has no jokes.

Then, to Gena: "Gotta take it. Gotta take it on the button here. There can't be any defenses. One thing you gotta be afraid of is, don't be corny. Don't be a self-pitying person at all costs. If it gets, 'Oh, what am I going to do?' – then you're in trouble. So no feeling sorry for yourself – you just know the way things are. Be calm about it. If you get excited, it's because you get excited, not because you're frustrated."

John goes to her and whispers so low that even in this small room we hear nothing. Then, "So that, all your behavior is the mannerisms of a real crazy person, but you're not crazy – it's that you don't want to tell him. 'Sex? I don't have any, and the funny thing is I really don't need it.' And it's true, you don't."

There's some noise beyond the walls and John calls out, "I don't want anybody back there! All I hear is clink clonk clink clink clink!" Eddie Donno shuts everybody up.

John calls action. The scene begins incisively, in the middle of a thought. I'll bracket in italics lines that will be cut in the editing room:

"So what do you think it is?" the doctor asks Sarah.

"Loss."

"You don't own anything – so how can you lose something you don't own?"

"Love – is a – *stream*. It's continuous. It doesn't stop."

"No, it does stop."

"Oh no," Sarah says, firm, "it does *not* stop. [*I am the first one to wish that it does stop. I would be the happiest person in the world if it did, but it doesn't. Does that make me crazy?*

"No. Imbalanced. Not crazy.] Your love is too strong for your family."

[*"I know. I've heard that before. Do you have any cigarettes? Would you hand me my purse?" He does.*

"Obsessed," he says. "You have to let them go."

"No."]

"I want you to describe your sexual life."

A pensive pause before she says:

"I don't *have* a sexual life."

"You do."

"I don't – need – a sexual life."

The psychiatrist lights a cigarette, then: "What other interest do you have beside your husband? You speak continually of him, and he doesn't love you."

"That's not true."

John breaks in, we're still rolling, "*Is* that not true? Does your husband not *love* you?"

[*"He loves me, he loves me,"*] she improvises to the doctor.

"NO AD LIBBING!" John shouts.

Without needing to be told (he's acted with John before), David Rowlands reprises the line, "What other interest do you have beside your husband? You speak continually of him, and he doesn't love you."

"It's – that's *not* true – it, uh –"

John interrupted to get that rhythm.

"And of your daughter," says the doctor, "who chose him over you?"

John again, "Gena, put your hands all the way through your hair, both of them, now throw it front of your face." She does this, then says her line:

"No."

"If – you don't let go, and if you don't get some balance in your life, something creative, some sex – I don't care with whom – you're going have to go back into the bug-house – where you don't belong."

Her line now is supposed to be a mocking, *"No, please, no, not that, please,"* but John breaks in before she speaks it: "Don't move. Don't do anything. Just look at him."

This will be one powerful close-up.

David Rowlands continues: [*"Balance.*

"Balance, ok, balance. Balance what?"]

"Go to Europe. They don't know you there. You have money,

see something. Be alone. Meet someone, you're attractive. [*Go to Paris, go to the river, and –"*

"Jump."

"Paint."]

John will reject the snappy ending in favor of a hard cut from "you're attractive" to Gena's difficulties in a Paris railway station.

John: "Let's do the whole scene over again right now!" Gena throws her purse into David's lap.

They'll do several more takes – takes that will incorporate the changes and gestures that John's called for in this take. John gets informal on some of these takes, just letting them go without calling "Action" – but Gena doesn't like that, snaps, "Would you call '*Action*'?" "Alright, I'll call 'action.' ACTION." Her animation is all for the camera. Between takes, between set-ups, her protective energy-field encloses her, she looks off into space, often without blinking, mouths lines to herself. Once she slowly sinks her face into her hands, saying, "I can't *do* this." Then she does it.

When they retake David Rowlands' close-ups, no one can quite remember exactly when he lit his cigarette. John, "It worked before we started discussing it."

Later Gena will tell me, "John has a great affinity for characters that are perceived by the world generally as crazy, or cuckoo, or whacko, or at least eccentric. The character that I play is one of those characters – that most people think is, well, quite crazy. But we don't see it that way. But then, I didn't think Mabel Longhetti in *Woman Under the Influence* was crazy either, where everyone else saw her as patently so. It's just that they have a different dream – a different thing that they wanted out of life. And they're confused as to why it doesn't happen, and how they found themselves in this position where they're marching out of step to everyone else.

"Personally, I don't think anyone is crazy who isn't cruel. To me, cruelty is crazy. Anything short of that, I wouldn't consider crazy. Of course, sometimes if you have a very strong dream and you follow it no matter what, you are inadvertently being cruel g to, because you ride roughshod over others. t actual cruelty, to me that person isn't insane at

tes, he's happy. The scene has clarity and stery of personality and the force of belief. He started loving this film when he watched the ilies from Gena's first scene, because he saw en Jack, Sarah, and Debbie. "In spite of all the ers – *they* don't know about these people, *we* ning about these people – but we know there's between them, that even after all this pain is everything. And the only one who loses is the e's a kid, she has no control. But when her floor, she goes right to her, no matter *what* lo.

calm at the end of the shrink scene because it's nows she loves them, she knows they love *her* bout that, not defensive, not trying to prove it. to that – what she knows."

re's always a devil in John's laugh.) "This is a . I love this picture." He laughs more. "So I o be a bomb! It's a disaster when you love

scene is almost Mack Sennett slapstick: a t of luggage tries to convince an indifferent me to her aid. He doesn't understand English, she doesn't speak French. Gena wants to know where the camera is. It's about a hundred feet away, taking in the entire action. So she acts with her whole body, like a silent movie – Mack Sennett would have approved. One take.

Al, for the only time in this picture, says "Excellent." He then adds, as though to appease his own natural skepticism, "As a matter of fact, it really was kind of nice."

John exults, "One take! The only thing we ever did one take of!"

"The shrink scene," as we call it, plays much longer than it reads – John's emphasis is on the pauses more than on the lines. It's central to the final cut. But John, over the weekend, without even viewing dailies, rejects the "excellent" one-take Paris scene. He'll re-shoot Monday.

MONDAY, JUNE 13 – *He wants you to do it in your way*

Sarah Lawson is frantic in a Paris train station – rather, she's frantic in a somehow-deserted passageway of a station, trying single-handedly to haul two carts loaded shoulder-high with luggage. She's late for a train and can't speak the language to the only other soul around, a porter [Francois Duhamel-Mega] taking a cigarette-break. Using wild sign language and made-up French, she convinces him to help her.

Cut to Victoria Station, London, where again Sarah is frantic, late, needy. At least here she speaks the language. She asks a surprised porter [Jaimie Horton] to place a collect call to her husband in Chicago. She speaks to Jack. It doesn't go well. [Seymour's part of the call will be filmed next month.]

She hangs up and suddenly 'sees' a vision. [John will call this "a dream," also to be shot next month: Sara driving a car, Jack running away. She crashes into him as the car turns over. She gets out, dazed. Jack is dead. But now she sees that the car has killed her daughter as well, Debbie's bloody under the fender. Sarah's 'dream' is clear: her anger at Jack can't help but hurt Debbie too. She can't go home.]

The porter sees she's in quite a state and asks if she's alright.

While they're setting up I hear that tonight at dailies George Villasenor will show the 'assembled footage,' or 'assembly,' a very rough cut of *Love Streams* as it's been shot so far. Most who are usually welcome at dailies are being uninvited. *I'm* uninvited, Eddie tells me. But I don't know if that's coming from Eddie or Al or George or the man in the moon, so I go to the man in the moon to ask if I may attend.

John squints at me, a little angry, a fighter's look, cunning, not sure whether to attack or defend: "No."

Then without missing a beat, gently: "No, you can see it. I just don't want you to be as depressed as I am."

He hates the film's beginning.

As has become usual after a weekend – this one spent editing the assembly – his belly's more swollen, his skin's pale and lifeless. This time his face is much more drawn. Once he starts directing he comes to life, gets more color, and we don't notice his condition; but away from the set, life seems to drain from him. One can only imagine how this hits Gena.

I'm scribbling notes about this and suddenly somebody's grabbing my arm, it's John, laughing his crazy laugh, "What are you always writing for?! What?! You're making me nervous!"

"I'm doing my job!"

We're laughing.

He grabs my notebook.

"I wanna see what you're writing!"

"No one can read my handwriting."

He sees I'm right. "You can *read* this?"

"Just me. No one else. That's how I like it."

He gives an approving look.

I tell him, "I'm getting so much material I'm starting to be selective."

"I'm getting so crazy at night, I'm starting to be *un*selective."

Phedon Papamichael says, while they're setting up, that he spoke with John all night until five in the morning. (No wonder John looks like shit. It's not 9am yet. I don't say what I'm thinking, which is, "You should know better, Phedon, and let him sleep.")

John asked him, Phedon says, "How does a man our age, his age, my age, be with very young women?" Phedon told John his attitude toward his much younger girlfriends: "I try to be lover, father, to help them."

Darkly Phedon tells me that John puts into his films what frustrates him in his life – adding, conspiratorially, "Even the divorce."

I don't want to know that. And I don't assume it's true. I've come to like Phedon a lot, but I've seen that he doesn't always speak the truth. (Remember "We have a way to get it out"?) Yes, continues Phedon, John puts in his films what he's frustrated with in his life, "and I would say this to *him*."

Gena is placing herself for the shot. "Am I in the right place, Al? Or is it crucial, or not?"

"You're fine, Gena," Al answers from behind the camera.

Throughout the film, Al and Eddie are exquisitely solicitous toward Gena. One or the other will bring her a chair, or see she has water. And John will go to her, silently squeeze her hand, then go off about his business.

Now John says, "Al, this can be good – you can pan and dolly at the same time. The pan will be fast and the dolly will be slow."

The 'pan' is a movement of the camera on its stand; the 'dolly' is the camera mounted on a moving cart. On screen we'll see the camera moving slower than Gena as she runs with her slapstick-like business (the dolly), while the focus of our vision begins behind Gena and ends in front of her (the pan). John needs all this movement so the viewer notices the movement rather than that there's nothing to suggest a Paris station except the oddly-uniformed porter at the far end of the passageway. There's nothing in this warehouse to suggest one, much less two, European rail stations, nothing but fences, walls, posters, a phone booth, a Frenchman (Francois) and an Englishman (Jaimie Horton).

Cassavetes actually enjoys not having much of a budget, but I suspect that's because he can blame his innovative techniques on something other than his artistry. John's conversation is unpredictable except in one way: he consistently refuses to acknowledge that he's a fully conscious artist – though on the set it's clear he's seeking specific effects, consciously, *every* time. As he often says, he doesn't know what's going to happen, as a director, and that's true; but the not-knowing is contained within a strict framework of possibilities, a framework he's conscious of and certain about (yelling "NO AD LIBBING!" yesterday, for instance). When he really doesn't know what he wants, he'll explore; but when he sees what he's looking for, he knows it and knows what he wants to do with it. That he always claims the opposite baffles everyone.

Nobody he's worked with believes John's pose, as Ted Allan told me outright. In Alan Pappe's book on Paul Mazursky's *Tempest,* in which John and Gena starred, Mazursky says, "He's led by instinct and he does his best to pretend that intellect is not working, but it is working." Savvy Eddie Donno puts John's directorial method most succinctly: "John wants you to give him what *he* wants, but he wants you to do it in *your* way."

Later I'll question Cassavetes about his influence on cinema. His answer is typical: "Influence? That *I've* had on films? Ahhhh… I think the *films* have had something of an influence, *but we don't have that much to do with the films!* I'm not in that much control of the films that we make. You know?"

"I know that every time things don't go your way you let people know it. That's not control?"

"I think everything you do is an accident. On *Shadows* we didn't have any equipment, we didn't have a dolly. And we had all this movement, so we used long lenses. And photographing in the street because we couldn't afford a studio or couldn't afford even to go *inside* someplace, you know? And our sound – when we opened *Shadows* in England, they said, 'The truest sound we've ever seen!' Well, at that time, almost all pictures were looped. You know, all the sync was the not the sync the actors actually spoke on the stage. It was cleaned and made to be absolutely sterile, so that there was no sound behind anything. If you saw traffic, you wouldn't hear it. But we recorded most of

Shadows in a dance studio with Bob Fosse and his troupe dancing above our heads, and we were shooting this movie. So I never considered the sound. We didn't even have enough money to *print* it, to *hear* how bad it was. So when we came out, we had Sinatra singing upstairs, and all kinds of *boom, boom,* dancing feet above us. And that was the *sound* of the picture. So we spent hours, days, weeks, months, *years,* trying to straighten out this sound. Finally, it was impossible and we just went with it. Well, when the picture opened in London they said, '*This is an innovation!*' You know? Innovation! We killed ourselves trying to ruin that innovation!"

"But you didn't have Bob Fosse dancing in your home in *Faces.* There weren't any dancers in *Husbands* or *Woman,* I don't see any dancers in this picture – and the sound-style is the same."

Raised eyebrows, blazing eyes. I will get no answer.

I get instead, "All the innovative things that you do are just the best that you can do with the limited materials that you have. And so you create an innovation through no fault of your own. And many people have done the same.

"If you don't have the money, you figure out a way to create these things. Some people spend a fortune trying to create a reality by building a set and trying to light it like it's a dump. It seems very easy now, in retrospect, to say, 'Hey, if you're going to shoot a dump – go shoot a *dump*!' So you become a genius!

"I think that money has nothing to do with film. And I think that, in the end, it *kills* you from being creative, and from inventing. Finding a way to do it *makes you think.* It makes the crew think. It makes everyone think. You say, 'We're in this room, how do you make this a palace?' And somebody says, 'What if you put this here?' And everyone else goes, '*Noooooooo.* That would be awful!' 'Alright, just do it, see!' So some fool like me, I say, 'Okay, fine, this is what we're going do: We either make the picture – or we don't. If we're going to make it, let's make this room a palace. *Or* – let's not make it a palace! Look [he makes the motion of scribbling on a page] see how easy this changes?! It's no longer a palace. It's a room.' You know? And you make the adjustment. But the *emotions* stay the same.

"So the emotions guard you. The sense of humor guards you. Saying, 'The hell with life' guards you. 'Go ahead, kill me!'"

He's just admitted, in a roundabout way, everything he usually denies.

I guess somehow I telegraphed that I'm about to make that point – this canny street fighter sees I might land one and laughs, "Gotta go, kiddo, got a meeting."

We're setting up to shoot Sarah's conversation with Jack in the phone booth . John's direction: "Gena, accept nothing."

"What?"

"Accept nothing – this time."

"I don't understand."

He tries to explain. Can't. Waves the idea away with a flurry of his arms. Gena shrugs.

Now he wants her to try new lines for the scene. The script reads, "Let's not divorce, I'm almost not crazy." Now he wants: "Jack, let's not divorce. I can't make it without you. If I've made mistakes, I'll rectify them. I'm almost not crazy now." Then, after Jack's reply, she's to add, "Jack, don't cut me off, please. I'm at the end," also not in the shooting script.

After a few takes suddenly John shouts to Helen Caldwell, "New scene number! Gimmie a new scene number!"

Every scene in a script is numbered. If John wants to create a substantially different moment in this scene he needs a new number. If the entire scene is numbered 19, this might be 19F. When takes of this shot are printed they'll be labeled 19F, in front of 19E's takes and before 19G's, so the editor will know where these takes go within the scene as a whole.

Jack has just hung up on Sarah, and Sarah has had her 'dream' of killing Jack and Debbie with a car. Now John gets a new idea and directs Gena to stand in the phone booth, breathing hard, and to bang her head, hard, against the booth. Tells her to stamp her foot when she hits her head. "You just killed your daughter, in your dream." After she bangs her head the porter is to say, "Are you alright, Ma'am," and she's to say, "No, I'm not alright."

Gena takes some time to sit down in her portable invisible isolation booth and mouth the new lines. Then they shoot two takes that John doesn't print. (If the director doesn't print a take, it never shows up in the editing room.) On the third take when the porter asks "Are you alright?" Gena, brushing her hair off her forehead, says, "No." Slight pause. "I'm fine. I'm fine. I'm fine. Just fine."

After John cuts he tells her, "Don't say 'I'm fine,' say, 'No, I'm not all right,' or just say, "No, no," but *be* alright, you know what I mean?" But, on a hunch, he prints that take anyway.

He cuts on the next take. "No good. You can't wait for your cue, Jaimie [the porter]. Take your *own* time. You too, Gena. Do it again."

"Reload!" the camera assistant calls out. They're about to run out of film.

"No, you have enough," John insists. Then turns to the man and asks, "Don't you have enough?"

They decide they do. They shoot and print a take with John's preferred dialogue.

In the editing room, for the final cut, John will discard Gena banging her head. The entire phone conversation will consist only of Sarah saying, "Jack? I'm almost not crazy now." Jack will answer, "I just don't get it." She'll place the receiver on its hook, and it will be unclear who hung up on who. She'll have the dream, won't bang her head, will exit the booth, the porter will ask if she's alright, she'll say the line John didn't (at the time) think was right: "No. I'm fine. I'm fine. I'm fine. Just fine."

John's in control, there *is* discovery but there is no 'accident' – there is room for the actress's conception, both her sense and his sense of the line are printed, and one is finally chosen in the editing room, after careful consideration, viewing both takes many times. Not improvisation. Not accidental. He's in control.

But he'll never admit it.

There is another creative aspect to this approach: There is no way to anticipate what John will concoct on-set. He'll often throw something unexpected into a scene while shooting, which means there is no way for any actor to prepare *enough.* The actors work in an atmosphere of the unexpected. So their performances don't have the sealed-off quality which is the trademark of most professional acting, the sense that nothing can get in or out of a performance but the specific requirements of a given scene, a given concept.

"Sometimes lying looks good," John says. "That doesn't make it any good."

John demands of his actors that they play their characters in relation to an always changing world – the world he creates on the set – rather than in relation to a given written story that can have only one outcome.

"The movie is made by – an atmosphere that is a particular kind of atmosphere that fits that picture, you know. And so, to me, the director's job is to make sure that that atmosphere is never the same from scene to scene and day to day. And you can do that."

In this sense, he's not being duplicitous or evasive when he says he "doesn't know." He knows a lot, but he doesn't think anyone can know it all; so he creates an atmosphere, shooting in sequence, in which discovery is possible – discovery within the framework of the whole, a framework he's considered and brought to the set as script, shooting schedule, and so on, a framework that leaves room for the entry of what he *doesn't* know.

"A lot of people – know what they're doing. I don't know till the next day. If our films are supposed to be something like life is – some vague thing that life has, that films can contain – then how can you determine what's gonna happen tomorrow? Unless you live such a proscribed life that you're bored with it. We live an exciting life. I mean, this is exciting stuff. So I can't tell what's gonna happen tomorrow. Even if you can read it, you don't know how somebody's gonna interpret it."

Driving to dailies John is worried that the beginning isn't tough enough, Robert Harmon isn't tired enough, we don't get enough of a sense that Harmon takes chances. He's thinking of calling up Tim Carey – a tall, spooky, funny scene-stealer who performed briefly but indelibly in *Minnie and Moskowitz* and *The Killing of a Chinese Bookie*. They'll go to some nightclub with a minimal crew, maybe just Bo on sound and George Sims on a handheld, and shoot something crazy with Carey. (He never calls Carey.) And that party scene he shot in the house, with the little girl, and Leslie singing – that scene is "editorializing," he hates it. When he shoots Seymour's side of today's phone call, he wants to make clear that the husband "has the freedom, has what he thinks he wants, but can't leave the house, can't leave." At the same time, Jack doesn't want her back "even though he knows she's right."

John, the director, never breaks faith with Sarah. The pain of this film for Sarah Lawson is that Sarah's right, but being right doesn't help.

At dailies, either the uninvited people were never uninvited or they said the hell with it and came anyway. Nobody throws them out. After yesterday's takes are run, and the 'rough assembly' is about to be screened, John doesn't wish to make a big deal of it and order an exodus. Instead he announces, "Anybody who's gonna stay, you gotta be very quiet now, 'cause this has nothing to do with anybody but *us*."

"Us" is John, George the editor, and Al.

Yes, the beginning doesn't work yet. But there are fine things throughout, really fine things. And Gena's stuff is incredible.

Afterwards John asks if I like it. "I didn't like or dislike it, that's material you look at to get an idea of what you want it to look like, not for itself."

He squeezes my shoulder. Goodnight.

Today's scenes will be in the final cut.

TUESDAY, JUNE 14 – *Nothing to hide behind*

The film thus far (in its final cut):

It opens with Robert Harmon arguing with this secretary about the girls. Then Harmon in the club, with Susan, then back with the girls – intercut with Sarah Lawson's court, therapy, and train station scenes, and a brief visit to Robert Harmon's home by the singer Susan [to be conceived and shot later]; then the arrival of Albie, and the girls' exit; then Harmon and Albie alone, in the morning, cleaning the house. In the final cut, by now the film's run 50 minutes.

There follows approximately six minutes of conversation and drinking between Harmon and Albie [Shot today].

Then Albie, drunk, lights a cigarette in the living room and notices two cabs coming up the driveway – he calls his father, Harmon tells him to go see who it is, Albie doesn't move [shot last Tuesday].

One cab carries luggage; the other, more luggage and Sarah Lawson [to be shot next week].

We have as yet no clue that Robert and Sarah even know each other. We're about 57 minutes into the film.

When Sarah arrives there's a shockingly brief exchange between Robert and Sarah [to be shot next week] that tells us nothing but that they are very familiar with each other, then Robert whisks his son off to Las Vegas [to be shot this Wednesday, Thursday, and Friday in Vegas].

*

John will spend the afternoon editing while the crew prepares for the move to Las Vegas tonight. This morning's shooting schedule, at the Cassavetes home-set, is just two set-ups of Robert Harmon conversing and drinking with his son Albie. Last night John re-wrote and lengthened their scene. (And slept when? I recall Gena telling me, a couple of years ago, "John never sleeps that I know of. I'm sure he must sleep sometime, but you can't catch him at it.")

When I arrive, Casssavetes and Jakob Shaw have just finished rehearsing their scene. John greets me, then turns to Jakob: "Now *you* – go and think about what we're gonna do. Go and think about it, and then forget it. But first you have to think about it. Just go through the beats."

Jakob goes his way. John tells me he's pleased with this scene. "It's so gentle. There's nothing to hide behind. It's all apparent – which is what you work for, to make things apparent."

The scene in the shooting script is half a page. It's mid-morning, Albie's finished his chores, Harmon's in his bar, Albie enters and says, "All done." Harmon says, "I'm going to have a whiskey. You're going to have a beer 'cause you're a kid." He pours his eight-year-old a beer. Breakfast. "When you get to be about 14, you go out on your own. Hitchhike across the country." "Why?" "I don't know, it's a manly thing to do." "I see." End of scene.

As re-written and performed, the scene's far more complex, and very demanding for the boy. (*Passages in italics were edited from the final cut.*)

Harmon pours a whiskey. When Albie enters his father asks, "Want a drink? Would you like a Coca Cola, a beer, or something?"

"A beer."

Now the decision is Albie's – he's imitating his father.

Harmon gets a beer from the fridge, opens it – and I'm standing close by thinking: It fizzes like beer, smells like beer, they're giving this little kid a beer, and at what, 9, 9:30 in the morning? Jakob's father, Larry Shaw, stands beside me, silent. They better get this scene in just a few takes or this kid's going to be out of it.

Harmon pours the beer into a goblet, hands it to Albie, saying, "Would you like – a little toast?"

But Albie starts in drinking. Harmon is delighted – the first such emotion he's shown. He smiles, shakes his head, laughs a little, a sincere laugh – his first of the film.

Albie blurts out, "Do you love me?"

"I don't know you well enough to love you. I don't think so."

He meets the boy's honesty with his own. I realize that Harmon's one hold on us as a character is that he never fakes. He's crazy, compulsive, selfish, insensitive, and sometimes cruel, but never self-pitying, never phony or hypocritical. Which may be why John can say, "I *like* the character I'm playing." The scene goes on:

"Do you love Mom? My mother?"

"No."

"Then why'd you marry her?"

"I was tired. I went to a party and I met her at a party. And she looked real nice. She had a blue dress on and those nice eyes. You know, those kind of eyebrows. And she looked real cute, cute little hips. And we laughed a lot and had a nice time. It was a very boring party. And she was tired, you know, kind of like – and I, uh, took her home and we touched, we felt each other and kissed. We got married rather than go back to that boring party."

To me, this seems a lot for a kid Jakob's age to deal with, whether he's acting or not. The speech mirrors a speech in Ted Allan's play, and, like most of Ted's concepts, it will be cut.

The boy asks, "Did you run away because I was born?"

"No. I didn't even know you were coming. I don't like men a lot, you know? I'm a writer, I don't make money on men. No one's really interested. They're kind of boring." A long pause. Harmon is baffled to be talking to this boy and has no idea what to say. He blurts out, "When you're 14, I think you ought to go and hitchhike across the country, you know?"

"Why?"

"To be a man. That's what I'm talking about. Go into a truckstop. Stop there and have a cup of coffee and see what men are really like, you know? Men. Not these people out here with the suits and ties and that kind of stuff, you know?" On that line he gestures to his own sports coat. Harmon always dresses formally, and we see here he doesn't consider himself a real man.

"I had a picture of you," Albie says. "My father tore it up. My mother cried. And they had a big fight and he hit her. And they changed my name to Albie Swanson like his. My mother cries all the time thinking about you. Please come back to her."

"She, uh, sleeps with another man at night. You know what that means?"

Albie nods. We don't know if he knows or not.

"So that part of… that part of… is over. I don't really like women anyway, you know. I really don't. I like *kids.*" A rare attempt at sensitivity! "And I like older people. 'Cause they seem to have the secret, to just, you know – they don't need anything. *You* don't need anything." The kid's expression is as needy as can be, so Harmon is telling his son not to need *him.* "They just want – you're innocent, and so are older people, they're innocent, that's what I like about them. Drink your drink, here, drink it down."

And Harmon/Cassavetes gestures to down the beer, and Albie/Jakob gulps the entire glass in one guzzle.

They got the scene quickly, both John and Jakob hit it dead on, and it's fortunate that they did because Jakob is unsteady on his feet and tells his father the beer made him nauseous.

Is there another father-son scene in American cinema that shows so nakedly the distance between a man and a boy?

I lunch with Gena. In her robe, in her kitchen-nook, she's relaxed, cheerful, completely at ease – nothing like the actress on the set. We're talking books, California authors, she mentions Joan Didion, saying, "It has to be a very good day before I'll read Didion, a very good day with the promise of a very good week to come." (Yet she'll spend many weeks in service to the psyche of a tortured character. No wonder she's as she is on the set.)

Then I drive John to the editing room at Cannon in Hollywood. On the way he says, "All editors are cocksuckers, 'cause they have to please the producer or they don't work. They're on the producer's side, not the film's." But not George Villasenor. "Stands his ground, tells it like it is to *anybody* – even me!" And he laughs that devil-laugh.

Unbelievably, George and John edit on a Moviola – a machine in use since the 1930s, motor-driven, a hunk of metal about the bulk of a fire-hydrant. The motor makes a racket, the film rattles on its sprockets, you can barely hear the dialogue. Operated by a peddle on the floor, you can run footage backwards or forwards, and the film flickers across the very small viewing screen like a newsreel from, say, 1910. In fact, a Moviola looks like nothing so much as the earliest film-viewers in the turn-of-the-century's nickelodeons, before movie theaters. And you think, 'They edited *Citizen Kane* on this?!' *Citizen Kane,* and every film John's made. Cannon has many state-of-the-art editing machines that are simpler to use, have much better screens, and make much less noise. But that's not for John and George.

Holding a spool of film, George feeds the machine by hand. Strips of film hang everywhere in the dark little room, there's one dim lamp, and bright light beams from the Moviola's viewing screen. For uncountable hours during the coming months, John and George will bend over this noisy antique and perform the most delicate surgeries upon this most delicate and abstract of John's films.

John is saying, "I'm not worried about her entrances, the sitting, the itsy bitsy things, we can play all that in master until we come to the *main text,* and then we'll select what we like." George records everything John says on a small tape recorder. When working alone, he tells me, he often must listen to the tape several times to understand what John means.

Me, I have no idea what John just meant.

They disagree about a scene. George wants a logical sequence, John wants uncertainty, doesn't want the viewer to quite get it.

George looks at me. "I like John, I don't like all his pictures."

John laughs.

George finally accedes.

"Well," he says, "God hates a coward."

"Mightily," says Cassavetes.

Today's work will be in the final cut.

WEDNESDAY, JUNE 15 – *Cuisine of Tony the Ant*

Six scenes will be shot in Las Vegas:

On the Strip, a cab carrying Robert Harmon and Albie pulls up to the entrance of the Imperial. They're greeted by the hotelier [Dean Shendal] – Harmon's a regular and a high-roller. [Shot today.]

Harmon and Albie enter their room, assisted by a porter. The dazed and frightened Albie soon learns that he'll be spending the night in that room <u>*alone*</u>*. Harmon explains he can't sleep unless he's with a woman. [Shot tomorrow.]*

Harmon leaves the hotel in a tux (it's still daylight). [Shot today.]

Albie is alone in the room after dark when a housekeeper [Carolyn Baker] comes in to turn down the bed. She's disgusted that the kid's been left by himself, asks if he's hungry, and calls down to room service for his dinner. [Shot tomorrow night.]

The next morning, Harmon pulls up to the Imperial in a car with two hookers [Kathryn Donno and Geraldine Hofstetter]. They're all laughing hysterically. Harmon writes their checks and stumbles out of the car, very drunk. [Shot today.]

Harmon staggers to his room, knocks on the door; Albie opens the door crying, begging to be taken home, begging to see his mother – and for the first time Harmon understands how deeply he's hurt this boy. [Shot Friday.]

On Friday, Cassavetes also shoots a scene he has no intention of using: Harmon and Albie touring the Imperial's exhibit of vintage automobiles.

Las Vegas, a city of about 200,000, has had a decade or so of hard times. Older hotels are in poor repair (the showroom of The Sands leaks in a hard rain). Not long ago the Aladdin was dark. Unless there's a major boxing event, or Sinatra's in town, you don't need a reservation at any hotel in any season. Except at the high-rolling Desert Inn, gone are the days when men without ties and women not in evening dress look conspicuous on the gambling floor.

In daylight the town looks desolate. Residences and shopping centers extend for a mile or so east and west of the Strip, then it's raw desert from those backyards to the mountains that ring this valley. On the Strip, swathes of desert separate most of the casinos, desert spotted with motels. Some motels are brand-name, some are what I call 'felony motels' – cheap seedy joints usually occupied by folks who have recently, or will soon, commit felonies. And there's an occasional fast-food franchise, pizza parlor, or gas station (offering free aspirin). Daylight is a bleached burning sheen.

Night is brilliant isolated neons shining out to each other. The colored jagged lettering of The Stardust, the gaudy pinks of the Flamingo's entrance across the street from the white-lit fountains of Ceasars Palace, the up-and-own moving light pattern of the phallic Dunes sign, the Alladin's lit huge magic lantern, then, nearly a mile south, the bright façade of the Tropicana, with desert at its backdoor.

This town feels neither like a city, a theme park, a resort, nor a combination of the three – big enough for you to get in trouble, not big enough for you to hide out. But there's something about it. Just being here makes you feel a little crazy.

This is Leslie Hope's first time in Vegas. She's now a production assistant. Since she's only 18, it's against the law for her to drink, gamble, or walk in the gaming area, but beautiful young women can do pretty much what they want in Vegas. She's never carded or restricted by its powers-that-be. Several times, on the crew's first full day, Leslie looks about her and says to no one in particular, "Can you *believe* this place?"

Jakob Shaw is becoming a pro. The boy has learned that on this set you never know what's next and you have to look out for yourself. He asks, "John, am I gonna say anything in this scene, should I get miked?"

John gives him a brief look of admiration and tells him it's not necessary.

The crew's setting up in front of the Imperial, to shoot Harmon's and Albie's arrival. It's 105 in the shade, but the brutal sun doesn't stop a crowd of onlookers, mostly retirees, from hanging about and gawking all day. Their faces change, but not their comments. "Come on, honey, we gotta go," a guy tells his wife. "Let's see who it is first!" "Who *is* that guy?" "I think – it's John Cassavetes!" "Who?" "John Cassevetes!" "I don't know 'im," and the husband takes her arm and pulls her away. A guy next to them says, "Sure, that's John Cassavetes, that's who I just said, it's gotta be *some*body! And a woman bubbles, "*John Cassavetes*, I'm tellin' ya! This is a thrill." She tells her girlfriend to get his autograph for her; her friend goes to John, who flashes his best Mephistophelean grin, "Of *course*, darling!"

When we start shooting a husband will grouse, "They do the same thing over and over!" His wife replies firmly, "*That's* the way movies are made." After a take Al Ruban calls out, "That's a print!" The wife: "'That's a print' means they *like* that one!" The husband: "They all look the same to me."

The production's negotiated a great deal, I understand, on rooms and shooting-privileges at the Imperial. It stands near the Flamingo, across the street from Ceasars, but has no fame and could use the publicity of being in a movie. It won't get any. In the final cut, its name is never mentioned; there are shots of Ceasars and the Flamingo as the cab pulls in, but we never see the Imperial's sign. Its hotelier, Dean Shendal, will greet Robert and

Albie at the door, John saying his name so fast you can't catch it, and you never see his face – they use a take shot from off to one side, focusing on Harmon and Albie, and the moment passes swiftly. Part of the agreement is that John shoot a scene amidst the Imperial's vintage auto exhibit, of which the hotel is very proud. A deal's a deal. John shoots the scene. But a hustle's a hustle. The footage never makes it to the editing room.

Dean Shendal has never acted before. Out of his earshot John tells Al and Eddie, "He can say what he wants, he can say, 'Uh huh, uh huh.'"

"He *can't* say 'uh huh uh huh,'" Al says, "you can't do that to him, you've gotta talk with him." It is Al, after all, who negotiated this hotel deal.

So John gets into it, shoots Shendal talking with a pretty girl, makes up banter between he and Shendal, shoots lots of 'coverage,' does the scene from different angles, it takes a while. At least the guy knows he's been on a movie-set.

Next scene: Robert Harmon in a tux, cigarette in hand, leaving the hotel, hailing a cab. At first they clear the area and shoot Harmon by himself. John hates it, says, "Let the people walk through, it looks like a mausoleum here with me all by myself, this never happens."

They let people walk through the shooting area, prepare to shoot, and John suddenly starts approaching the passers-by, saying hello, he opens a door for a woman, people start avoiding this crazy man, he calls to the crew, "Ok, cut!"

But he never said "Action."

Bo Harwood on sound says, "Hey, Eddie – nobody told me to roll."

"Ask *him,*" Eddie points to John, "nobody told me either."

John calls "Action" and cuts up again, asks a passer-by, "Would you hold my cigarette, please?"

The guy just stares at him.

"What's with *you,* boogie?" says John, all crazy-eyed.

Al and Eddie are getting nervous.

John tells the guy, "Ok, get the hell out of here then! TAXI!"

The next take, John is almost expressionless. I'm thinking,

"Cut, this is dead," just before John says, "Cut, this is deader than Kelsey's-I-don't-know-what!"

(Kelsey?)

Finally, John settles down and they get the shot.

Somebody's put a sticker on the camera that reads: SOUNDS LIKE BULLSHIT TO ME.

Now John takes me aside, very earnestly, tells me that he and George cut the rest of the picture yesterday, all the footage, including the transitions. He explains that up until he and Gena meet, the shooting and editing must be 'formal,' well-lit, linear cuts, good composition. But that all changes when he and Gena meet, it gets looser, rougher, no restraints, natural light, "because it's family." "*So,*" he says with his eyebrows arched, it's very hard for him to do this Robert Harmon section in Vegas, because he has to be so stiff, "walking and eating stiff," to show the constraint of being without close family. Gena, too, has played her scenes much tighter than she'd prefer "because she's got to, because it's all got to burst out when he and she get together."

John works up business for the next scene. It'll be a hooker's car, she's driving, the other gal sits beside her, and Harmon's scrunched next to them in the front seat, they're laughing insanely. One's holding a coffee cup that spills as they laugh and Harmon writes their checks.

In prep, with John watching the procedure, Eddie soaks Harmon's checkbook in coffee, spills a little coffee on the pavement, daubs a check in the coffee. "Like this, John?" Eddie asks.

"Yeah, but I need the one under it wet too."

Eddie daubs another check, very carefully, on the pavement puddle.

"That was very artistic, Eddie," I tell him. He hits me on the arm, lightly, laughing.

They're to shoot. Before Eddie hands the coffee cup to the hooker at the wheel, he dips his finger in it to make sure it's not hot. The hooker is played by his wife, Kathryn.

*

I convince John that I know the best Italian restaurant in Vegas – in fact, the best west of New Orleans and south of San Francisco. He says, "You're on!" and gathers a troupe: Phedon, his girlfriend Geraldine (today's other hooker), Bo, Leslie, Robert Fieldsteel, and a couple of others whose names I still don't know. We're walking, John and I in the lead, south on the Strip – and I learn that desert distances are deceptive, because it takes us a half hour, the walk is over a mile.

He tells me of disagreements with Eddie and Al – that he sometimes lets them win because they need to, and he respects them, and he doesn't want to offend them. "They have to be able to think I'm an asshole."

John can't believe our destination: The Tower of Pizza! Fronted by a neon Leaning Tower of Pisa, the logo of the joint glowing above it.

"*This* is your great restaurant?" John says, with heavy eyebrow-language.

"This is it."

The décor is simple as can be: square tables covered by red-and-white oilcloth. A waitress and bus-boy push four tables together for us. John obviously expects someone on the staff to recognize him. If they do, they don't care.

We begin to drive the waitress nuts. Phedon wants absolutely no garlic – he will, he promises, *die* if there's garlic. Cassavetes wants a discussion with the cook. Phedon insists that any *decent* restaurant will prepare special dishes that are not on the menu, even if the cook's never heard of them. Of course everybody (but me and maybe the waitress) has been drinking.

The waitress dismisses John's protestations with, "You're a real ball-buster, mister."

This lady is tough. Really tough.

"You ain't goin' near that kitchen, mister, believe me."

John looks hard in her eyes and – decides to believe her. It's the only one-on-one argument I've seen him flat-out lose.

As she walks away he says, "She's *great*."

During all this I've felt like hiding under the table. I'm the guy who brought them here. They know it, the waitress knows it.

Tensions ease when the food is served. It's as good as I said it would be. Everyone's amazed, delighted. Even the waitress. In honor of my taste, John echoes a line of Ben Gazzarra's from *Husbands:* "The man is right. When the man is right, the man is right."

Leslie explains to John why she can't stand Robert Harmon. "He's a creep with the kid," among other things. John explains that he understands everybody in the movie but the kid and Robert Harmon, and he doesn't *want* to understand them, and that he, John Cassavetes, doesn't want to understand John Cassavetes either, "because I love *motion,* change, and I hate answers because they stop change."

"You're a phony sonofabitch." Phedon says that as calmly as he'd say, "There's a spot of sauce on your tie."

"I'm phony?!" John laughs. "I feel sorry for *you,* because *you're* phony, because *you* think you know what's right, what's good. I don't know and I don't *want* to know."

"You put your life into the movie," says Phedon, "and then you say you don't."

"What?"

"You know! Don't tell me like you don't know."

"I put *everything* into the movie. What I know *and* what I don't know. And that's as far from phony as Kelsey's-you-know-what."

Kelsey again.

And so it goes, back and forth, around and around, and John ends the argument, with no logic, getting up, leaning across the table at Phedon, John's swollen belly crushing his bread-dish, saying very loudly, "Actors are the most beautiful people in the world, because they take on the problems of anybody!"

When it's time to leave John insists on picking up the check for all of us – $107 total, plus a generous tip for the fearless waitress. We make hubbub in protest, but he's not about to lose two contests in one night. As he walks to the cash register he wipes the money across his behind as though it's toilet paper. "I *like* to pay the check, because it embarrasses everyone! And the only reason it does is because money is so goddamned important to everybody!"

Later I'll learn that the Tower of Pizza is owned by, and is a favorite hang-out of, Tony "The Ant" Spilatro. Spilatro is a gangster who might justly claim to be the craziest, most unpredictable, and vicious Mafiosi ever to hit Vegas. No wonder the waitress is tough. No wonder the food is great. No wonder "you ain't goin' near that kitchen, mister." I will be forever thankful that I was not the inadvertent cause of a meeting – with what consequences, no one could foresee – between John Cassavetes and Tony the Ant.

In Love Streams the entrance scene with Shendal will be minimal. For Harmon leaving the hotel, John will choose a shot in which he shakes his head as though at some unpleasant thought, a suggestion that Harmon knows leaving the boy is wrong. In his return with the hookers, the May 13 shooting script has the business with the coffee, the checks, the laughter, and the girls spelling their names so he can write the checks, all of which are in the final cut. But John will discard the take with these written lines: one whore says to the other, laughing, "I ***love*** *him!" and Harmon says "Love, what the hell is love?" Instead John will select a take he improvised: "Gotta see my son, you know, love is everything, just remember that, remember the Alamo, remember Smoky Joe," and, laughing, he hits himself hard on the forehead.*

THURSDAY, JUNE 16 – *Keep it a secret, ok?*

Harmon and Albie talk. At night, the maid finds Albie alone and orders up some food.

John Cassavetes likes to shoot rooms. He likes to shoot *in* rooms. Confined quarters for confined people. The crew hates it – 'cause there's no room. For a very small crew, as John had on *Shadows, Faces,* and *Woman,* small rooms don't present large problems. But for a crew this size, another small room means another nightmare. Even John agrees they'll have to rent the room next door, to attach more cables, get more electrical power, and so that Bo Harwood can set up his sound-mixing equipment out of sight of the camera. One problem. There are two old ladies in the next room and they won't be checking out till noon. The morning's wasted. Gone is the prospect of an early get-away tomorrow afternoon. The crew rose early to shoot three scenes today, two in daylight and one at night; we can't count on that now, and must plan on shooting a scene tomorrow morning (and then the phony scene at the automobile exhibit). The production office must change plane tickets, people call their families about the changes – hassle all around.

Amidst the grousing, standing in the middle of the room nobody likes, John grins.

"A *perfect* room," he says with relish, "for this character. A room where people have lost. Lost things important to them, not just money."

Nothing to do this morning, so the crew spreads out, mostly to the gambling floor. I'm walking across the casino and the focus-puller, Sam Gart, catches my eye, waves me over. He's sitting at roulette and losing. He just wants to say, "*Fuck* the company that took us to Las Vegas! Put that in the book."

I'm getting a lot of that. Several crew-members have introduced themselves and told me their life stories because they want to be in the book. I'm interested, I take notes, but I can't break it to them that I don't have space in this book for 50 life-stories.

In the lobby I run into John. "Come on, kid, let's go get some ice cream."

Over ice cream he says, "It bothers me that he [Harmon] doesn't change. All this happens, and he doesn't change." (I have a feeling *that's* going to change.) "She *does* change – and that's a shame. Because you're [her husband] never gonna get her back. A woman like that – one in a million – who can love so completely, yet keep her individuality and her strength." Then John's onto his "my favorite part of the picture" riff. Every day it's something else, and it's always something small, small but important. The daughter pressing her face to her mother's shoulder in the meeting-room, Jakob Shaw's openness when he asks Harmon to come back to his mother, how Gena plays with her cigarette in the shrink scene.

He smiles gently, and suddenly looks exhausted: "I had a good time last night." At the restaurant, he means.

I'm alarmed now – as we speak the color's draining from his face, his skin goes gray. I say nothing, but he reads my expression. "I'm tired. Tired."

"What do you expect, man, you've been up for days on end, working like mad?"

"Always."

He's always pushed this hard. But he's never been tired.

*

In the afternoon, we shoot Harmon's scene with Albie. First a porter delivers Harmon's tux, complete with shirt and shoes – that little bit is why we needed the whole room. For the meat of the scene, all that was necessary was the window where Harmon talks with Albie, the desolate daylight of Vegas bright behind them. (It's possible that this morning John didn't know he'd stage their talk there.)

In *Love Streams'* final cut this scene will be brief – though it doesn't *play* 'brief' because, in this film even more than his previous work, John structures his scenes not around words but around the pauses between them.

Harmon asks Albie how he feels. "Okay." "Still a little drunk?" "Uh-huh." "Stomach all upset?" "Yeah." "You ought to go to sleep." Then Harmon springs it on him: "I'm a man. And a man – is different from a little kid. I find it very hard to go to sleep alone. You know what I mean, don't you? Do you?" "Yeah."

As viewers, we don't quite realize what is to happen. We won't know until the next moment, when we briefly see Harmon leaving the hotel. And then we'll see Albie alone in the room at night when the maid enters.

The Harmon-Albie scene in the May 13 shooting script is much more sympathetic. First Harmon offers to play cards with the boy. They sit down to cards. Albie says, "It's very hard to tell you that I'm going to be a writer." Harmon attempts an honest, sober conversation. When the boy asks if Harmon loves him, Harmon says, "I don't know what love is. I thought I did, but I don't." He tries to have a conversation, and at the same time is resentful of the need for conversation. The boy asks if his father wants to go for a walk. No. The boy tries to take care of his father, asks if he's hungry. No. The conversation is a failure, but in the May 13 script it's attempted.

Last night John re-wrote the scene. (Cassavetes may be tired, but he refuses to give in to his fatigue. He works as he always has, no matter how he feels. He must know it may be killing him, but right now the picture is more important. What he said days ago takes on another meaning: "I figure, if you work on a picture *that's your life*.")

The new scene begins as I describe above, but, as written and shot today, it goes on: Harmon indicates that he knows he's giving the kid a raw deal. He keeps asking the kid if it's alright with him, that Harmon go out on the town all night. The kid, of course, keeps saying yes, it's alright. Then *Harmon* offers to play cards. The kid says no. Harmon offers to take the kid out on the town. The kid says no. Harmon is almost sympathetic.

But even when Cassavetes is tempted, as he clearly was, to present his character sympathetically, in the end he doesn't. Except for his Gus in *Husbands*, he never has. This sets Cassavetes apart from every actor of his star caliber. He never goes the least bit out of his way to make his audience like or approve of him. Even when starring in a TV series, *Johnny Staccato*, he played a complicated man with an existential point of view who never pretended to be a hero. Thus far in *Love Streams*, all we can admire about Robert Harmon is that he never says what he doesn't mean.

This time of year, the sun doesn't set in Vegas till about 9pm. After dark we shoot Albie's scene with the maid, played by Carolyn Baker. She's learned the function of the guy taking notes (me) and asks, "Am I gonna be in your fuckin' book?"

The scene: the maid comes to turn down the bed and finds Albie alone, immobile at the window, looking out at the lights of Vegas and the black desert beyond. She asks is he hungry? He says no. "Big boy like you not hungry?" She asks, "Where's your mother?" "In Los Angeles." With an expressive look of disgust she does the only thing she can for the boy: calls room service. Almost the whole time the camera is on the center of the scene: Albie's desolate expression. (In the script we hear her order and hear her verdict on folks who'd desert a kid like this: "Sick people." John shoots it, but decides he doesn't need it.)

As they prepare, John says, "Jakob, do you know what this scene is about?"

"Yes."

"You do?"

"*Yes.*"

"Don't tell anybody. Keep it a secret, okay?"

"Okay."

As Jakob turns to hang out elsewhere during the setting-up John says, "Hey, Jake." The boy comes back. "Give her some help when she comes to the door. The maid. It's her first day, she's nervous. Remember how you were on your first day? So give her some help. Be believable for her."

The boy smiles a proud, weary smile.

"You tired, Jakob?"

Jakob nods.

"That's okay, be tired. You can use *that*, too."

This very short scene takes a very long time. Carolyn, as John observed, is indeed anxious. On the first takes she muffs everything – lines, movement cues, everything. She says "I'm sorry" a lot. Very gently John says, "Carolyn, sit down a few minutes, sit down and relax."

The room is a suite. The action is in the bedroom. After several fruitless takes, John won't watch. He sits in the living room. Eddie and Al ask John to attend where they're filming, but John can't watch this woman's anxiety anymore. "I concentrate better in here, I see her in the bar mirror."

After a take Al asks, "Was it alright?"

"Alright."

"A little fast?"

"A little wooden."

They do it again. John won't watch.

Carolyn Baker is keenly aware that John doesn't even want to watch her. It makes everything worse. She walked in scared, now she's terrified, but she sticks – while Jakob is fine, take after take, consistent, not thrown by any of this, an extraordinarily patient and fair-natured little boy, nothing fidgety or snide about him. He's become a pro, alright.

The takes go on, John doesn't watch. He hears Eddie call "Action." He calls Eddie into his room, tells him, "Eddie, let me say 'Action,' will you please – for her sake."

I've never seen Cassavetes so tired. Maybe nobody has. He slurs his words. Every movement seems an effort. I realize he's sitting down in the other room not only because it's taking too much out of him to watch her, but because the man can't stand up.

Nevertheless, as the takes go on, he rouses himself. He must. He's the only one who can fix this. He goes and speaks gently to Carolyn, finishing with, "Deal with the *scene,* darling, not the script." She's a little better on the next take. He smiles. "Carolyn, I got it, I get it, and you got it, so let's just do one more for fun."

In the final take she's just right.

Late, late that night, John, Robert Fieldsteel, and I, sit in John's room. John jokes about the bathroom. He hates its mirrors – everywhere he turns he sees his belly. He laughs that devil laugh. Fieldsteel and I laugh with him.

You can't help it. John *really* thinks it's funny. His sense of absurdity is catchy. We really think it's funny too. With him. For now.

John turns serious discussing his film. He knows it's not the sort of picture most people want to see. But: "What people *like* is different from what they want. You have to give them what they want, not what they like. They see insincerity and they hate it – but they don't say what they really feel. Why do people throw away all their mentality, all of what they really feel, in lieu of a promise – fake, made by the society – of how everybody's supposed to live?"

Today's work will be in the final cut.

FRIDAY, JUNE 17 – *You stink*

A very drunk Robert Harmon staggers down the hall, knocks on the door, Albie opens in tears, angry tears, and wants to go home. Harmon gets angry, but, in his own way, breaks down as well.

Then, very quickly, an exhausted Jakob and an angry crew shoot the useless vintage-car-exhibit scene.

By the time Robert Harmon takes the elevator to his floor, his hilarity with the whores has vanished as though it had never been, as though it meant nothing. In a long dolly shot down the hallway, the camera recedes before a staggering, pathetically drunk, unhappy man. John is satisfied with his performance on the third take.

The next scene is Jakob Shaw's most difficult. It is terribly hard for a proud boy to break down, weep and whine, over and over, "I wanna go home, I want my mother, I want my mother." This is precisely what any boy Jakob's age is most afraid of feeling and most afraid of doing, especially on camera, and most especially infront of more than a dozen gawking witnesses. The shoot is interminable and excruciating. At first the kid just can't get those emotions going. John goads him, pushes him, gets angry at him – trying to crack the natural reserve, the unusual dignity, that has served Jakob's performance so beautifully in his previous scenes.

This kid's tough. It takes a lot even for a Cassavetes to shake him, but finally John does, the kid loses it – and, admittedly, the performance (if, by now, you can call it that) is terrific.

But it will require three set-ups and a total of 15 takes – more like 20 actually, and probably more than that, because on two takes John runs the action through several times without a cut. In other words, the boy is called upon to be in this state, and in this situation, for almost two hours.

For the rest of us, it's the most difficult scene to watch. Quickly we lose all objectivity. There are maybe 15 of us in the hall, crowded behind the camera, and nobody is on John's side. Toward the end Jakob, really angry and *really* wanting to go home, ad libs, "You *stink!* I want to go *home.*"

We cheer and raise our fists in solidarity. (However, none of us dreams of interfering, and that says whatever it says about us.) John gives us a severe look, rolls his eyes. They go again.

"Didn't I tell you, didn't I tell you I was gonna go out all night? DIDN'T I! I *told you* I was goin' out all night, I was gonna *be* with somebody, didn't I?"

"Yeah."

"And you said ok, right?"

"Right." (The boy is breathless, he can hardly say the words.)

"You said you were gonna be a man and I was gonna be a man, right?"

"Yeah."

John/Harmon sinks to his knees, clutches the boy, the boy struggles, really struggles, doesn't want to be held, John is repeating "Didn't I" and the boy's repeating "I wanna go home, I wanna see my mother," and John/Harmon, on his knees holding the boy, stops speaking, closes his eyes, buries his face in the boy's chest, presses his cheek against the boy's heart, and John's face, turned toward the camera, is a study of agony and grief. Robert Harmon – at tremendous cost to someone else, to an innocent – has finally felt something genuine.

Do I need to note it? That scene makes the final cut.

MONDAY, JUNE 20 – *The worst I've seen him blow*

The scenes today occur just before Harmon and Albie go to Las Vegas. We've seen Albie, drunk, alert his father that two cabs have arrived; we've seen his father, also drunk, telling Albie to shoo the visitors away, and the boy immobilized [shot June 7] . Now:

Harmon goes outside to see what's going on. One driver [Phedon], standing by his car, tells Harmon, "There's a lady in the cab." Harmon opens the passenger door and we see Sarah Lawson smiling at him, a smile we've not seen before – relaxed, happy. Harmon lunges into the cab, throws himself on her, embracing her! He's spontaneous for the first time. He says a muffled exclamation – "God!" – into her shoulder. She clutches him with closed eyes and an expression of fulfillment. Cassavetes has constructed his film such that this is its most shocking moment thus far. We've not yet seen, nor have we been led to expect, these aspects of either character.

From their embrace, the camera pans to a confused Albie standing by the cab, near Sarah's open window. Harmon explains, "This is my son from the second marriage." Sarah is delighted, wishes she'd brought Albie a present, says she hasn't seen him "since he was in the hospital being born." Harmon tells her that's the last time he saw Albie too.

Harmon tells the cabbies to take Sarah's luggage inside. He also tells them (in her hearing) to wait, he's going to the airport.

Sarah, out of the cab, grinning, looks at the house in a way that makes clear she's never seen it. As they go into the house, Robert kisses her on the cheek. Spontaneous again. Just inside the house they embrace again, very happy, she's saying, "This is wonderful! I can't believe I'm actually here, can't believe I'm actually seeing you!" While he hugs her he's grinning, "You NUT, you're nutty as a fruitcake, I love you."

There's no doubting his sincerity. This is the first time he speaks with no hint of irony or disgust.

After Vegas and the raw Mojave, it's soothing to drive up winding leafy Laurel Canyon Boulevard, take a right onto Mulholland at the top of the hill, then another right, and after a few curves there's the steep circling driveway to the Cassavetes home, surrounded by foliage. If John and Gena wished, they could cut the greenery in front of their house and view a great vista of Los Angeles, miles and miles of it. But that's not for them. They prefer enclosure, their home surrounded by thick plant-life. Gena tells me that sometimes in the early morning she'll go out with her BB gun and scare off the coyotes.

Not that she needs a gun to be scary. Seymour Cassel says, "She has such a dignity about her that she can intimidate you if you let her."

They're shooting the cab scene in front of the house.

From inside the cab Gena calls out a clipped, "Hey! Cassavetes!

He's all attention.

She's concerned that when Robert Harmon opens the cab door the reaction-shot – a shot showing a character's response – is of Sarah. Gena wants a reaction-shot of Harmon too, before they embrace. "I think it's very important to see what you're thinking at the moment."

John resists. She pushes. John says, "I say what Marty Ritt once said when I had an idea on *his* set [*Edge of the City*, 1956]. He said, 'When the Indians start making the pictures then –'"

"This Indian *is* making a picture, *honey*."

The rest of us freeze in place. No one breathes.

Between John and Gena, a thick silent moment – then she shrugs, "You're the director, but I think it's a mistake."

(I realize later John doesn't want to tip off Harmon's feelings with a reaction-shot before Harmon's spontaneous lunge at Sarah in the cab. He wants to surprise us.)

The nine outdoor set-ups take forever. The sun goes in and out behind the clouds, ruining the matching light. Film magazines jam. The boom man (who's working for no pay but experience) doesn't aim the boom correctly. John is even critical of one of Al's camera moves – a first for this shoot. Al smiles sweetly (sweetly for Al) and says evenly, "John – I'm *glad* you're getting older."

Then, horrors, a take goes too smoothly. Gena complains, "We did it so smoothly and easily it's like a *plan* that's unfolding."

As Gena knows better than anyone, there's nothing worse you can say about a John Cassavetes shot. They do it again.

The cabbies, Phedon and Jim (a Teamster on the production), must tote all her luggage into the house. John tells them to do it any old way, so it looks real. They take forever and it's a mess. There's no way for amateur actors to improvise such a seemingly simple, but actually quite complicated, activity. After their useless take, Gena says chirpily (getting her licks in), "We had a very good scene that time, John, one that you hadn't written. You said be free, they were free."

John's glare would blow anyone away – anyone but Gena.

"Now you're mad at me," she chides, and, as an offering to his bruised dignity, she puts her arms around him, then rubs his shoulders. He's still mad.

Into the midst of this walks poor Priscilla.

Pert and pretty, with long blond hair and lovely features dulled by a dour expression, Priscilla McDonald is the efficient, snappy head of publicity at Cannon Films. What happens next takes a little background to understand.

One evening about two weeks ago the phone rings at John's house. John takes the call, gets quietly angry, hangs up, tells me it was Al Ruban: Priscilla wants to 'can' Larry Shaw. Hates his on-set photos. I'm thinking, "Fire Sam Shaw's son, Jakob Shaw's father, on John Cassavetes' set – do you know how to spell 'fat chance'?"

Within days another still photographer appears on the set, hired by Priscilla: Francois Duhamel-Mega. He's a good guy, Larry's a good guy, and to their great credit they get along, asking each other about light-readings, shooting angles and the like. But Francois is confident, while Larry – a large, gentle, affable man – is insecure. Several days later he shows John some of his color prints, saying hopefully, "Something you could use?" His eyelids flicker as he says it. John smiles – when Larry was little, John took him to ballgames. "Sure, Larry, sure." Around that time Al Ruban tells John that so-and-so, a Cannon executive, swore to him that he didn't know about the new photographer. I tell John that so-and-so is lying. The day before Francois showed up I heard so-and-so say "They're getting a new guy tomorrow." Al smoothes it over with Cannon: the new guy can stay but his salary will be paid by Cannon directly, it won't come out of *Love Streams'* budget. That's when John assigns me to write a synopsis of *Love Streams* – he thinks the film will "take a bath" with reviewers because they won't know what to do with it, and he doesn't trust Golan's people (Priscilla) to get it right.

Priscilla is expected today. There's an appointment. John's gone through all Larry's black-and-whites, selected a stack he likes, and he'll show them to her when she arrives on-set. The woman's mistake: she wants to prove to Cassavetes that she's right. Priscilla's had a victory, she's gotten her man on-set. She should have left it that way.

I'm eating lunch, I miss the first round. Bo Harwood tells me, "He really gave it to her, man, that's the worst I've seen him blow on *this* shoot." Bo says John handed Priscilla the stack of black-and-whites, she flipped through them like a pack of cards, he said she passed up a great shot, she looked at the great shot and sniffed, then kept flipping. And (nobody tells me why) John thinks she's been rude to *Gena.* Oh my God. So Eddie was directed to get Priscilla off the set – non-violently, if possible.

John hasn't counted on Priscilla being almost as stubborn as he is. (Give her that.) While John tells me what just happened, Priscilla steps up and asks if he'd like to see Francois' shots now.

"I don't wanna see anything you have anything to do with! I

don't want to see your fucking face again, as long as I live, you and your rude fucking attitude, what do you think I am, your fucking messenger boy, get off my set, GET THE HELL OFF RIGHT NOW, rude fucking cunt."

Midway through his rant Priscilla's walking down that steep driveway as fast as she can manage without actually running.

John wins the battle, Priscilla wins the war. Humiliated by this public brouhaha, when his son Jakob's scenes are done Larry Shaw will quietly disappear.

Cassavetes is pissed at Priscilla, pissed at Gena, pissed in general. He takes me aside to vent. "It's a fucking *production*! I can't say, 'Just backlight it there and throw a reflector up there and it'll be alright.' They've gotta do *this*, they've gotta do *that* – they're professionals. I need amateurs. And I can't get it with this crew without being a prick all day. I could have killed Gena, those cab shots – because she'd just come to do it well, to do the part and not be in the way, keep distance, handle it, and that's not this kind of picture. This kind of picture, you've gotta get on and own it for yourself, get *on* there, it's *your* picture. Like she did in the warehouse scenes."

His memory is plenty selective. He neglects to remember Gena arguing for his close-up – and neglects to consider that, after he put her down in front of everyone, she might not feel like getting more involved than necessary. As for the lighting, Al's in charge and Al does it John's way. This is just John being temporarily insane.

I say none of this – not because it would just make him crazier, but because it's become clear that my prime function is to be John's sounding board, so he can think or vent aloud without affecting anyone who has a real job on this picture. (This book is my job, but it doesn't get the picture made.)

Most of all John's pissed at himself and he knows it: "I've been shooting so *slow*. I don't know how to speed it up now."

The outburst at Priscilla is expensive. It costs him embarrassment with Menahem Golan, Priscilla's boss and (technically)

John's. It costs precious time, having to work through intermediaries because he and Priscilla are not speaking. Finally it costs him the chastisement, later in the week, of going to Priscilla's office and making an official apology. "And she was very sweet to accept the apology," he'll tell me. Then that devil-laugh: "I would have thrown me out of the office!"

Later I'm at Cannon, in the *Love Streams* production office, where Carole R. Smith (official title, Production Office Coordinator) wants an eyewitness account of the tussle. She's heard of nothing else all day, but at second- and third-hand. A small round-ish woman with direct eyes and a no-nonsense air, Carole's the person who *must* be telephoned for most production decisions to be actually accomplished. If a Cassavetes film is like a neighborhood bar, Carole's the bartender. Tough in the best sense, if you ask her about John her first reaction is, "John who? I know lotsa Johns."

I give her a blow-by-blow of the brouhaha. She laughs. She knows John well. On *A Woman Under the Influence* she was Production Office Coordinator and "paid the bills, did a lot of cooking and shopping, was the Transportation Coordinator, ordered the film, took care of children, did props, wardrobe, all kinds of things. It's so funny, because when we were shooting *A Woman Under the Influence,* every time something was going really, really bad, John would yell 'Carole! Shut up!' Like I was making all the noise. And it wasn't me! Now he hasn't got a Carole to yell at. Poor darling, he hasn't picked a scapegoat on this picture, because there's nobody there who would take it as well as I did.

"One day on *Woman* John was yelling someone down at his very best, which is his very worst. I felt sorry for the guy, I said, 'John! *Stop it*!' He turns to me, big smile, says, 'Carole, you're spoiling my act."

Ten set-ups, 41 takes, about 21 minutes of printed film, for two minutes of the final cut.

TUESDAY, JUNE 21 – *All that jazz*

Harmon, Sarah, and Albie have gone inside the house, Harmon and Sarah have embraced [shot yesterday]. Today we shoot how Robert Harmon suddenly switches gears, gets hyper, excited, insists she has a drink, then goes upstairs to supervise where the cabbies are to put her many, many pieces of luggage. Sarah, alone with Albie, asks, "So, how do you like your father?" Albie answers with sullen silence. Sarah says, "Well, he happens to be a wonderful person – everybody likes him."

When Harmon comes back downstairs he springs on Sarah and Albie that he's taking the kid to Las Vegas. The kid is surprised, so it's clear to Sarah that this plan has just been conceived. She hasn't been there 10 minutes. Harmon's genuinely happy to see her, yet he's leaving her flat. Given that he's already told the cab to wait, he made that decision before she entered the house. To smooth things over, Harmon asks if Sarah wants to come to Vegas too. Before she can answer, Harmon asks Albie if he wants Sarah to come. Albie says no.

As Harmon gives Sarah the keys to his car he asks, "Can you drive?" "Sure I can drive." He gives her directions to the nearest shopping center.

They embrace again, at the door. As they embrace she says, "I read all your books. They're all about women." "I know." They stand there, he ruffs the kid's hair while he looks at Sarah – the only affection he's shown the boy. She ruffs the kid's hair as they leave.

Slowly, with deliberation, she closes the front door, stands there, runs her hands through her hair. Though we view her from behind, Gena's body-language is so eloquent we don't need to see her face; her slightly bent legs, the gesture of closing the door, how she stands a little stooped, then straightens her posture and runs her hands through her hair and seems to sigh – all eloquent of a desperate woman, left alone again, but in a place that may be a refuge.

Then Robert and Albie talk in the cab. Albie asks, "Who was that?" Harmon says, "You mean Sarah?" Who else could Albie possibly mean? "Do you love her?" "Not the way you mean." "Do you kiss her?" "Not the way you mean I said."

Interestingly, John rewrote yesterday's and today's scenes (revision dated June 20), cutting any hint of specificity, even the vaguest clue to their relationship, and cutting anything concrete about Sarah's attitude. In the May 13 shooting script, when Harmon sees all her luggage he says, "That means you've left your husband?" "Yes," Sarah answers. A few beats later Sarah says, "I see you don't want me here." And when Sarah asks Albie if he likes his father, he says "Yes" and she says, "That's amazing. No one else does."

Also in the May 13 script, Harmon is apologetic about leaving her, asks if it's alright, promises that "I have a whole book to write about you when I get back," and doesn't ask if she can drive.

Cassavetes is consistently excising anything that might let a viewer define the relationship between Robert Harmon and Sarah Lawson. And he adds lines ("Can you drive?") that deepen the mystery. He's often written new lines that play against the content of a scene, as in having Sarah say what viewers know to be untrue, that Harmon is "a wonderful person" whom "everybody" likes. Cassavetes addresses the questions Albie naturally would have; Harmon could easily tell the boy who Sarah is, but refuses. As near as I can tell, he's made most or all of these changes without consulting Ted Allan. Every change makes the film more indefinite and abstract. At this point it seems John has something in mind, he's driving the film in a certain direction, but as yet I have no idea where, what, or why.

A guy on the crew announces to everybody, "It's the summer solstice!" Then, to himself, "I wonder what the Hopis are doing right now."

Right now Cassavetes is bemoaning yesterday's work. "I even shot coverage of Gena looking into the living room – and she never looked into the living room!"

We're slow getting started because a fuse blew on the sound equipment and Bo Harwood has ridden off on his motorcycle to buy a replacement. Phedon and Eddie argue elaborately about the rules of solitaire. Several crew guys sit at John's kitchen table playing poker. And John's telling me that *Love Streams* is really a musical.

Really a *what*?

He explains at length, motions me to follow him, we go into a kind of walk-in closet, almost large enough to be a room – John all the while explaining that, *really*, the movie's a musical. I have no idea what he's talking about. I'm so befuddled, I neglect to take notes. (Nor would notes help – after all, it's not as though he's speaking in complete sentences.)

In the little room, or big closet, are stacks of old records. Literally, 'stacks,' LPs (mostly without jackets) piled on shelves, rubbing scratches into each other, collecting dust. John quickly flips through several, then, breaking off his incoherent 'musical' explanation, he gets very excited about one record.

"You gotta here this, Michael, this is a *beautiful* record."

The record is titled 'Top Brass,' on the old Savoy label, the small company that recorded Charlie Parker.

He rushes out of the room and I follow, up the stairs, into a bedroom where Gena is applying her make-up. Part bedroom, part make-up room, part wardrobe room, there can't help but be a mess. There's a circa-1960s phonograph atop a stand in the corner of the room.

Excited, he shows Gena the record.

"Oh that record!" she says. "It's so elegant."

As John brushes the dust from the vinyl and turns on the phonograph he explains, "It's just these jazz-guys, trumpet players, nobody famous, and they're playing together, not to compete, to *listen* to each other, enjoy each other." He places the record on the turntable, sets the needle on the first cut – a blaring up-tempo bebop tune.

"Not that one," Gena says, "the next one."

Several others are in the room now, drawn by John's and Gena's enthusiasm. The music begins. It's so wonderful I will spend most of next Saturday hunting it down in Los Angeles' record stores, finally finding 'Top Brass' in the used bins of Rhino Records on Westwood Boulevard. The trumpeters are Donald Byrd (who recorded with John Coltrane), Ernie Royal and Joe Wilder (whom I've not heard of), Roy Copeland and Idrees Sulieman (both recorded with Thelonious Monk) – first-rate bebop horns, none famous enough to front his own recording, gathered together by an astute producer for a unique session. The cut John and Gena love, and have remembered so vividly since they bought the record in 1955, is a medley that spins for 15 minutes. Backed by Hank Jones on piano, one by one each trumpeter renders a ballad – *Willow Weep for Me, Imagination, It Might As Well Be Spring, The Nearness of You,* and (not usually played slow) *Taking a Chance on Love.* (It's interesting that *Imagination* was a featured number in *The Killing of a Chinese Bookie,* and later in *Love Streams* Gena will sing a line from *Taking a Chance on Love.*) Each melody, connected by Hank Jones' modulations, is interpreted with restrained, meditative loveliness, each trumpeter's style a different language of longing, intelligent and beautiful. As the music plays several of us sit on the edge of the bed, or lean against the bureau, or stand in the doorway, while John rubs Gena's shoulders – all of us suddenly as far from the hectic making of this movie as though we'd risen together unexpectedly in the basket of a balloon.

No one says anything when the medley is done. Cassavetes leaves the room, everyone remembers they have jobs to do, the spell is broken. Call it a brief example of art's healing, restorative power.

Today's eight set-ups and 31 takes go comparatively smoothly. The work is essential in the final cut.

WEDNESDAY, JUNE 22 – *A movie, not a moment*

This evening we'll shoot what directly follows the Las Vegas sequence: Robert Harmon takes Albie back to his mother.

Just as twilight turns into night, Robert Harmon and Albie pull up in a cab across the street from a dilapidated working-class house in the Echo Park neighborhood of Los Angeles. The ground rises steeply from the sidewalk to the front porch; there are stairs from the sidewalk to the porch. The boy looks like he's about to cry. Harmon says he's sorry "the vacation didn't work out." As soon as Albie is out of the cab he bolts across the street, runs up the stairs, pounds on the front door. When the door doesn't immediately open he bangs his head against it. His father Eddie [Eddie Donno] opens the door, sees Albie's bloodied head, asks, "Did he do this to you?" Eddie tenderly leads Albie inside where Albie's mother, hysterical, exclaims, "What did he do to you!?" Harmon watches from across the street, is concerned, goes up the stairs and knocks on the door. Eddie opens the door. Harmon says, "I'm Robert Harmon," Eddie instantly commences to beat the shit out of him – punching, kicking, while Agnes tries to stop it and Albie says to Harmon, "I love you, Dad," over and over, as Agnes and Eddie pull the kid inside and shut the door.

Set-ups won't begin until early evening. John spends the day with George Villasenor in the editing room. John will tell me, "When you're making a film, you're not conservative at all. I'm not. But when you're *cutting* a film you suddenly say, 'Oh yes, I want it to look like a *film.* And you have terrible problems. I mean, we do a scene, and on one side it's marvelous; and on the other side it's marvelous, and then you start cutting it up – and it's no longer marvelous! You miss it. 'Cause you're either on *that* person's side, or with this person's side, and I look at it and I hate it. What happened to Gena? What happened to the other actors? What happened?

"And so, in getting a guy like George Villasenor, it's so wonderful, I don't have to go through those emotional turmoils. *He* goes through them. And I say, 'Wonderful, George, it's really great.' He says, 'Yeah, but I shoulda been on a Gena a little longer there.' 'No, no, no, it's alright,' I tell him, 'you're indulging yourself.'"

In the editing room John explains, "You get fooled by the picture."

I ask what he means.

"Sometimes you see a good moment, and you just watch the moment. But when you put it together it's soft, it's not coming from anywhere."

"You fall in love with one piece," George adds, "and it doesn't fit with the others."

"See," John says, "I don't want one fake look in this picture. That's why we don't help it along with the camera. It's all straight shots. The beauty has to come straight out of what we're *doing.* That's why it's such a tough picture."

A working editing room is always dark, the better to see the screen. John and George stand over the rattling Moviola watching Robert Harmon get out of a cab.

"Let him go a little more," John tells George, "let him go a couple of steps. There's something very free and nice about that walk, you know?"

"Yeah – it still has energy, you know? On the other takes, it's dying. But there's a little match problem there." The take doesn't quite match what comes before or after.

"I dunno," John says. "It doesn't bother me."

"But I have to agree with you," George admits, "that shot fits the character better."

They watch Albie and Robert Harmon in the Vegas hotel. Over the Moviola's clatter we see Harmon hug his son, the boy struggling to get free, crying, "I want to go home, I want to see my mother." We see Harmon's grief as, on his knees, he presses his face to his boy's chest.

"George, I don't want that to be too smoothly cut. Because it's such a disturbing scene, it should rock you. And if it gets too well-timed then it starts to look like a *movie,* not a moment. You know?"

That is the most succinct statement of Cassavetes' aesthetic we'll ever hear – Cassavetes, the guy who insists he doesn't know what he's doing.

Now they're looking at footage of Sarah entering Harmon's house for the first time, and Harmon and Albie leaving so quickly.

"I just love Gena's timing," John says. "I know she'd go through with a scene no matter *what* happened – if she were hanging off a cliff!"

John watches her reaction to Harmon's exit several times.

"George, I wanna pop that film, so that her entrance and our leaving happen so fucking fast we don't know what's happened."

He means he wants to jump the transitions, show the emotions with as little connective tissue as possible. "I don't like to pop the emotions, but I like to pop the other stuff right there."

"I'm not going to let you do that too often," George says. "Everything's worked so far. It's when things don't work that you try to shock them into action. But let's try it."

During a break John and I run into Eddie Donno in the hallway. This is not the Eddie we're used to, the indefatigable Eddie in shorts and T-shirt bellowing instructions to the crew. He's dressed for his role tonight as Albie's stepfather, and his mood is subdued.

"So, Eddie, you know all the words you're gonna say tonight?" John asks with mock archness.

"No, but I know the character. I'll look at the lines later."

"Everybody imitates *me* now! I *know* all my lines! You know that, Eddie, don't you? Don't you know that?"

"I know that."

"I just refuse to *say* them."

Both men crack up laughing.

You don't notice that it's getting dark until 8:30 or even nine in the evening at this time of year in Los Angeles. This Echo Park neighborhood has eaten its dinner and is coming out on the streets to cool off. Hispanic mostly, kids mostly, hovering about our *Love Streams* vans, our power generator, our portable dressing rooms, our canteen truck, the scaffolding we've built for the lights, the cops directing traffic – even a small production like *Love Streams* comes on like a circus in a neighborhood like this. A couple of ice-cream trucks make their rounds, each broadcasting its incessant jangly jingle.

When we start shooting a crowd gathers. Crowd control will not only be easy, it will be a lesson in how seductive is this awkward business of making a motion picture. As the crowd starts edging up to the action, a local Hispanic kid, maybe 15, starts yelling, "Quiet!" and "Please step back, outa the way, *please*!"

When they call "Cut!" because of a muffed line this lad shakes his head and says under his breath, "No good, no good."

When the take starts again, our production's crowd controllers yell, *"Silencio! Silencio!"*, but this good and serious lad yells "Quiet! Quiet for the next shot!"

As the crew sets up the next take, Robert Fieldsteel and I discuss the evening's scenes. Fieldsteel's a young, capable man with a sometimes baffling array of gestures. When he's excited, his two arms will do different movements in different directions. He walks with a little waddle, like Chaplin playing a professor. He has huge, utterly frank eyes. He's a gentle, intelligent man.

Tonight he's mad. The scene about to be shot is all wrong. The action is too emotional. The kid shouldn't say "I love you" to Harmon. After the stepfather beats Harmon up, the kid should just look at him, then we should cut. We shouldn't see Agnes running after Harmon and screaming, shouldn't hear Harmon say "It's too late." Playing this John's way "makes Gena look silly," because a love stream stops here, and she says it doesn't stop. I ask Fieldsteel if he's told this to John, and he says he doesn't like to volunteer his opinions that freely, he prefers to tell John only when John asks.

"So what do you think, Robert?" asks John.

Cassavetes hasn't exactly materialized out of thin air. When our conversation began, I noticed him half a block away at the ice-cream truck. He had no reason to walk our way except that he felt like it. He had no idea what we were speaking of, but that question was the first thing out of his mouth – "So what do you think, Robert?"

This is a quality of being a director that isn't taught in film school because it can't be. It's the quality of being tuned in. From down the block John saw an energy in our conversation that might be worth his time, so here he is.

Fieldsteel tells Cassavetes what he's just told me. John's expression darkens in disagreement.

"You might be right," he says, "but everything you're saying is purely literary."

"What does *that* mean?"

Fieldsteel and Cassavetes are arching eyebrows at each other. Fieldsteel has learned the art of arching eyebrows from the master, and he's learned well.

"That's just writing you're talking about," John says. "I'm not a writer! What you're talking about hasn't been performed yet, and there's no way to know how that's gonna go until it's played."

As for cutting the scene when Albie is looking at the prostrate, beat-up Harmon, Cassavetes thinks it's "important" to see the whole scene, see the consequences of what these people do, Agnes running after Harmon, Harmon leaving in the cab.

"We have to see the whole painful emotional thing – otherwise, it's just a movie."

Some of tonight's work will make the final cut.

THURSDAY, June 23 – *My dinner with Cassavetes*

We re-shoot last night's scene. Then:

Harmon staggers back to the cab with Agnes chasing after him, hysterical, yelling "He's your son, he's your son!" In the cab, Harmon says flatly, "It's too late."

Interestingly, Robert Harmon's son is playing a scene parallel to what we saw Robert Harmon do early in the film. Harmon stumbled up a flight of stairs to Susan's little house, fell, bloodied his head, and needed to be helped inside. Now Albie runs up a similar stair to a similar house, bloodies his head, and must be helped inside. For Cassavetes, the quality of "family" is something that plays itself out mysteriously, inevitably, out of control of anyone's intentions. After Albie's stepfather beats Harmon and Harmon lies on the ground, Albie stands over him, his face bloody, and says hesitantly, "I love you, Dad." Visually what is being said is, "I am you, Dad."

Tonight John adds a long close-up of Robert Harmon lying on the ground after Albie and the others go back in their house. It's clear he's following a train of thought and coming to some conclusion, though what these are we can't know.

Tonight is Jakob Shaw's last scene. Between set-ups John says, "Gena told me, 'Why are you so mean to that child? I can't work that way.' But he's starting to think for himself. If everybody's telling him how great he is, he'll never have to think for himself."

They're shooting Albie at the front door, banging it with his fists, screaming to get in. Jakob is supposed to fake hitting his head on the door (he's been shown how) and break a blood-pack concealed from the camera under his hair. But Jakob gets so caught up in the scene that when the blood-pack doesn't break (as sometimes happens) he slams his head against the door to break it, before anyone can stop him – and all the while he continues to deliver his lines!

The rest of the night the boy will be a little wobbly on his feet. He gave that door quite a shot with his head. That's the take they'll use in the film.

It's pushing midnight when we wrap the day's work. John invites Phedon and I to a late steak dinner at the Pacific Dining Car on 6th Street, one of the city's finer restaurants, and the only really good restaurant open at this hour. We're quite a bit more rumpled than the other diners, but you can get away with that when you're a star-plus-entourage. John's slacks and sports coat look slept in. I'm in jeans, a shirt I've sweated through twice today, and cowboy boots. But Phedon dignifies us. Trim and thoroughly European, he has a trace of elegance no matter what he wears. His true clothing is a precision of gesture which rarely fails to command respect, especially in good restaurants.

We're seated, we order, and John says he's concerned about Phedon. Gena brought a psychic to the house yesterday and the psychic said that someone close to John, possibly a relative, very different yet very like, was going through a deep change right now, making a decision or shift that would be very important, and it sounded like something Phedon might be going through. John is careful not to mention specifics in front of me. Phedon graciously tells him, "You can say it – Ventura is not a stranger."

John shakes his head. Ventura may not be a stranger but Ventura is a writer, and John knows that writers can be merciless about their material, though I have been trying mightily to respect the privacy of these people. Still, it is a very thin line between writing only what reveals them as creators and writing what reveals them as men and women to their intimates, which is neither my business nor yours.

Thankfully we slide off that subject and start bemoaning – I don't know how it came up – the lack of English art since World War Two. How they've had no great poet and no native novelist for a long time. Laurence Durrell was born in India, after all, and Doris Lessing comes from Africa. "They never *had* a novelist," says Phedon, and I say, "What about Dickens?" and both John and Phedon cry "Dickens!" enthusiastically, and we agree that Dickens has been carrying England's honor in literature for a hundred years. This generalization is gross, unfair, and all but illiterate, but we relish making it, and it starts Phedon to remembering England during the war – how, at the age of 19, when the Nazis occupied Greece, he escaped, went to England, and joined the R.A.F. He served for a year and a half before joining the free Greek forces and spending three years in combat on a destroyer. "I saw hell during the war – not in my private life only, but the hell of war. When the war ended it was not possible for me to be afraid of any man."

In England he had married an Irish girl with whom he was deeply in love. They had a child. While Phedon was on the destroyer, his wife and child were killed in an air raid. After the war he returned to Greece where his father, a major industrialist, wanted him to join the business. "I said 'Fuck you' to all that – went to Africa, to Europe, all over, turned down many jobs and lots of money, in order to paint. I tried to be an artist, do you see? Now – I am myself, and that is enough."

Our talk turns, for one of the only times this summer, to movies. John says he saw "an *incredible* film" today, or yesterday morning, on television, "with one of those English actresses who always looks like she's about to have a breakdown," whom we soon establish is Susannah York. He doesn't know who directed it, he was flipping through the channels and the film was already well begun when it hooked him. As he describes the picture I realize it is Robert Altman's un-Altman-like *Images,* never widely distributed in the United States. Altman made it during that intensive period that included *M.A.S.H.* and *McCabe and Mrs. Miller. Images* is a frightening picture about a woman losing her mind, one of the few movies I've seen where the viewer truly loses the distinction between reality and unreality. John thinks it's a little like "that Garfunkle picture by that English guy," which he also loves. I fill in the blanks: "*Bad Timing,* Nic Roeg." John loves every Roeg picture he's seen. "I wanted him to be the cinematographer for this picture, but they said, 'You can't do *that,* he's a director!'" John speaks glowingly of Roeg's technique, and how *there's* a man who knows what it's all about. (Later he will express similar enthusiasm for Oshima's *Merry Christmas, Mr. Lawrence* – it convinces him that the Japanese will love *Love Streams,* "even if the rest of the world hates it.") Then, out of nowhere: "Maybe we should go home and watch *The Godfather.* Or *Failsafe.* That picture made me cry, when they decided to bomb New York."

Phedon says he's heard that the cinematography of *Return of the Jedi* is supposed to be very good, but John just expresses disgust. "If I directed a picture like that, or even *worked* on one, I would faint – I'd faint, and I'd never get up again, I'd be so ashamed."

(Later, when reminded of the comment, he'll say, "I love George Lucas. No, no, I meant I couldn't handle all the technical stuff and keep from going crazy." I'll allow these comments to abut each other and let it go at that.)

John speaks with special reverence of Kurosawa, then bursts out laughing. "I love him, but I can't ever meet him – I've been avoiding meeting him for years." Kurosawa once wrote a letter to John about how much he admired *Shadows,* and how it had inspired him to make a film about street-life in Japan. (None of us can remember the film's title.) Kurosawa had written how Cassavetes' use of locations in *Shadows* had been very thrilling to him as a filmmaker. "And how could I tell him that we hardly *used* locations! I mean, we did a lot of shooting in the *street,* if you want to call that a location, but we had this one little room, just a room, and we made that room look like anything we needed it to look like. I felt like such an asshole when I got the letter."

Kurosawa sent John a script once, "but I couldn't, it was all *hi, hi,* whatever it was. I could never face the man now. *Great* filmmaker, though, that man."

Filmmaking is an adventure, John says, one of the only adventures left. Phedon says that he's sorry for his son, age 21, because it's not possible today to have the sort of adventures that he had as a young man.

"There are still adventures," I say.

John bemoans that there are very few artists now.

"There are still artists," I say.

John brings up the 1920s, and the French art movement of the late 19th Century, and the New York scene of the 1950s, and says that there's no camaraderie among artists now. There are no vocal colonies, no artistic circles that are making a difference, nobody giving art a special voice, "that special force." He refrains a thought he often says: that artists have to be young; that there's no such thing as an older artist. "Artists *ought* to be young" – because when you're older, calmer, wiser, you begin to see things "in a *general* way," and that's good, but it's not the passionate particular way that you see when you're young. And that's what makes the most exciting art, Cassavetes says.

Now he bemoans how, in his own eyes, he can't spark this crew, doesn't have the infectious energy he once had, to make the whole thing a party so that everyone will go and go and go. (Phedon and I don't say the obvious: John, you're *ill.*) John recalls *Shadows,* how they'd go to bed at five in the morning and get up at seven and get straight back to work because there seemed nothing else in the world more fun or more worth doing. Or *Faces,* when he'd get an idea at four in the morning and call everyone – there were "about 10 people" on the entire picture – and they'd come over, and by the time they got there everybody would be too tired to work, but they'd drink and talk and take the next day off, and maybe the next, and then *do* it, with sheer headlong excitement.

"The god of *this* picture is money," John says of *Love Streams.* Phedon and I exchange exasperated looks. What Cassavetes *means* is that *Love Streams* has a shooting schedule! Unlike

Shadows, *Faces*, and *A Woman Under the Influence*, there are people on this crew who insist on going home sometimes; and, also unlike those pictures, there will come a pre-scheduled day when no one will show up, and the picture had better be done by then. So he can't have the utter freedom he prefers and craves, though on *Love Streams* he must know that he has more freedom than most directors ever dream of.

If he knows, he's not admitting it tonight. Tonight he's complaining that on a shoot like this "you can't really *do* it." He talks about how he should have spent five days shooting the scene he's just done in two, so he could really "get out of that kid [Jakob Shaw] all that the kid has to give. Just worked and worked and got down and down. Because in daily life he's such a fantastic kid," and he should get *all* that on the screen. Jakob probably won't act again, at least not for a long time, and this was his chance to have that experience. "Because as long as you really have the great experience, the film doesn't matter."

Nothing matters but the intensity of the experience. Remember how on *Faces* there was that old woman [Dorothy Gulliver] who had been a silent movie star – "And I was gonna *kill* the next person who was so thrilled that she'd been a *silent movie star*." And he'd asked her, "Can you do 10 minutes with a chair? Just you and a chair?" And she'd said of course she could, and, with John paying for the film out of his own pocket, they shot 10 minutes of that woman playing to a chair. John mimes how first she came out and touched the chair's back, then its rim, then sat in it – 10 minutes of film, and it didn't matter if it ever got on screen because "*the impact of that experience*" would get in the film some other way, would be felt.

"I had those four women in that house and I'd get them drunk and think, *I'll drive these women so craaaaaazzzzzyyyyyy!* And that would all get on film."

And he and the silent movie star, the energy between them so vibrant, "and even sexual," so that one night he told her, "You can chase me for 30 minutes, or two hours, or whatever you say, and if you catch me, darling, I'm yours!" And around and around the house they went, the house where we're filming *Love Streams*, she calling out, "Svengali! Svengali! Oh, Svengali!" while Seymour Cassel was outside shouting through the windows, giving the old woman fake directions, Seymour climbing up on the roof to yell false leads, and the chase went on and on until:

Gena, pregnant, who'd been asleep upstairs, finally came down and said, "John, if that old woman dies I'll divorce you. Let her sit down and rest for 20 minutes before she chases you again."

Phedon and I can say nothing. It's like that moment in *Opening Night* when John turns to Gena and says, "I'm getting *older.* What do we do about that?" His real answer, his *life* answer, is that he will try to make a film, *Love Streams,* different from anything that he or anybody has ever done – a film about two people who in their separate lives have come to the end of love, the end of family, the end of any illusions about creativity, and who in the not-too-distant future will be old, two people beyond any possibility of what we generally take 'meaning' to mean, two people whose truths are raw and immediate, beyond words. A film in which a male and female archetype fitfully illuminate one another, a stormy illumination where every emotion leads to something beyond itself. A film which many are sure not to like, because such intensity and such risk gives them motion sickness.

Phedon and I say nothing. We both know enough to know that Cassavetes carries with him that special Hell reserved for the artist, the knowledge that no matter how hard you work and no matter with what faith and skill, what you create will never be as good as what you saw once, in the beginning, in the fires of your imagination, when you set yourself the task of bringing this work to life in the all-too-real world. There's no comfort for this, and there shouldn't be. So Phedon and I just listen, feeling almost as exhausted in one way as John says he feels in another, and John continues disjointedly speaking of *Love Streams,* and the check comes, and he pays, and we three stand, Phedon and I feeling rather helpless.

John looks from Phedon to me and back to Phedon, and says, quietly, "It's... it's still going to be a helluva picture."

And as though rising from the depths, he starts to laugh that cackly wheezy Mephistophelean laugh, and Phedon starts to laugh, and me, our laughters building into guffaws, all of which rather disturbs this sedate dining room and its proper clientele, and arm in arm we walk the length of the restaurant, grinning, suddenly enormously happy with ourselves and with each other – and, not the least, with this *Love Streams* in which we're sharing so strangely – for no nameable reason than 'because.'

And as the valets are getting our cars, Phedon announces, with that friendly dignity that is his special gift, "This has been a beautiful evening," like a benediction, and I get into my car as they stand there, and I drive off as John Cassavetes and Phedon Papamichael, cousins and fast friends, as the saying once went, speak of what they can only speak of when alone.

Footage shot these two nights will be interweaved in the final cut.

FRIDAY, JUNE 24 – *You can't hide anything*

After the debacle with his son, Robert Harmon steps from a cab in front of his house. In the cab, we see him smoking and very still. As though dazed, he walks through his dark rooms – suddenly he smashes his fist into the framed photographs of girls in the hallway. His hand bleeds. This passage is the bridge between Robert's encounter with Albie and his next moments with Sarah Lawson.

Yet again Cassavetes will edit this scene to make it less definite, more abstract. We won't see Robert Harmon punch the framed photo. We'll hear glass break and see that Harmon's hurt his hand – he might have hit it, but in his state of mind he might also have stumbled into that wall. The viewer can't be certain.

Another night shoot. John spends the day in the editing room with George Villasenor. In the evening, while John and the crew work, Gena and I talk about Ingmar Bergman. "I love him," she says, "I do love him, but *Scenes from a Marriage* – a MARRIAGE?!" She laughs. "There are no children in that film. Where's the marriage?"

Then she asks, "Am I right, is this one of John's finest performances?"

"Honestly, I think it's his best. It's a performance of tremen-

June 2. Robert Harmon (John Cassavetes) watches his son run away. Courtesy of Cannon Films/RGA.

June 10. Sarah (Gena Rowlands) speaks to her psychiatrist (David Rowlands): 'I don't need a sexual life.' Courtesy of Cannon Films/RGA.

June 14. Robert Harmon (John Cassavetes) drinks with his son Albie (Jakob Shaw). Courtesy of Cannon Films/RGA.

June 15. Robert Harmon (John Cassavetes) with two Vegas hookers (Geraldine Hofstetter and Kathryn Donno). Courtesy of Cannon Films/RGA.

June 20. Sarah Lawson (Gena Rowlands) arrives at the home of Robert Harmon (John Cassavetes). Courtesy of Cannon Films/RGA.

July 1. Margarita (Margaret Abbott) parties with Robert Harmon (John Cassavetes). Courtesy of Cannon Films/RGA.

July 7. Sarah (Gena Rowlands) looks for sex in a bowling alley. Ken (John Roselius, centre) watches. Courtesy of Cannon Films/RGA.

July 18. 'These are miniature horses! Aren't they small?' Sarah (Gena Rowlands) is followed by cabdriver John Finnegan. Courtesy of Cannon Films/RGA.

July 18. Cinematographer Al Ruban discusses a shot with John Cassavetes. Courtesy of Cannon Films/RGA.

A Lawson family portrait: Seymour Cassel as Jack, Gena Rowlands as Sarah, Risa Blewitt as Debbie - for the still camera only. No comparable shot is in the film. Courtesy of Cannon Films/RGA.

dous conviction. Robert Harmon isn't likeable, yet he's sympathetic. He's empty, yet he's fierce and even passionate. A very, very strange character, hard to figure, but with a presence that's definite, forceful. I can't think of another performance like it, not John's, not anyone's." Then something occurs to me. "You never go to dailies. You don't – what's the word? – you don't want to monitor – terrible word – your performance?"

Gena considers. "I love – the actual performance. That's a very happy time for me. Watching the result is not, for me. In the first place, when you see yourself on film you see a giant image of yourself, which other actors don't seem to mind. I've never talked to any other actor that it seems to bother. The fact that your head is 12 feet across and you're 18 feet long, doesn't seem to bother them. It does bother me. The actual size of seeing myself on film – it seems like a bunch of giants! I never see it in perspective. So I don't go to dailies, I don't enjoy that part so much."

In an interview some time ago I'd asked her, "Do you study your performance when a picture is finished?"

"Once a picture is finished it sort of just… makes a lock in my mind. I only see it once usually at the end, or maybe twice. I don't want to remember it that way. I still remember it from the inside looking out. It's very difficult for me to be an audience to it *ever.* It's sort of disturbing to me, so I usually don't see it except just to see how the whole thing turned out. But that's the last of it."

I'd asked how it was disturbing. She answered, "Changing sides, I guess. It's as if you would be asked to suddenly step out and observe your life. I don't feel that it's necessary for me to be an audience – so I don't see why I have to if it disturbs me. I guess, I wish to think of it on the other side – I wish not to lose the character, the private specific character to *me.*"

Remembering that conversation I ask, "Do you feel like, when you're seeing your character from the outside, on the screen, that it's not yours anymore?"

"I think you're right, yes. Then it has gone. It's been taken away from you at that point. It becomes something a little different."

Later Gena will tell me, "You can't hide anything, if you're a performer, from film. Anyone who has eyes to see can tell almost anything about your life from watching you on film. You just can't hide it. No matter how much you are into a character, you can just see an actor's *soul* on film. And actors know that. It's sort of unnerving sometimes."

She's lit her third cigarette. She pauses just a little before lighting it, as she has before lighting the others. Finally I understand that she expects *me* to light her cigarette. Sheepish – oh so sheepish – I stammer that I am *really* ashamed to be of a generation that doesn't think of lighting a lady's cigarette until receiving several hints.

"It's a generation gap, isn't it?" Gena says flatly. "That about says it."

"It really is. Frankly, I feel stupid."

"You know, when I was growing up, you just didn't *dare* light your own cigarette. It had nothing to do with you, but it commented on the churlishness of someone else – the man you were speaking to. So you'd have to sneak and try to light your cigarettes in a convenient place in a conversation. I'm really happy for that particular emancipation."

"Your films and John's – not the outlook, but the style – are very much of quote-unquote your generation, which I take to be the generation that started – "

"– the War of 1812?"

"I'm not sure – what I'm trying to say."

"I'm so glad, because I never know what I'm trying to say either." She laughs. "It makes me love you."

Six set-ups, 18 takes, roughly 21 minutes of printed film, cut to about two minutes in the final cut.

MONDAY, JUNE 27 – *It's a dream*

With his bloody hand wrapped in a towel, Robert Harmon walks quickly and purposively into his dark living room [shot on June 24]. Upstairs, Sarah has heard the breaking glass and his loud walk and, very slowly, she comes downstairs. In the dark living room, Harmon turns on his jukebox, a classic from the 1940s, cased in colored glass, glowing bright pinks and oranges – an entirely unexpected and surreal object in the life of Robert Harmon. He lights a cigarette, selects a record, the music plays. [Shot tonight.] Sarah watches from the hallway. [Shot tomorrow night.] He sees Sarah watching and silently gestures an invitation to dance. She goes to him and they gently dance for a few moments. [Shot tonight.]

John is in a state. More intense than usual, nervous, preoccupied, talking more to himself than to me about how maybe after *A Woman Under the Influence* he had no more to say and should shut up as far as directing is concerned – then his face lights up, his eyes brighten, he's looking straight through me at some idea he's seeing:

"It's a dream."

I'm a little worried about him. "What's a dream, John?"

"It's a *dream,* this picture. All weekend I'm thinking, *It's a dream,* we're making a dream."

"I don't understand."

"You think *I* do?!"

But that's just his standard response. I'm certain he's understanding *something,* somehow, but I haven't a clue what.

Again he says, with real satisfaction this time, "It's a dream."

Only seven set-ups. 17 takes. Things go slow. John's reluctant to shoot the dialogue that follows Sarah and Harmon dancing. Can't make up his mind. Decides not to shoot it tonight. Says he has to think about it.

Gena is patient, Al Ruban and Eddie Donno are frustrated, but there's nothing anybody can do: John is thinking.

Meanwhile I'm thinking about "It's a dream" jotting down notes.

Maybe he's right. Consciously or unconsciously, he's been shooting *Love Streams* like a dream. The acting is scrupulously realistic, but the action is not – from the first, the action is dreamlike. The strange atmosphere of Harmon's house filled with beautiful sexy girls… the nightmarish activity with Susan the singer… intercut with Sarah's crazy behavior in the court's meeting-room, all that strangeness with her family, and the shrink scene, she in the doctor's chair, the doctor in the patient's chair, yes, that's dreamlike too… then, the sudden appearance of a son Harmon's not seen since the boy's birth… their bizarre conversation, getting drunk with a little boy, and at that very moment the sudden appearance of Sarah, who's no stranger but who has no identifiable relation with Harmon… the craziness of leaving a boy in a Vegas hotel room alone all night, the wrenching grief of the next morning, the fight between Robert Harmon (the failed father) and Albie's stepfather (who's really raising him)… and the boy enacting and imitating Harmon, getting drunk, lighting a cigarette, getting bloodied… a man telling such a dream to a therapist might be told that the boy in the dream is himself, is everything in him that's failed to grow up, and that everyone else but Sarah are objects of his failed desires and constant fears, and that Sarah represents some last wild hope…

Alright, John. Maybe it's a dream.

John prints nearly 18 minutes of tonight's takes. They will be but moments – about half a minute – in the final cut.

TUESDAY, JUNE 28 – *I don't dance unless I have a drink*

John re-shoots some of last night's work – Sarah's entrance into the living room, and their dance. Then he shoots the remainder of the scene as he's re-written it:

Sarah watches Harmon smoke and awkwardly move to the music, a song he selected deliberately, a 40s rendition of 'Where Are You?' The singer asks the question plaintively, she wonders where "you" have gone without her, where's her dream, where's her heart, "must I go on pretending," she longs for a happy ending. Harmon sees Sarah watching him, silently gestures for her to join him, she goes to him and they dance. In the final cut we see the dance in an unbroken shot from down the hall: Sarah and Harmon dancing gracefully, smiling, sharing a lovely familiarity, lit by the eerie gaiety of the jukebox's pink and orange lights – it's clear they've danced before, long ago. For these moments, as the singer croons her lament, these two are very happy. Which, in itself, is shocking in this picture: moments of unalloyed and sober happiness (neither has had a drink).

Sarah breaks the spell by telling Harmon that Susan's called. Harmon strangely asks, "She called me*?" (As though Susan could be calling anyone else at his number!) "Yeah, that's your girlfriend, isn't it?"*

The music's still playing but Harmon abruptly stops dancing, turns on a lamp, calls Susan. Her mother answers. Susan's not home. Harmon tells her mother that he's coming right over anyway, he'll be there in 20 minutes, he won't take no for an answer.

By now the tune has finished. Sarah says, "Fought with Albie, huh?" (So she knows Harmon well enough to know, without being told, what's happened.) Fiercely Harmon says, "Yeah, well, life is a series of suicides – divorces, promises broken, children smashed, whatever. You oughta go to sleep."

"It's only about 9 o'clock."

He tells her she looks awful, needs rest, needs sleep and sun – as he speaks he leads her toward the stairs. She's trying to tell him what's happened to her, she stops walking to tell him, he says, "Can we walk and talk?" – and leads her up the stairs.

She complains, "Hey, I don't want to go to bed."

"No more emotion, let's go."

"I'm not being emotional. I'm not tired. No. You're right. I'm going to bed. Very tired." Very angry. She marches up the stairs without him.

Now Robert Harmon does what he's not yet done in this film: he's indecisive, walks down the stairs, pauses, walks back up, pauses, then goes quickly to the bedroom. Sarah's lying on the bed, won't look at him. He buzzes her cheek noisily, kisses her arms and hands noisily, makes her smile, then he fibs: "I have to go, I have to see this old lady about a house, I have to have a drink with her." (He doesn't have to and his visit is not "about a house.") Harmon tells Sarah, "I'll have breakfast with you in the morning." Sarah smiles. And, again, she is left alone.

Sarah must be very special to him indeed. There's no one else in this picture to whom Harmon would, in effect, apologize; no one else he'd try to appease; no one else to whom he'd promise his time.

The revision is dated yesterday but John wasn't certain yesterday, couldn't bring himself to shoot it. Even tonight he's calling the changes "tentative." They're major. At this point, 65 pages into a 134-page shooting script, John drastically changes direction.

The Ted Allan-John Cassavetes script we all carry to the set every day has Sarah telling Harmon that Susan called and that she, Sarah, has invited Susan and her mother to dinner. Shooting-script pages 106 to 129 (23 pages, the film's climax) relate that dinner party: Sarah hasn't gotten enough food, the food she's bought hasn't been cooked, she's quite nuts, Harmon is nuts, and

Susan and Margarita are thrown into a classically Cassavetes, *Faces*-like, *Husbands*-like free-wheeling, emotionally volatile, embarrassingly funny evening. This is the play as Ted wrote it. This was the section that followed Ted's vision "totally," as he would say. In a fashion reminiscent of *Who's Afraid of Virginia Woolf?*, the invitees are sacrificial victims whom the major characters use as foils in order to confront each other and themselves.

A "tentative" decision? Then why not do a take or two that includes the dialogue setting up Ted's scenes? Easier to shoot that dialogue and not use it than to re-shoot later.

John answers that he doesn't want to "tie the film to that plot," to the complications arising from Sarah's invitation. But shooting the dialogue doesn't tie the film to anything. He's shot plenty of dialogue he won't use. He's often shot scenes he *knows* he won't use, just for the experience. So this decision doesn't feel tentative to me.

Tonight I'm appalled at the barest suggestion that John wants to jettison the party scene. I've been looking forward to a 'classic Cassavetes' time, to watching him do that wild stuff he *says* he's been missing so much, getting a bunch of people in a room and making them craaaaazzzzyyyyy. I don't yet want to admit that such a scene doesn't fit what he's been shooting – doesn't fit the mood, tempo, or content of what he's shot so far. John says, "We're making a picture about inner life." That party isn't inner life. And if it's a dream it's Ted's, not his.

Cassavetes' revision of tonight's scene, and his refusal to shoot the original scene, has enormous implications for the film – that's obvious. But, for reasons unknown, John is downplaying the changes as though tonight is business-as-usual.

During the takes of Robert Harmon at the jukebox, almost the entire living room is in the shot. So Bo Howard and Leslie Hope (now assisting Bo on sound) work from behind the piano, which has been pushed out-of-shot into a corner. Fieldsteel, Francois (the new photographer), Helen Caldwell and I sit scrunched under the piano. When the jukebox is off, before the scene starts, the room's nearly pitch black. Crew people milling about outside, or on the porch, must be careful lest, with this delicate lighting, someone's reflection appears on a window in the shot. In this dim light the reflection would be hardly noticeable to us but the camera would pick it up. This dimness gives Al Ruban trouble knowing the boundaries of his camera frame, especially when the camera moves. So Al complains about "all the arms and legs along the floor" – we folk under the piano, and others crouched behind furniture. It gets ridiculous. For one of John's close-ups I count 24 people in the room besides John. That's half the crew.

Of course the film magazine starts to bang again. (It's been behaving lately. Not tonight.)

On Gena's shots Al, who is rarely 'off,' keeps calling cuts and apologizing to Gena. "I made a lousy move. Gena, I'm *very* sorry."

Gena's attitude toward these technicalities is stoic. She tells me, "You can either learn all about that or forget about it. I do what I do – and they can do what they do."

Before the dancing shots John heads for the bar. "I don't dance unless I have a drink."

"It's the only way I can *get* you to dance," Gena calls after him, "only in a movie." To me she says: "Now you've met a Greek who will not dance."

We head for the bar. Two drinks later Eddie Donno comes in: "Rehearsal, guys?" As they go to rehearse Gena tells John, "Just be sure you're doin' exactly what you're gonna do. No tricks."

John dances easily and gracefully when they shoot – but each take differs. A lot. Helen Caldwell, whose job is to keep track and take notes, asks John, "Are we gonna try to match cuts on this, or do you just want me to keep track of them?"

"Yeah, that would be nice."

His answer tells her nothing. Should she simply note the changes, or should she keep him informed shot-by-shot right now?

Helen tries again. "So – do you want to know?"

"No, I don't want to know. Because I can't control it."

I whisper to her, "You asked the wrong question. If you use the word 'know' in a question to John, he'll always say he doesn't know and doesn't want to."

From under the piano, we watch many takes of John and Gena dancing. Between takes, they are two work-harried people. Call "Action" and something else happens. Gena, as Sarah, fills with a gentle, secretive radiance. Suddenly. To see this moment on film is to see what you paid to see. To see it from five feet away sitting under a piano, is to see magic. One moment, I see a woman – gorgeous, yes, but also fatigued and distracted. "Action." That same woman radiates something precious, rare, complex, an essence of beauty not to be defined. John radiates a similar essence in a darker hue. They meet, embrace, dance a slow circle, mingling radiances.

"Cut." They're just people. Extraordinary people, but people nevertheless. "Action." Angelic, gentle, glowing joy.

John decides they need a close-up of Gena's bare feet as she dances.

This, I understand. Gena has the prettiest feet.

"Get the vacuum cleaner," Eddie commands, "we're gonna get a shot of her feet!"

As they vacuum the rug, and set up the lights, Al laughs: "What does it *mean,* when we put more light on her feet?"

"Than we do on the faces, right?" John's laughing too.

"Watch it," Gena warns, "I always overact with my feet."

She enjoys the take and laughs after they call "Cut."

Rare for Gena, laughter on the set. "I'm not a lot of fun on the set. I'm – uh – known for that."

Thirteen set-ups. Twenty takes. (Most of these are 'complete takes,' that is: the entire scene is shot.) Twenty-five plus minutes of film printed. A little over five minutes makes the final cut – a great ratio even by studio standards.

WEDNESDAY, JUNE 29 – *Let him do it*

In the film's final cut, now we see Robert Harmon in front of Margarita's house, lifting a cardboard box out of the trunk of his car, going up the steps, to be met by Margarita – the box contains champagne, crystal glasses, and ice. Music plays in her house, sounding like a cross between jug-band and vaudeville. [Shot tomorrow night.] Cut to tonight's shoot:

A very quiet exterior shot of Robert Harmon's house, dark but for the lit kitchen area. The camera moves very slowly and nothing happens for nearly 20 seconds. Then, through the window, we see Sarah Lawson enter the kitchen, dressed beautifully in black eveningwear, her hair flowing. She's carrying a bottle of whiskey and a pack of cigarettes. She puts down the whiskey bottle, drops the cigarettes, picks them up, lights a cigarette as she sips a drink (almost at the same time), she shakes the match to douse it, she's flustered. Cigarette in her mouth, she picks up the phone. She calls her husband Jack [his end of the conversation to be filmed next month – it's two hours later in Chicago, he's in a robe, he's smoking too]. The conversation goes nowhere. After he hangs up she stands with the phone to her ear for some seconds. Puts it down. Then we see her leave the house, there's a cab waiting, she gets in and tells the cabbie, "I want you to be patient with me because I don't know exactly where I'm going."

When Cassavetes is done with that scene he'll shoot a transition shot: Robert Harmon returns from Margarita's in a cab and enters his house.

*

John explains the scene to Gena: "When you do it, everything should be messed up. Don't worry about the confusion, just light the cigarette, do the drink, all the stuff at once. Don't worry about how everything's going – just take your time."

(Gena doesn't know he's directing her to do this cigarette-drink-phone scene exactly as Robert Harmon did an earlier scene. In that scene – excised from the final cut – he dialed the phone as he lit a cigarette and sipped a drink at the same time. At the very same time. He inhaled the cigarette, drank whiskey, spoke into the phone, *then* exhaled.)

In the breakfast room Gena looks at the glass that the props people left for her. She examines it, puts it back in the cupboard, takes out another, holds it up to the light.

"I think I'll use this glass. That one –" she gestures toward the shelf – "is such an ugly glass, I'd never drink out of that."

"Sweetheart – sweetheart –" John is trying to get her attention while she's deciding about the glasses. "Gena." She looks at him. "When you come down the stairs, just – slow. Take your time. Don't be going somewhere because you *have to* go somewhere."

"Do you want it to resemble – when I went down and saw you dancing? Just subliminally?"

"Yeah."

(Film critics take note. Improvisation? Lack of intent? "Just subliminally," yet!)

Outside, lights and dolly tracks have been set up for the exterior shot. The house is bright with light, and as we prepare for the shot each window is a tableaux of some activity. The night is fragrant and (thankfully) chilly. It's nearly midnight.

John comes out in short sleeves, oblivious to the chill, to rehearse the camera-move with Al Ruban.

"Do you know when the zoom starts?" John asks.

"What zoom?"

"Shit, Al, I forgot to tell you about the zoom! I'm sorry, I'm *very* sorry."

"It's easily done," says Al, unperturbed.

When the zoom device is attached to the camera they go over the move once with Dermot, the tall usually-smiling dolly-grip. Dermot pushes the dolly while Al rides the camera with the focus-puller. John stands by, tense, watching everything.

"I think the zoom should start sooner," Al says. "I'm seeing the staircase. The lens sees it before your human eye can see it, because of the curve of the lens."

"The zoom should be so imperceptible," John tells him, "that you don't even know it's zooming in. It should be very slow." He laughs. "Anyway, it'll probably work if you don't do anything I say."

"Right. If I let the camera do the work," Al smiles.

"If it doesn't work it probably works the best," John says, ending the discussion.

When they shoot the take, John runs comically beside the dolly, hopping up and down to see Gena in the breakfast room. Then, disgusted: "Cut. That's bullshit."

She had entered the breakfast room and picked up the phone with a toss of her hair, very beautiful, very impressive. Which is exactly what John doesn't want.

I go inside with him to hear what he'll tell Gena.

As he personally dresses the set, putting a vase of pink roses on the breakfast table, he says, "I just don't want any definite moves. Gena, you've got to do everything in no particular time, with no drama involved. Light the cigarette, do the thing, all at once, don't throw your head back."

"I *have to* put my head back when I light the cigarette because otherwise I'll light my hair on fire."

"Just keep moving. She can't *think* of what to do."

I stay out-of-shot in the kitchen. John goes outside. He cuts the next take quickly, comes back in. "It's still one thing at a time," John tells her.

Gena is aggravated. "How can I light a cigarette and drink at the same time?!"

He leaves, and as Gena goes upstairs to begin her entrance again she says in a stage whisper, *"I hate that man."*

Another take. John says, "It's great, 90 per cent there, but…"

The next take, anything Gena picks up she puts down harder, slapping things around. The cigarette dangles from her lips, she lights it, snuffs the match, pours a drink, takes a sip, *then* exhales – and dials with the cigarette awkwardly pointing straight out from her lips.

"Gena, super! That was great, that was beautiful."

Gena says nothing, goes quickly upstairs, steaming. John walks down the hall with long energetic steps saying to himself, "*That* was fantastic, *that* was a distraught woman like I never saw!" A pause and then: "Drama sucks."

They move camera and lights inside to film the phone conversation. While they set up, Cassavetes works in his bar. Robert Fieldsteel reads the scene to John. John doesn't like it. He cuts five pages of dialogue in half, changing the exchange from a specific argument to a kind of mutual helplessness. In the scripted version Jack and Sarah are still 'with' each other to the extent that they can at least argue. In the revised version, they can barely speak.

Originally, this is one of the moments when Sarah tells Jack, "I'm almost not crazy." In the shooting script the line is repeated in three scenes. In the final cut, the line is said only in the London phone-booth scene. Tonight Fieldsteel tells John that tonight Gena wants to change "I'm almost not crazy" to "I'm almost ok."

"No, I don't like that." John takes a drag on his cigarette, changes his mind. "If she wants to say, 'I'm almost ok,' let her – I don't want to mess up her performance."

Gena comes in, sees what's going on, tells John, "Don't change *anything*."

"Sweetheart, the change doesn't affect what you do. It's really the inserts [Jack's dialogue] that we're changing."

They read her the changes and John sees he's changed her lines more than he's realized. Gena takes a deep breath:

"Can we do it both ways? Because this'll throw me higher than a kite."

"Of course," John says gently.

"We can do it twice," says Gena.

"We can do it 10 times," John says, again gently.

When they shoot Fieldsteel reads Jack's lines off-camera. Perhaps some branch of quantum physics can delineate the complications of Gena as Sarah speaking to Sarah's husband Jack, who's really her friend Seymour, who isn't here, Fieldsteel's here saying his lines, while Gena's actual husband is also her director standing behind the camera.

After shooting the scripted scene, Gena goes over the new lines with Fieldsteel.

"Oh – let's try it," she says, "it's interesting."

Suddenly John tells her, "I love you, you dumbohead."

Her smile's a little confused. They don't speak like that on the set.

John laughs, "No, put that in, say it on the phone. 'I love you, you dumbohead.'"

Now Gena really smiles.

That line will make the final cut.

Earlier in the evening Cassavetes said to Eddie and me, "I called Frank Yablans today." Frank Yablans is head man at MGM/UA, with whom Menahem Golan has a distribution deal. "I said, 'Frank, are we really gonna be out in December?' He said, 'What picture are you working on?'" John's eyes start tearing with laughter. "'I say, *Love Streams.*' 'That's a great title,' he says. TWO MINUTES LATER he says, 'What's the title of this picture?' I tell him again. 'Who's doing that?' 'Cannon. Golan's Cannon,' I tell him. 'I'm meeting with him in 15 minutes!,' says Frank. 'You are? Then will you do me one favor, will you, Frank? When those two Israelis come in, no matter how long they say the picture is, tell them, 'How can you possibly make such a short picture?!' He was off the phone in a breath."

Through laughter John adds that he likes Yablans, Yablans has always supported his work. "He was going to play a gangster in *Mikey and Nicky* but there was some scheduling problem."

Love Streams producer and money-man, Menahem Golan,

wants *Love Streams* out in December for an "Academy® outing": releasing a picture for a week in December so it qualifies for this year's Academy Awards®, then giving the picture wider release a month or so before the awards ceremony, hoping for publicity generated by possible nominations for Gena, John, and/or the picture. John hates the idea. Shooting runs into mid-August, which means he'd only have about three and a half months to edit. That would be short for any picture; for this picture, John fears it's far too short. (Fast-forward: John will talk Golan out of this notion, and the picture will finish editing and lab-work in late January.) John's nervous about confronting Golan on this. He's also nervous that his picture is running too long. His contract stipulates a two-hour film. John's thinking more like three hours. (The final running time will be 2:22.) Hence his joke with Frank Yablans, wanting Yablans to tell Golan, "How can you make such a short picture?!"

Tonight, for the first time since shooting began, Menahem Golan visits the set. They sit in John's bar, painfully attempting conversation. What they have in common is that both are fighters, risk-takers and film directors. (Golan has just wrapped an engaging little comedy called *Over the Brooklyn Bridge,* starring Elliot Gould.) They're roughly the same age – John 53, Golan 50. Both dress in baggy clothes, neither shaves every day, both know what it means to win big and lose hard, and both know the immigrant experience in America. Golan is experiencing it now. John is the son of immigrants; though born in America, John's early years were spent with his family in Greece; when he returned here at the age of seven he spoke no English. There, all resemblance stops. Golan is a big Israeli bear, Cassavetes is a small New York cat. Golan is an entertainer (he'd be the first to say so); Cassavetes is an artist (he'd be the last to say so). Golan, the most successful director in Israel, has no prestige in Europe and America; John has an outlaw's prestige in America and is revered in Europe. (He'll tell me, "I'm a street-person so I don't care about being esteemed in Europe or here.") Golan is smart and savvy; John is (he'll make me pay for saying this) a genius. Their personal styles and preferences couldn't be more at odds. As men, they have nothing to say to each other.

John's game. He's trying. "The last living relative, that's what this film is about. You know, my mother died this year. [This is the first time he's mentioned that in my hearing.] My father is dead, my brother – my elder brother. Every morning I wake up, I want to call somebody –"

"Call me," says Golan.

" – to find out how they are."

"Elliot Gould calls me twice a night, you can call me."

John's *really* trying. He's saying things he doesn't often speak of, things of great importance to him.

"So, in this picture," John goes on, "this man constantly thinks of his sister, and never sees her. Finally, she comes to his house. But the audience doesn't know it's his sister! We're on page 80 and we haven't said it's his sister."

"I still can't believe you shoot in sequence," Menahem says.

John shrugs. "It's all I know."

Menahem introduces an edgy topic of business. A few weeks ago in the *Love Streams* production office I heard Carole Smith say on the phone that "John doesn't *want* the documentary." When I asked Carole what that was about she instructed me, in humorous but firm fashion, as to what was my business and what was not. Hearing no more mention of a documentary, I forgot about it. Now Golan tells John, "I have good boys from Israel, very good, they'll do the documentary, we'll start next week. It'll be good for the picture, play in festivals, help sell the film."

John can (as my mother would say) "talk the handle off a coffee pot." When he turns on the charm, there's no finer charmer. And he can be sweet! I haven't seen much of that, what with the strain he's under, but he can be sweet as a little boy. Now he turns it all on. For the most convincing, charming, sweet reasons, he'd rather not have another film crew on his set, each day is a new creation, Gena is giving an Academy Award® performance but she's a very delicate actress who can't bear distraction… and anything else that sounds remotely convincing, true or not. But Golan – also charming, also unexpectedly sweet in a bear-like way – won't budge. He wants the documentary.

John whips around on his barstool, points a finger at me: "Ok, have *him* do it."

Golan's never seen me before. Probably figures the-guy-with-the-notebook is doing a magazine article or some such thing.

Golan turns to me, doesn't miss a beat, "Good, *you* do it. Tomorrow you go to Cannon – you know where Cannon is? – talk with so-and-so, he'll give you cameraman, editor, sound, *you* do it. Shoot lots of film. I don't want 'the making of,' I want *Cassavetes.*"

I feel like a poker chip. John raised and bluffed. Golan raised and called.

I'm saying sure, sure, writing down names, instructions, directions, but really… *Am I dreaming now? Am I the only person to come to Los Angeles with no intention of directing a picture and now suddenly I'm given a picture to direct – without even asking?! Does this happen to anybody outside of dreams?*

Six set-ups, 22 takes, 15 minutes of printed film, for nearly three minutes in the final cut. The Sarah-Jack phone call will be further abstracted to a mere five lines, about half a page of revised dialogue, nothing like its original five pages.

THURSDAY, JUNE 30 – *A quick yes*

Robert Harmon arrives at Margarita's house.

Also scheduled to be shot, but instead shot tomorrow:

Harmon and Margarita have a little party. She wraps herself in a sheet and bedecks herself in costume jewelry and flowers to show Harmon how she looked long ago when a showgirl. She mentions her age – 53, Harmon's age. [This will be cut.] They dance, get very drunk, she teaches him to play the kazoo, they kid around, he kisses her, but only "teeth-kissing," he kisses only her teeth. It's almost all improv – transcribed into the editing script from a "rough assembly" of the film, the scene runs nearly 11 pages.

We're to shoot in the evening. I'm to spend the afternoon at Cannon preparing for – this doesn't sound real to say, it's got to be in quotes – "preparing for *my* film."

These madmen, Cassavetes and Golan, have given responsibility for directing a documentary to someone who knows nothing about the job. Golan's willing to spend real money on this craziness. Yet – forgive the capital letters, but it blows my mind – I'M NOT GIVEN A BUDGET! I'm to have carte blanche, apparently, all the film and all the time I require. Given the salaries of my crew and myself, filmstock (we'll shoot a lot), the cost of our equipment, use of the editing room (we'll edit for two months) – I'll never know for sure (NO BUDGET), but Golan's shells out at least $125,000, probably more. Entrusted to me, a guy he never met before a few hours ago.

I can't sleep, I keep hearing Carole's words in my head: "John doesn't *want* the documentary."

I'm not sure *I* want a documentary. It's exciting, sure: I get to make a film! In another way it sucks: I'm a poker chip, I'm part of their game, I don't know what I'm doing, what the hell is going on?

So, first thing, before my meetings at Cannon, I drive to John's house.

I'm not terribly pleased at how amused he is to see me.

"Hi, kid."

"John – what the fuck is going on?"

"You're making a movie."

"Look. Understand. *Your* movie is a lot more important to me than 'my' movie. If you don't want me and a bunch of other amateurs tripping over your wires, just say so. The *book* is important to me. The documentary…"

A beat. John is loving this. Why, I don't know.

He laughs: "I'll give you a quick *yes*."

A moment.

"So – I'm a director."

John, through arched eyebrows, darkly: "You better be."

I'm driving to Cannon and John has me, the director he wants, on his set. Through my assent – which is a little different from *consent* – he's outfoxed Golan. Yet again, Golan won't have his boy in a key position on John's set. John Cassavetes, master director, ringmaster of his reality, has cast me instead. As always, he favors amateurs. I'll undergo his precious sense of *experience.* ("The experience is more important than the film!") And, no small thing, he knows I won't (one of John's favorite words) "double-cross" him. A stranger just might.

*

Tonight's location is a small house off Sunset Boulevard in Silver Lake. The dressing-room trucks, generator, and equipment truck seem massive on the small scale of this old Los Angeles street. They shoot Harmon's entrance and Margarita's greeting – one set-up, nine takes, mostly improvised. They use the last take, where Margaret Abbott takes the cigarette out from between John's lips to give him a friendly greeting-kiss.

While the crew sets up for the first interior shot, Cassavetes, Helen Caldwell and Robert Fieldsteel sit on the floor of the living room amidst the foot-traffic of electricians and set-dressers. Cassavetes is re-writing, putting in a bit with a kazoo, playing with dialogue. "Just give Margaret the kazoos and tell her she has to play them. And has to make me play. And give her that speech. Let her sweat over that awhile. Give her that, tell her John is drunk, he has some things, he doesn't know what he's doing."

None of which is true but it's an interesting 'direction.'

John gets up off the floor and looks around. He doesn't like what he sees, tells Phedon, "The place – is too austere. It's not a place where entertainers live."

He thinks it needs photographs on the wall, and more decoration, plus a stereo and a record collection.

Phedon's not happy. He's the production designer, this room was his idea.

"I know it's a lot of work," John tells him, "but we're a long way from building a scene."

Bo Harwood is uncertain about the appropriate music for when Harmon and Margarita dance. Over the years he and John have composed many tunes together, and he's going through tapes to select one. John tells him, "Let's not make it easy to make the scene work, because then there's no scene."

It's soon evident that the set decorators will take hours to collect stuff that will make this a convincing abode for entertainers. If they search out the accessories tomorrow they can shoot this scene tomorrow night. John calls a wrap.

"Why should we have to be the way people aren't?"

*

They use the last take of Harmon's entrance, 1:27 minutes in the final cut.

FRIDAY, JULY 1 – *Not afraid of being bad*

Harmon parties with Margarita.

Cassavetes has been looking forward to this party with Margaret Abbott. "I'm gonna throw *everybody* out of that house! It's gonna be nobody but her and me and camera and sound. And then I'm gonna get her so drunk! She's a great woman, a wonderful woman, and if I can just get her loose enough she'll do great."

John throws nobody out. Everybody in the crew, with no duties elsewhere, watches the scene. This is the Cassavetes they've signed on to see, a scene reminiscent of *Faces* and *Husbands,* long takes of wild and somewhat inebriated improvisation. In John's films there's rarely anything more overtly sexual than a kiss, but in his party scenes there *is* something orgiastic, like some pagan revel around a fire in a forest.

This character, Margarita, is an aging version of women who've always inhabited Cassavetes' cinema. She could easily be the young woman of *Shadows* 35 years later, or one of the partiers of *Too Late Blues,* or even Gena's Jeannie in *Faces* during lonely middle-age, or the women picked up in the casino in *Husbands,* or the showgirls in *The Killing of a Chinese Bookie* (Margarita is presented as an ex-showgirl).

It's worth noting that *Love Streams,* a film about love, is a film in which the characters are almost empty of sexual energy. Even the 18-year-old Joanie tells Harmon that sex is useful for money but she doesn't enjoy it. Harmon is revolted at the sight of two beautiful young women naked in a shower. With Susan, played by the superbly sensual Diahnne Abbott, Harmon is too drunk for sex. Sarah tells her shrink, "I don't have a sexual life – I don't *need* a sexual life." (When John spoke of that scene he said, "She's right, she doesn't.") She will pick up a handsome guy at a bowling alley and presumably sleep with him – John tells me she sleeps with him, but that's not clear in the final cut. In *Love Streams* sex is always a possibility, but it's also only a possibility; it has little to do with what's really going on with these characters, and even for Sarah it would only mean a final break with her husband.

In fact, after *Minnie and Moskowitz* sex disappears as a force in Cassavetes' cinema. *Shadows, Faces, Husbands,* and *Minnie and Moskowitz* are about characters to whom sex is terribly important, either in itself or as a romantic ideal. (However, Leila Goldoni says in *Shadows,* after her first love-making experience, "I didn't know it could be so awful," and for Stella Stevens in *Too Late Blues* sex is compulsive and degrading.) *A Woman Under the Influence* occurs at a point in the characters' lives where sexual energy has been thwarted but not crushed. Then *The Killing of a Chinese Bookie, Opening Night,* and *Gloria,* are inhabited by people for whom sex has become peripheral. If *Love Streams* is *Minnie and Moskowitz* 15 years later (an echo Cassavetes clearly intends), its verdict on what some call "the healing power of sexuality" is bleak. Cassavetes sees no help there for the crises that overwhelm our inner and social lives. He locks people inside rooms, without special effects, without plot and almost without a story, without even sex, and examines how they face and/or fail to face each other and themselves.

Yet *Love Streams* pulses with an energy, a power, that is not at all bleak. John expresses it to me this way: "This story can't take any melodrama. Whatever happens, *happens.* And when it happens, they laugh, or get angry, but they don't..." His voice trails off, then comes back strong: "They don't give in. *They don't give in,* and that's what makes them likeable. They get it, and they grit it, and go on."

Tonight John is very concerned that Margaret Abbott must have a good time – and "an experience." "I can't put somebody through [a scene] without an experience, because then it's not worth it to make the movie."

Now he's telling Al Ruban, "The light should be shitty."

"Shitty?" Al questions, smiling with his eyebrows.

"Not shitty – I mean –"

"No, I know," Al says tenderly. "I know not to listen to you but to hear you."

Al turns to his crew, says, "I don't know where we're gonna wind up, we oughta run this cable to the other side of the chair." On anyone else's set it would be surprising to hear a cinematographer say he doesn't know where actors in a scene are "going to wind up." On John's set, he's not supposed to know. They set up their cameras and lights so that they can cover the whole house. John tells Margaret that while they're playing the scene she's to say "I'm going into the kitchen" before she goes into the kitchen, or "I'm going to put the record back on the shelf" before she does so. "That's to warn the camera guys, so they'll know what we're about to do and they can do the shot. We'll edit the lines out of the film, so don't worry. Do anything, anything you want. If we dance, we have the time to dance. If we talk, we have the time to talk. It's our stage."

Long, long takes, covered by two cameras – seven, eight, nine minutes a take. One runs more than 10 minutes. John doesn't want a cut, even for technical interruptions.

Al calls a cut. "We blew it, we really went soft," meaning that they went out-of-focus. John tells him, "When you go soft, keep going, just get in [focus] as fast as you can."

Bo Harwood calls a cut because a low-flying helicopter ruins the sound.

John's people aren't getting the point.

"Listen, guys, we've got a 1000 feet of film, so nobody cuts. I'm the guy who cuts."

Even when one camera runs out of film John keeps the scene going as long as the second camera can shoot. John and Margaret, Harmon and Margarita, drink, dance, teeth-kiss, play the kazoo, with maybe 30 people watching from behind the furniture, from the bedroom, from the kitchen, through the windows – watching an intimate revel that feels terribly private, except that we're watching. Is this acting? Is this theater? Is this movies? This woman is so vulnerable, and she's enjoying this so much, is she a good actress, a bad actress, an actress? (John tells me, whispering between takes, "She really knows how to act because she's not afraid of being bad.") We spectators feel like kids the first time they watch the grown-ups get drunk.

And they're dancing to such a strange tune! A Harwood-Cassavetes composition, a soft easy beat over which a reedy tenor sings with a bewildered air, *I'm almost in love with you… I almost like your eyes… What can I do/ I'm not/ But almost/ In love with you…*

(When you don't look at her, Margaret Abbott's voice sounds like the voice of John's late mother Katherine. A voice as shrill and piercing as if she had a cicada in her throat, and New York to the bone. "Robert" comes out as *Raah-but.* It makes me queasy.)

Margaret Abbott has had her 'experience.' After a take she tells John, "I wish I could do this every day. I wish I could have done this 30 years ago. I'm so happy! I'm been waiting for this."

One set up (two cameras roving the space), 11 takes, almost 48 minutes of printed film. In some 'rough assemblies' this intimate party will run nearly 10 minutes – it's funny, sweet, sad, its everybody's favorite scene, and it stops the film. Stops it dead. It's too unlike the rest, and… this is the one night when Cassavetes plays Cassavetes. Robert Harmon seems more elated than loaded. It jars the film. Which may be why Cassavetes finally cut the scene to play abstractly, non-linearly, in the three minutes selected for the final cut.

TUESDAY, JULY 5 – *No man's man*

Robert Harmon is teeth-kissing Margarita when Susan comes home with her date, a tall handsome man of her own generation named Frank [Tony Brubaker]. Susan is pissed, embarrassed, and a little amused; her date is pissed, embarrassed, and not at all amused. Susan checks on her sleeping son in the other room. Robert takes his leave.

Phedon tells me that John has worried all day about this scene, and predicts John will shoot several completely different versions "because he's confused."

John shoots different versions of the scene, but I wonder if he's all that confused. His madness usually (though not always) serves a method. John shoots take after take, none resembling the other, all freely improvised. In one take Harmon argues with Susan's date, in the next they almost fight. On one take her date leaves hesitantly, on another quickly. Finally: a calm, understated take, everyone but Harmon embarrassed, and everyone behaving anxiously but in civilized fashion. In the initial takes Cassavetes conditioned Diahanne Abbott and Tony Brubaker to expect *anything,* so that finally they perform with the uncertainty and hesitancy normal when confronting a situation so unexpected and weird. Cassavetes never tells them his purpose; he directs them through performance.

Diahnne Abbott knows John's intent. I will ask her if she thinks John intentionally throws her timing off, to which she says, "I don't see him as throwing your timing off – just keeping it fresh, keeping the scene fresh. Especially if an actor gets into a thing where they've memorized their lines, they know the scene backwards and forwards and they want to do that scene the way they memorized it. That gets pretty stale and it looks stale. John likes things to be fresh. It's great what he does. I think he's real shrewd like that."

This scene frames beautiful work by Diahnne. Gradations of Susan's feeling for her mother, Harmon, and Frank, pass across her face in waves, counter-pointing her spoken lines. Her reaction underscores an odd element in *Love Streams:* all its women are really on Robert Harmon's side. His first wife, Susan, her mother, Sarah, his assistant Charlene, her daughter, even the hookers, all try to be helpful, all want the best for him. While, in contrast to the men of John's other films and in contrast to John's own life, the men of *Love Streams* don't much like Harmon. Susan's date and Albie's stepfather actively dislike him on sight, while Albie wants the love of his father but knows he can't trust his father. Harmon tells Albie, "I don't like men." Men don't like him back.

Five set-ups, 15 takes. The takes John slowly built up to will be used almost in their entirety in the final cut.

WEDNESDAY, JULY 6 – *Building a house*

Now we see where Sarah Lawson goes after Robert Harmon leaves her alone.

Dressed for a fancy nightclub, she chooses a funky bowling alley – a woman of style, pricey clothes, pricey hair, in a working-class joint. She couldn't look more out of place. Yet for the first time she seems confident – "whacko," as Gena would say, but confident.

The scene plays as though improvised, but is shot as written in the May 13 shooting script, revised slightly but significantly. A dolly shot establishes the bowling alley and a pan reveals Sarah at the cashier's desk. She says: "Hello."

"How are you?" the cashier asks. ["Hello" in the original, changed to set up the next line.]

"To tell you the truth I am, I – I –" she stares off into the air for a couple of beats, recovers: "To tell you the truth I'm very concerned about my daughter."

"Well," says the cashier, unperturbed, "we're all concerned."

"Oh, you too. Oh, I'm sorry. Well, you now about it then too?"

"About it?"

"About the uh, balance. [Slightly changed.] Listen, to tell you the truth this is my first time and I, uh – I – I'm looking for the sex."

"Well – you'll need bowling shoes." [Inserted today.]

No, she plans to bowl barefoot – or rather, in nylon- or silk-shod feet.

Commentators have, in general, missed Cassavetes' strong absurdist streak because his cinema-of-the-absurd is filmed and performed with meticulous realism. It does not register as absurd because it's so genuine and raw, and there's nothing absurd in the sincere. John now repeats almost every day, "It's a dream." This scene could be subtitled 'I Dreamed I Went Bowling in Evening Clothes.'

John tells me, "Being a director, it's very like every day you build a house. And at the end of the day, you tear it down. And the next day you have to build another house, all over again. And sometimes you hate the house, sometimes you love it. And you can't build it alone."

He is giving instruction: today is my first as a director. I'm so nervous that the sense-of-direction I often boast of utterly fails me, I can't tell north from south, east from west, and it takes me over an hour to find the bowling alley. Well, John loves amateurs.

I'm on 'my' set, which is John's set, and I have my crew, guys in their early-to-mid 20s. Manning our 16mm camera is an Israeli, Gideon 'Giddy' Porath. He's a pro. Our soundman Peter Tullo is, like me, an amateur. Our editor has worked as assistant on action films: tall, unflappable, laconic Daniel Wetherbee. Giddy and Dan will save whatever slight reputation as a director I shall ever have – gifted and resourceful, every notable moment in our documentary belongs to them. This will be Giddy's first 'Director of Photography' credit, Dan's first as 'Editor' – important career steps. Today they politely conceal their dismay at my confusion. I don't know what I'm doing, and I'm not about to pretend.

Dan must leave before we start shooting, so not until our first dailies will he see that I'm not 'slating' my shots – the slate that slaps down in front of the camera, upon which is chalked the reel, scene, and date, which is also spoken, so that a sound reel can be matched with a picture reel. No slate, no notes. It'll take days for Dan and his assistant, Seth Gavin (whose suggestions will also prove important), to sort this out.

When, later, I sheepishly tell John my mistake, he laughs: "You did that too! I did that on *Shadows*! It set us back six months! We finally got the idea to go to a school for the deaf, deaf teenagers *lip-read* the footage and saved our asses. It cost you how much time? Just a week? You're a lucky director."

Today my sense of light sucks – and Giddy doesn't yet know me well enough to know I won't be offended if he tells me I'm screwing up. The film prints green-tinted because of the fluorescents. Of our first day's work, Dan salvages two or three brief shots as inserts during our doc's end-credits. There is one nice one, though: John and Gena sitting on bar-stools, Gena's legs stretched out and resting on his lap, John speaking to her swiftly, gesturing, Gena listening, both smoking – a tableaux of sweet intimacy spiked with intensity. What were they saying? We never could find that sound-reel.

As for John's film: Six set-ups, 24 takes, for 1:07 of finished cut.

THURSDAY, JULY 7 – *I love stupidity*

Beautiful Sarah Lawson takes off her shoes and checks out the bowling balls beside a noisy working-class group on the adjoining lane, including tall handsome Ken [John Roselius] and a tall, pretty, savvy-looking gal who's apparently his date, Dottie [Jessica St. John]. Sarah is noticed. Ken calls out to her, offers to keep score. Sarah flashes him a blazing smile: "You can if you want to, but it's not necessary. I don't keep score." Ken laughs, "You don't keep score?" "If I throw a strike, I remember." She bowls surprisingly well and is very excited – jumps and twirls! – when she almost bowls a strike (all pins but one). Ken and his friends cheer. On her second try she can't get the ball out of her hand at the end of her swing, she falls down with it. Ken, Dottie, and friends rush to help her, she's apologetic and confused, they're all making a fuss. Dottie tells her to take deep breaths, Ken knows what to do: he holds the ball, supporting its weight as Sarah stands, then he instructs Dottie to chalk Sarah's fingers. Dottie does so and Sarah's hand is easily freed – and all the while she's giving Ken what used to be called 'big eyes.' Big smiles too. Dottie shoots Ken a look, knowing a flirt when she sees one. Cut on Dottie's look.

The scene is shot as written but for the particular business as Ken, Dottie, and friends come to Sarah's aid – that's improvised and established through a series of takes. But again Cassavetes has deleted a specific motivation: in the shooting script, "a telephone RINGS as she starts her forward motion swinging the ball." She falls, then explains to the people who come to her aid, "I just heard the telephone, and I was afraid it was my daughter." In the scene as shot, she falls only because her fingers are stuck – or perhaps to become the center of Ken's attention.

"I thought blonds didn't perspire, Gena," John says while her forehead's daubed.

"Hey, *Greek*!" she calls to him before the next take. "You wanna start me looking at the ball, or what do you want to do?"

Exchanges between them are terse, the takes are difficult. John's written Gena some lines for the finger-in-the-ball scene, which she's to deliver amidst the improvised lines of John Roselius and friends. Through a series of takes, John, from behind the camera, goads the bowlers into noticing Gena, yelling at her, getting raucous with her, while she comes in with her scripted lines at different moments in their action. It takes time and work to build up to the beautifully realized scene we'll see on-screen.

After John's gotten what he wants he says to me, "Wasn't that stupid? I love stupidity. *Wasn't* that stupid?! It was nice. And – they all went to each other [to help her]. You *never* see that in movies."

The bowling alley shoot ends with Bo Harwood needing to record 'room tone,' background sound, to be added as needed to edited footage (for instance, in case a line must be dubbed). John says, "Quiet everyone, don't move," as he and Bo put on headphones and we all… listen… to the hum of the bowling machines… the dimmer, almost subliminal hum of the fluorescents… muffled voices from the bowling alley's bar… and Cassavetes raises his arms, waves them, pointing this way and that to each source of sound, like the conductor of an orchestra, intent, serious, eyebrows arched, as though bowling machines, bowling balls, fluorescents, and distant chatter are instruments that somehow obey his precise conduction.

*

A comparatively light shooting day. John, Al, and perhaps Sam Shaw (I wasn't there) attend a meeting at Cannon with Golan and his people. Later I'm given a copy of the meeting-report, dated today, July 7.

On June 20, Priscilla McDonald initiated the fracas that caused still photographer Larry Shaw to quietly retire from the set when his son Jakob's work was done. I wrote of that argument, "John wins the battle, Priscilla wins the war." In light of this report, that must be revised: "John wins the skirmish, Priscilla wins the battle" – today John and Larry's father Sam win the war. One casualty on each side: Larry and Priscilla. In the meeting Priscilla and her team lose all authority and control of publicity of any kind, not to mention the prestige of working with world-class names.

From the report:

"A.1. Every interview request to go to Production [Al Ruban]: John for okay, copy to Sam Shaw and Al Ruban. EXAMPLE: ...Priscilla (June 24) [scheduled] Foreign Press interviews for August 4 and August 5 – not listed for John. These interviews were made without his or Production's (Al Ruban's) okay. Suppose the set location is changed on that date?

"B.1. A copy of every P.R. proposed interview and creative marketing ideas regarding publicity and production to be given to John Cassavetes and Sam Shaw.

"B.2. The tight schedule does not allow for distractions of any kind; e.g., being considerate to interviewers from press would be tough for John and Gena.

"B.3. Michael Ventura on text. [Underline in original.] Ventura is writing an in-depth text on the picture. He is the only one John is now talking to when he is free to talk (e.g., lunch breaks). Ventura will do the press kit text – Plot/Theme, John-Gena sequence, Diahnne interview (bios)."

The report goes on to give John and Gena rights "of photo censorship/selection and stills. Final selection by Sam... Sam and John to get a set of all contacts [photo contact-sheets] – including Cannon Prod. (Francois)." Then the report singles out Diahnne Abbott for a special publicity push ("she is due for a major break"). "A set of selected stills with universal captions (by

Michael Ventura) for story line and picture." Of the posters: "John and Sam approval."

Priscilla learns the hard way that you do not mess with friends of Cassavetes.

Then the report goes weird:

"After seeing the assembled viewing this week, I've [John, that is] changed my thinking. It is a major, across-the-board, American movie that will reach the widest audience." And more in that vein. John can't possibly believe this.

In an added note: "An out-take from Michael Ventura's documentary of the bowling ball sequence for the Bowling Association and the numerous bowling TV shows." John hadn't yet seen my botched footage.

A comical footnote: Several weeks ago (long before this meeting) John asked me to write the 'in-depth' text for Cannon's publicity packet in order to educate critics whom John was certain would not understand *Love Streams* (despite its "across the board" appeal). Many years later scholars and documentarists will quote my text as John's own words. Very flattering to me, I must say. They quote the following:

"The photographic-negative quality of the brother-sister relationship [in *Love Streams]* was graphically portrayed in the interracial family of *Shadows.* The awful emotional isolation in which artists trap themselves was a subject of both *Too Late Blues* and *Opening Night.* We have seen Sarah and Jack fall in love and get married as *Minnie and Moskowitz...* We saw the process of alienation of husband and wife, much like what Sarah and Jack speak of in the divorce hearing, in *Faces.* The freedom that the three friends dream of in *Husbands* is the freedom Robert Harmon has and finds empty. A female intensity bordering on madness was explored in *A Woman Under the Influence,* with the difference that Mabel Longhetti's lunacy was accepted by her family while Sarah Lawson's is rejected. The nightlife that Robert Harmon finds so fascinating was the subject of *The Killing of a Chinese Bookie*. Even the combination of love and discomfort that Robert Harmon feels toward his son is not unlike the woman-child relationship in *Gloria.*"

John approves my text, so he may agree with these notions. But anyone attributing such a paragraph to John Cassavetes might better have noticed that its style of analytical comparison is as unlike Cassavetes as Kelsey's you-know-what.

Seven set-ups, 13 takes, for 2:40 in the finished film.

FRIDAY, JULY 8 – *Hours of beginnings*

Robert Harmon, home from his revel with Margarita, gets panicky when he can't find Sarah. He climbs the stairs two at a time calling her name. Upstairs, he sees a car pull into the driveway and watches "the dim figures of Sarah and a man (Ken) as the man helps Sarah out of the car" – so goes the script. Sarah is happy, girlish, she leaps on Ken, throws her arms around him, "I had a wonderful time, a wonderful time!" Ken, dazed to be with this classy beauty, says a humble "Thank you." She kisses him – not a full lover's kiss, but playfully, affectionately. "You're the cutest guy I ever met!" More little playful kisses. Twice as she goes to the front door she stops, turns to him, grins, waves, while the benighted Ken looks on, baffled but delighted.

Again and again in *Love Streams* we watch its characters negotiate a house that is made to seem labyrinthine – the labyrinth in which one lives, be it a mansion or a one-room studio. Again John speaks of how "formal" all these exits and entrances must be, because, with dialogue cut as minimally as possible and specifics abstracted as often as possible, coming and going is the film's major activity. The combination of formality, abstraction, spare dialogue, and unpredictable comings and goings, give *Love Streams* its quality of "a dream, it's a dream."

It's dream-like how people keep showing up out of nowhere – Albie and Agnes, Sarah, now Ken, and later a menagerie of animals. *Love Streams* is about how it does no good to hide in your own shell, your own house. Life will flush you out sooner or later. When Robert Harmon went cruising for experience, he found only the inconclusive episodes with Susan and Margarita, which he controlled and limited. All his deepest experiences literally drive up his driveway and ring his doorbell, quite beyond his will.

Tonight John is very pleased to have conceived a flowing, tracking and tilting shot from outside: it begins by looking through the dining room window, picks up Harmon as he enters the dining room, tracks his walk into the kitchen, moves back to the stairs as he climbs them, zooms out and tilts up to pan into the bedroom to see Harmon turn the lights on and off, then catches the shine of Ken's headlights on the house as his car pulls up. A very pretty piece of film, complex yet smooth, a minute-and-five-second shot that they get in only five takes.

Then a much easier set-up – in Harmon's bedroom, showing his point-of-view of Sarah and Ken. But it takes forever (11 takes) as minor things go wrong again and again. By contrast, the more complicated Sarah-Ken scene needs only three set-ups and 10 takes.

At the end of a long night, Cassavetes seems more peaceful than usual – and less tired than anyone else. He tells me happily, "I've got 75 beginnings, no ending. At the beginning of a picture you're always on sure ground. Then you get 10 pages in, and that's when the *movie* starts, the phoniness, the plot. So I try to be always at the beginning of a picture. That's why my pictures are so long! Hours of beginnings, no endings."

Again Cassavetes deletes specificity: we won't see Harmon panicked at Sarah's absence. The lovely, smoothly elaborate tracking shot won't appear in the final cut because, John says, "it draws too much attention to itself." The three set-ups and 19 takes of Robert Harmon's action are cut to 11 seconds in the bedroom: Harmon enters the upstairs bedroom, goes to the window, looks down at Sarah and Ken, to whom the remaining 49 seconds of the scene belong. By contrast, Sarah's scene couldn't be more specific "because it's so unlike her at any other time. Gotta see she's capable of this, she's not just a depressed nut."

MONDAY, JULY 11 – *Did I kiss you off a little abruptly?*

Sarah Lawson comes to the kitchen, stands in its doorway, looks at Robert Harmon. He stands in his tux at the window, so she knows he's seen her with Ken. She pauses, gives the barest hint of a shrug, accompanied by a slight smile that seems to say, "So?" As she walks past him into the kitchen she asks, "You want some coffee?"

"No, no thanks, babe."

From the kitchen she says, "I had the most wonderful time tonight. I'm getting my balance."

"Yeah! You look happy."

"What is creativity, Robert?"

"What's creativity?"

"Now I don't mean, you know – I know you're a writer and you're creative. People paint – but I don't paint. Would you consider, uh – cooking – an art?"

"Cooking?"

"Yeah, I – [she goes to the table, stands facing him] I, I'm trying to find something – something that, eh – just something I *can do. I don't mean that I'm the only person in the world that can do it, you know, but just – something that I could, eh – something special, you know, like cooking or –"*

"Writing – you could do some poetry, write poetry?"

She walks back into the kitchen, prepares coffee.

"No, I – poetry, I love it, but it's just so depressing. I always get so low. No, I don't think that's healthy. Uh – I don't even know what I'm talking about!" She steps back to the table. They both sit down on: "Would – would love be considered an art?"

"Well, some people think so."

"Well, you're a writer, you're always writing those, eh, those books about sex. Maybe you could write one about love. I could help you with that."

"Ok, we'll see how that works out."

"I love you."

"And I love you."

"You know, I'm going *to do this damned thing, I really am. I'm going to find balance. And – I think you should do it too. You know, I'm going to do something for you. I'm going to – I'm going to buy you a baby. Really! You really need some – living thing that you could love, Robert, you know? It could be just a little, a little animal that you could take care of and kiss and sleep with."*

"Please, don't."

"And you'd be balanced, and I'd be balanced –"

"Please –"

"– hon – then I can go back to being obsessive about my family."

He reaches out and takes her hand. They hold hands during:

"I think –" he says. But she interrupts:

"You know what Dad always said?"

"No, what did Dad always say?"

"'For every problem there is an answer.'" A pause. "I'm not gonna have coffee." She stands and leaves the kitchen as she says, "I'm gonna take a bath and I'm gonna go right to bed. I'm gonna get up at dawn! Ok? Goodnight, honey."

He gets up and turns off the flame under the pot. The phone rings.

"If this dialogue is all we've got to go on, would we know Sarah and Robert are brother and sister?" John ponders this question as the crew sets up and we wait for darkness. He's toying with never stating their relationship outright. I'm not quick on the uptake tonight, I don't realize until later: if he's toying with that, he's toying with revising the entire ending, because the fact that

Sarah is Robert's sister is central to the last 20-or-so pages of the shooting script. Tonight John's explicit only about revising tomorrow's dialogue, where the relationship becomes clear. So he's pondering. "What do you think," his finger drift's over today's page, "if *this* speech is *it*?"

I'm usually his sounding board, his way of thinking out loud. (Even his thoughts often must be 'performed'!) He rarely asks my opinion. I say, "That's hard for *us* to figure, 'cause we already know. Also, like the man says, it depends on the performance."

"To the world," John says, "they look completely crazy. When they're with each other they're normal – but *that* looks crazy."

There is a sense in which form *is* art, for art achieves its power through form. What Cassavetes accomplishes with form is too consistent, too subtle and yet specific, to be (as he's so fond of saying) an "accident."

Love Streams, obviously, has almost no narrative, no plot. Yet it does have a story. The distinction is crucial. Orson Welles once said, "Who needs a plot? But who can live without a story?" James Baldwin, in *The Devil Finds Work,* defined the difference in a way I think Cassavetes would approve: "A story is impelled by its necessity to reveal: the aim of the story is revelation, which means that a story can have nothing – at least deliberately – to hide. This also means that a story resolves nothing. The resolution of the story must occur in us, with what we make of the questions with which a story leaves us. A plot, on the other hand, must come to a resolution, prove a point: a plot must answer all the questions which it pretends to pose."

John says, "Any time there's a plot point, I go crazy. If we can't do it without letting the audience know that we know it, screw it! And everybody gets very angry because they want the plot, you know? I say, *They'll be watching the plot, they will not be watching the people.* So we're making a picture about *inner life*. You know? And nobody really believes it can be put on the screen. I don't believe it either, but I believe that if you put it out there then people are capable of understanding and wanting to understand *feelings* –

when they're sure that it's not a mistake, and when they're sure that you're not going to double-cross them midway in the picture and go streaking back to plot, I think they'll watch with great fascination and interest."

Most stories are founded on a scene that occurs at the beginning and most stories climax with a scene at or near the very end. We blindly accept this classic form, especially in film; most of us are unable to imagine an alternative. At the beginning we expect certain information – who are these characters, what are they doing in this story, what are their issues? In the middle, we expect elaborations and complications. At the end, we want resolution and some fireworks. Most dramatists get their effects by playing to, or playing against, these expectations – in this sense, the dramatist is assisted by the expectations of the audience. But if the typical structure of beginning-middle-end is cast away completely, the dramatist gets no help from our expectations. He can neither satisfy them nor develop his theme by teasing and playing against them. There is no more demanding form than that which dispenses with the classical beginning-middle-end structure – for without it, the dramatist's only means of holding our attention is to show something gripping, something interesting, something truthful, every moment. For these moments to cohere, finally, into an artistic whole, the dramatist must in the end establish what these moments elementally share.

Cassavetes recognizes that life does not happen with dramatic unity and linear regularity. He sees the artificiality of beginning-middle-end structures, so what does he do? For its first half hour, sometimes even its first hour, a Cassavetes film is a series of moments, incidents. As in life, these incidents occur in a sequence in which they don't always appear related. They're only relation to each other is that they're happening to a given set of characters who've been, for whatever reason, selected for our attention. Cassavates arranges these incidents with a dramatic sense not unlike that of a jazz composer like Charles Mingus (whom John calls "a genius," a word he uses rarely): tempos shift suddenly, haunting melodies are juxtaposed with dissonant and jarring progressions which in turn flow into melody again. Then, a half hour or so into his film, Cassavetes reveals the nature of the characters' relationship with each other. That relationship is all the 'plot,' all the 'premise,' that he employs.

In *Husbands* we see the basic relationship at the beginning: three friends have lost the friend who was their social glue. But not until well into the film (the famous bathroom scene) do we realize that Archie (Peter Falk) and Gus (Cassavetes) have a strong relationship that Harry (Ben Gazzarra) is not privy to – the death of the fourth friend has left Harry isolated, and his isolation drives the remainder of the film. *A Woman Under the Influence,* a film about a marriage, runs 23 minutes before we see Nick and Mabel in the same room. There are four major characters in *Faces.* We meet two in the first moments of the picture: John Marley's Dickie and Gena Rowlands' Jeannie; but we won't see Dickie's wife Maria (Lynn Carlin) for 22 minutes and we won't meet the forth crucial character, Chet (Seymour Cassel), until the film's run for an hour and 15 minutes! (Film critics' quiz: name another film in which a primary character is not introduced for over an hour.) What precedes the encounters of Cassavetes' characters is raw material, presented without guideposts so that the audience must take an attitude toward the characters *before* the film's major themes and relationships are revealed.

Love Streams' two primary characters don't even cross paths for 57 minutes. They speak but briefly when she arrives, and briefly again when he returns from Vegas, but they don't have an actual conversation, don't fully relate to each other, until the film's run over an hour and a half – 93 minutes, to be exact. And we still haven't been told they're brother and sister.

How does Cassavetes establish the elemental relationship between these scattered moments? He supports his daring scenic placement with the oldest, most conservative device of storytelling: strict parallelism. In *Love Streams* we see Robert Harmon's ex-wife and Sarah Lawson's estranged husband; we see Robert's son, Sarah's daughter. Robert picks up a woman in a nightclub, Sarah picks up a man in a bowling alley – and these venues are the opposite of how each lives, a hetero man in a gay club, a rich woman in a working-class joint. Each pick-up scene ends at a front door. These parallels continue as the film progresses. As in *Faces* and *Husbands,* in *Love Streams* the major characters undergo different *experiences* of nearly identical *situations*. Thus the inner lives of the characters are expressed by the form of the film: when we see two people have entirely different reactions to similar situations, then it is their inner life, not the situations, that determines their reactions. It is through this *form* that Cassavetes lets the inner nature of his characters reveal itself. His people rarely tell us what they're thinking, and when they try they often don't make sense, yet we come away from a Cassavetes movie having been soaked in their psyches. We may or may not understand them, but we know them in the almost Biblical sense of having experienced them. And because, as John says, each moment in his film is a new beginning, we don't know what will happen next and we cannot judge these characters in terms of an unfolding story or plot.

Cassavetes' cinema is formless, some critics say? "I don't know what I'm doing," John says? Those critics are blind and John is devious. The proof is on the screen.

We've a scene to shoot tonight, it's hot as hell, the set-up's lights make it hotter still, and nobody seems to be looking forward to work of any kind.

"We're going to do a little rehearsal," John announces. "We may shock everybody, we may do two or three."

Gena's just been 'miked.' A battery-powered transmitter has been fastened under her dress at the small of her back, to support her hidden portable microphone. She turns her profile to John: "The battery doesn't show on me, does it?"

"No. It just looks like you're a little heavier."

"Thanks," Gena tells him.

In costume, with lights set and everybody quiet, cameras ready and waiting, they run through the scene.

"Let's try one more," John says when they're done. "I'm going to change my position."

They exchange places, he sits in her chair and she in his. Before they start again Gena tells him, "I'm having a hard time getting to the place where I say 'I love you.'"

It's a difficult jump. The lines go, *"Why don't you write a book about love, and I'll help you with it?" "We'll see how that works out,"* Harmon says. *"I love you,"* Sarah says. *"And I love you,"* says Harmon.

When they rehearse again they barely say the I-love-you lines, letting the words say themselves with no inflection. The moment is more powerful than on the first run-through. But now Gena is worried about the end of the scene when she goes upstairs. "Did I kiss you off a little abruptly, what do you think?"

They do it again, and she works on the moment of deciding that she doesn't want coffee and it's time to go to bed. They work with when to move and with the length of time it takes for the water to boil. Bo Harwood, on sound, says that the boiling water sounds like a waterfall through Gena's microphone.

"What the FUCK it's a fuckin' coffee pot!" Thus speaks John.

Silence. Everyone, including Gena, is shocked at the outburst.

John looks around slowly, at each and all of us. He smiles. "I'm getting so reasonable in my old age."

He says to Gena, "You want another rehearsal or you want to start?"

"No, let's try one on film, darling."

They do it.

"Did it seem, uh, reasonable?" she asks after the first take.

"It did to me," John says.

"You know – I can't tell."

At the end of the next take they just look at each other, in character as Sarah and Robert – it's not a John-and-Gena look.

And, still looking into her eyes, John's shoulders shake and he starts to laugh that laugh: "I'm so depressed I can't stand it!"

"I am too! Are we gonna rejoin the living?"

They smile at each other, smiles I've not seen before, smiles that don't take place in this particular room but in a part of their lives the rest of us will never see.

"I don't know what it is," Gena says, "every night I get depressed with this."

John changes the staging, not much, but enough to require a shift of lights and repositioning one of the two cameras. It means a short break. It's so hot that when a person passes you in the narrow hallway the brush of air feels almost like a cool breeze.

"Don't you just love hot weather?" Gena says. "It just makes you want to spring into action, doesn't it?" She goes outside so the lights' heat won't sweat off her make-up.

They do many more takes through eight more set-ups.

"There are more things to remember in this little scene than in any six scenes in the movie!" exclaims Gena after one take.

Before the next take John tells her, "Just make the whole thing a little harder to do."

"A little harder to do? It's too easy?"

"No, but – it shouldn't be easy for her. That way it's a real conversation."

"Maybe I'm getting too glib," Gena says.

"*Maybe,* but just a little. But we've got the other take, which was a good take, so let's try it this way now."

"Sure," says Gena, "it'll be fun."

I get the impression that their actual words don't mean very much in themselves but are a kind of code that they both understand very well. They seem to be coaxing each other toward something they already know, something they *know* they know. The next take has an excellent feel to it – the differences are subtle, minimal, but everyone in the room feels them and everybody's smiling.

"That more of what you meant?" Gena asks.

"I liked it a lot," John says.

"It's really hard to decide what it is, because out there [saying goodbye to Ken] I'm at this very high level, then I come in, and I see you, and..." Her voice trails off. "By the time the scene's over I *may* get it!"

"Take a longer pause at the door."

"Longer than the last one?"

"Don't be afraid to be embarrassed."

She leaves the room to prepare to make her entrance yet again.

George Sims, the prime camera operator on *Faces,* operates the second camera tonight – another manner of John 'directing' Gena, with old friends Al and George shooting her in this pivotal scene. John says to George, "This scene is breaking me up. All during the picture I can't stand anybody to talk about anybody but *me,* and she's talking about herself!"

While in this scene John's Robert Harmon is primarily reacting to Sarah Lawson, Gena must establish in one conversation both the nature of her relationship with him *and* the nature of her dialogue with herself. This scene and the shrink scene are Sarah's only calm conversations in the entire picture.

They do another take, then John calls for another one right away. "Let's go again, and just keep the whole thing *up*!"

"Up, how?"

"I mean, if you can."

"What do you mean, *if* I can?!"

And they share the laugh of co-conspirators.

Nine set-ups, 21 takes, for 3:40 of the final cut. (Plus three set-ups, six takes, to set up the next scene.)

At dailies the next afternoon I'm still uncertain if this scene is enough to establish the brother-sister relationship. What's clear is that only with each other are Robert and Sarah not 'on,' are not defensive, and are not trying to prove anything.

Except for a few seconds that establish where Robert is, John selects just one long take, one shot, for the conversation: from the dark kitchen we see Sarah enter, she speaks, she comes into the kitchen without turning on the light to make coffee, she speaks as she does this and that, goes into the lighted table-area, talks to Robert Harmon – but for the most part we don't see him. He sits out of camera-sight. We hear how relaxed his voice is (for the only time thus far) – a voice expressive and distinctive enough that we don't need to see him. Thus it's an especially forceful moment when his hand comes into frame to grasp hers. After she leaves, he stands, walks toward the camera, turns off the flame under the coffee water (another subtle sign of their relationship – he expects *her to leave her water boiling, takes it for granted, reflexively attends to it).*

Of course, even such a simple thing as making coffee is abstracted in this picture: we assume that's what she's doing, as we assume he's turning off the gas on the stove. But these kitchen shots are such that we don't see what they're up to; she says she's making coffee, but stove, utensils, etc., are either in near-pitch darkness or out-of-frame. Given only what we see, they could be stirring witch's brew, we wouldn't know the difference.

TUESDAY, JULY 12 – *Where were you?*

The scene as revised and cut goes like this:

Immediately after Sarah heads upstairs and Robert turns down the gas on the stove, the phone rings.

We see Sarah upstairs, on the phone's second ring. She takes off her shoes as the phone rings three more times. She notices a phone under the nightstand beside the bed and picks it up.

Downstairs, when Robert doesn't hear another ring, he picks up.

Upstairs, Sarah says "Hello" casually into the receiver as she sits in the chair beside the nightstand, still holding one shoe.

The voice on the phone is her daughter's: "Mother?"

"Debbie?" Sarah drops the shoe. Her voice goes tense: "Are you alright?"

We see Debbie in her bedroom in Chicago. [Shot July 25]

"How can you ask me if I'm alright? Did you find your sex, Mom, is that what you were looking for?"

"Ask your father to come to the phone."

"It's making me ill what you're doing to Dad. You wanted the divorce."

The rest of their conversation is on Sarah:

"Please call your father to the phone."

"He's asleep."

"Wake him up."

"You think I'm afraid to call him. Mother, please leave him alone."

Sarah gets fierce: "Debbie, listen to me." She holds the phone in her right hand, while her left gestures forcibly, forefinger pointed as though in Debbie's face. We're seeing another side of Sarah. "You do what I tell you, you do it right now. Call your father to this phone."

Debbie obeys instantly. "Alright, alright, fine. I will. Just hold on."

Sarah leans over, her head almost on her knees, as she waits.

In Chicago, Debbie runs down a hall, Jack is getting out of bed, Debbie runs back to her room and picks up the extension.

We see Sarah again. "Jack – you have no mercy. Alright, that's fine with me. But you leave our kid out of this.*" Her force surprises; it feels like Jack didn't win many arguments with his wife. "This is our biggest and it is our only problem."*

We hear but do not see Debbie break in with, "Hey, I'm 13, I'm not a child, honey. I know more than you do."

Sarah leans back, her head against a mirror, she's looking at the ceiling.

"Jack, would you answer one question for me? Do you believe that love is a continuous stream?" The quiet agony of her question is unlike anything we've heard from her until now. It registers that she's been thinking of this question continuously, posing it to herself over and over, since her talk with the psychiatrist.

We hear Jack, but we watch Sarah. "Sarah, we have a little daughter that's going through puberty right now. And she's more important than you are right now. I'm not taking care of you anymore, Sarah. We're divorced."

As he speaks she leans forward slowly. When he says "We're divorced" her head is almost on her knees and she puts the receiver back on its cradle on the floor.

Cut to Robert Harmon, on the phone downstairs, furious: "Jack – please have the grace not to explain to MY SISTER what a divorce is! And stop lecturing her!" He pauses, as though someone is speaking on the other end, but we don't hear. "Well – then," Robert yells, "don't call her and leave her alone! YOU'RE the bitch!"

As viewers we've no time to take in this information – this 'reveal,' as filmmaking shop-talk would put it, that Robert and Sarah are brother and sister, because immediately Robert runs up the stairs and down the hall, clearly afraid of this conversation's effect on his sister. She's gone into the bathroom, he knocks, but opens the door before she responds, "Are you alright?" We don't see her as she answers, "I'm washing my face."

"Well, love is dead." He's heard her "continuous stream" line. "Love is a fantasy that little girls have."

She tries to brush past him to her bedroom, saying, "OK, I'm tired, I just want to be by myself."

He starts speaking about her daughter, she turns on him furiously – suddenly they're arguing, an in-your-face family fight. Not five minutes ago they were gently, intimately conversing, but now she's telling him – with that forefinger slashing like a knife in his face – that she doesn't intend to discuss her daughter with him, he knows nothing about children. He's saying Jack is just a man, a man just like him who sleeps with lots of women, they talk over each other's lines till she cuts through with:

"What kind of BULLSHIT is this? [Sarah can handle herself when she's cornered]. Hey, you're talking about a guy I've been with for 15 years, who put the, put the food on the table and the clothes on her back. I mean, we've had experiences of the heart you couldn't even imagine. *You're talking about a guy who, who, who held my hand in the hospital, who CRIED when his baby was born. Where were you?!"*

Her "Where were you?" is sharp and quick. Sarah compresses into those words deep bitterness and resentment. We remember that she companioned Robert the night his baby was born.

Instantly after "Where were you?" they both, at the same moment, turn their backs on each other. She goes into the bedroom, he strides down the hall.

She leans against a wall, we see her in profile, she's exhausted.

He goes into his bedroom. It's dark, lit only by the hall light. He's lit a cigarette. He sits. Takes a drag. Turns on a lamp. Takes a drag. Turns it off. Another drag. We cannot read his expression. [Shot July 15]

So, just once, 99 minutes into his film, Cassavetes lets us know that Sarah and Robert are brother and sister. And he zips past the moment, Harmon literally running up the stairs right after 'the reveal,' and we're in the midst of a family-style shouting-match in which each denies the reality of the other until she spits out, "Where were you?"

That question stops the conversation, because it reveals the nature of their relationship.

"Where were you?" is not in the May 13 shooting script written by Cassavetes and Ted Allan. Nor is it in John's slightly revised version for today's shoot. "Where were you?" is Gena's.

There were three takes of 'the bathroom argument,' all of them printed, all of them the complete argument, save for the last take during which John and Gena went through the entire scene three times in succession without cutting. That totals to about seven minutes of film, seven minutes of an intense family battle. For once the cliché is accurate: the atmosphere *is* 'electric.' A static electricity of the psyche fills that little hallway and shocks the observers. These two know how to fight, and know how, as actors, to evoke in us every family fight we've ever experienced.

When Gena/Sarah shoots out her "Where were you?" John/Robert stalks off down the hallway yelling "I was in Poughkeepsie!"

Before the next take he tells Gena not to say "Where were you?" and she doesn't. But in the editing room John will see that Gena has understood the relationship, or the expression of the relationship, better than he and Ted. She's remembered that Sarah tells Albie that she hasn't seen him since he was in the hospital being born; with "Where were you?" she's created an opposition, that Sarah was there for Robert but Robert wasn't there for Sarah. The bitterness and resentment of her words conjures the dynamic of their relationship as we've seen it: Robert ran out on Sarah as soon as she arrived, then ran out on her again as soon as he returned from Vegas. Her outburst tonight suggests that's been their pattern all their lives – that, even with his sister, whom he loves more than anyone in the world, Robert Harmon's not there when it matters.

The scenes shot last night and tonight are *Love Streams'* hub – the basis not only of what's to come but of what we've already seen. The other scenes, backwards and forwards in time, only make sense in the light of these two scenes. Not until tonight's sequence is it clear why Sarah and Robert are in the same movie.

By not defining their relationship until this late in the film, Cassavetes' has invited the audience to project the entire spectrum of man-woman relationships onto Sarah and Robert. Is she an ex-wife, an old flame whom he never married ('the one that got away')? Thus Cassavetes lets us feel the undercurrent of sexuality between brother and sister without shoving it down our throats. We'd resist a blatant statement of such nuances, but there's no way for us to resist this approach – *we're* supplying the nuance. By the time we learn they are brother and sister, we've filled in the unacted aspects of their love. We feel they're platonic, but we feel a mutual electricity nevertheless.

The literalness of Cassavetes' style is only a surface literalness. His structure and form are non-linear, circular – a form expressive of the concept that we rarely catch up with ourselves, for one area of the psyche acts one way while another area of the psyche behaves differently, so that a single life leads separate inner lives. The most shocking moment is when an individual is faced with a situation that forces the disjoined areas of inner life together. These are moments of almost unbearable intensity, and they change everything. These scenes are the hub around which the film radiates.

Until we see the 'rough assembly' that includes Gena's "Where were you?" we won't fully appreciate her precision and subtlety. When Robert Harmon comes back from Vegas and turns on the jukebox, the song that plays as he and Sarah dance is 'Where Are You?'

Waiting to shoot the telephone argument Gena, in full costume, sits outside enjoying the night air – stifling hot, but not nearly as hot as the house. She tells me she's concerned about her house cats. The coyotes of the Hollywood Hills are bolder this summer, and cats are no match for them. Some nights, Gena's seen them in the driveway. Again she mentions the BB gun she uses to drive the coyotes away, "but if I sit here with a rifle on my lap the crew will think I'm going to kill John."

She remembers when she was little and her older brother David (who plays Sarah's shrink in the film) would make her dance with a BB gun by shooting at her feet. He always told her how ugly she was, and it was a rule that she wasn't allowed to see his friends. She had to run into the closet if they came into the house unexpectedly. "I can still remember the smell of mothballs." She'd hide until David and his pals went downstairs to the billiard room. She remembers that by the time she was in junior high she was picking her own clothing, because her mother said she had to develop her own style, but her brother hated her clothes. He would get so angry at what she was wearing that he would go to his room and not come out to go to school, "even though we didn't go to the same school!"

Her brother's first job was helping people get on and off escalators in department stores. Escalators were new then and at first many people, especially older people, were afraid to get on them. With the first money he made her brother bought her a coat of his choice so she'd stop wearing the coat she liked.

"I don't know how he turned into such a wonderful man!"

It's unusual for Gena to be social just before an important scene. Then I realize she's *working*, even now. Several days ago she said to me, "A brother and sister – that's *very* mysterious." Telling me these stories just before she shoots, she's keeping the mystery present and vivid.

Later Gena will tell me, "The thinking about it when I'm alone and private, that's the part I enjoy. I love it, as a matter of fact. I think about it a long time. It really isn't any *deep* thinking – I don't know how to put it. I never know how to put it. I just know that I like to think about it. The more time I have to think about my character, the happier I am. I'm very reluctant to let that part of it go.

"And my family's quite used to it. Zoe, the other day, she said, 'Every time you're doing a part, I'll be talking and in the middle of it you just sort of drift off.' And it's true. Because something she will have said will remind me of something, or make me think of something. And it just catches me so totally, when I'm working.

"And the children are so wonderful about it because they're so practical. They don't get alarmed when you drift off and are staring into another world. Zoe always says, 'Earth to Mother, Earth to Mother, come back.'"

When we include those parts of the scene shot July 15 (Robert alone smoking) and July 25 (Debbie's and Jack's part of the phone call), we're looking at 11 set-ups and 39 takes (21 tonight), for 4:10 of finished film.

Of Sarah's and Robert's lines, besides John's improvised "I was in Poughkeepsie!" only one line will be edited out – a line of Robert's on the phone with Debbie and Jack. John will write more extensive speeches for Debbie and Jack, then cut them in the editing room to the few lines transcribed above.

Cassavetes never even films an entire scene from the May 13 script: after their fight, Robert lies on his bed, Sarah comes in, sits on the bed beside him, strokes his hair. She says, "I love you, Robert. I know you're trying to help me. And I love you." The script then reads: She kisses his head, lies down beside him, puts her arm around him. *She says, "You're my baby." So she's his BIG sister. "I'm not," he says. "I'm happy with you. I never want to leave." "I never want you to," he says.*

These are the characters of Ted Allan's play, not the characters who've developed through the performances of John Cassavetes and Gena Rowlands. The scene is "too soft," John says. He's afraid it will sidetrack the audience from the core of the film. "It's giving them solace, when you don't want to give them solace. It's exploitation to give them a false solace." These characters "don't need solace either. Sarah's stronger if she doesn't go into my room, doesn't need to ask for comfort by seeming to give it."

Instead Cassavetes wants us to see Robert and Sarah each alone, reacting silently to their evening. After careful consideration, he's finally let us know they are brother and sister. But that's as specific as he's willing to be. If the qualities of the excised scene are to appear in the film, they must appear as performance, unsupported by dialogue.

WEDNESDAY, JULY 13 – *What are you doing behind the camera?*

The scene as revised and cut goes like this:

Robert smokes and paces in his living room. It's morning, bright sun shines through the dining room window, there are flowers all over the house, and he's dressed more casually than we've seen him. (We remember that before he raced off to Margarita's he said he'd have breakfast with her; he's there, now she's not. Another parallel.) The phone rings. It's Sarah. Robert says, "Sarah, what are all these flowers doing here? I mean, this looks like somebody died and went to a wake. Come on!" [Shot July 15]

We see Sarah in a shed of some sort. The shed is full of clutter. She tells Robert that she's at an animal farm getting him a baby, "I'm gonna change your life around a little bit." She listens to a reply we don't hear. She says, with great confidence, "Yeah, yeah, yeah, yeah, you don't like me now, but when I get home with what I'm gonna get home <u>with</u>, you're gonna be <u>crazy</u> about me."

After the call nosy Mrs. Kiner [Doe Avedon, the Cassavetes' secretary] echoes our former projections about Robert and Sarah, asking, "Was that your husband?"

"No."

"Your fiancé?"

"No."

"Well I must say I'm very curious as to know who it was."

"That was my closest and my dearest friend." [Again, a parallel: Sarah won't answer direct questions about Robert, as Robert wouldn't answer Albie's direct questions about Sarah.]

Outside the shed, Sarah adds: "And he doesn't want me to buy him a baby."

"What does he want you to do?" asks Mrs. Kiner.

Sarah answers with a discouraged, "Oh, I don't know. Actually, we're both pretty screwed up. But I really think that he's in more trouble than I am." [Shot today]

Sarah's gives up on the idea of a pet, but Mrs. Kiner, a good saleswoman, keeps plugging. She shows Sarah a goat, ducks, a mallard, a rooster, and finally sells Sarah on Jim the dog. Sarah gets so enthusiastic about the dog, she decides one animal isn't enough, she wants to see more. [Shot tomorrow]

We're at an animal farm in Topanga Canyon – a place that wrangles animals for filmmakers. In the sun the heat is terrible. In the shade it's not much better. There is no breeze. Smells of beasts and sweaty folk just hang in the air. Baying animals, baying people. John is preoccupied, as though he's having a conversation with himself and filming is an interruption. He shies away from production questions about next week – Eddie Donno's, Al Ruban's, anybody's. Should they lock down this or that location? "Ask me later." Diahnne and Margaret Abbott want to know when we'll be shooting Sarah's dinner party? "Tell them I don't know yet."

Most of us won't find out until next week – John himself may not yet be certain – but today and tomorrow we'll film the last scenes that refer to the May 13 shooting script in any way.

John sits on the back of the equipment truck, chain-smoking. Giddy Porath sets up our 16mm on a tripod. Peter Tullo holds our sound-boom out of the shot near John's head. I'm standing next to Giddy behind the camera.

"Everybody ready?" I say, trying to sound like a director.

John says, "Michael, what are you doing behind the camera?" He gestures with his cigarette, "Come 'ere. Sit with me."

"In the shot?"

"In the shot, yeah."

(I'm glad *somebody's* directing my picture.)

We'll shoot two more interviews with John. Each time he'll insist I share the screen with him. Giddy tries to fool him and usually shoots only his head or his gestures. I appear, but briefly.

At the moment I'm feeling very, very young, I'm embarrassed to say "Action" in front of John Cassavetes, but I manage it. Again we forget to slate. John sees my mistake, no doubt, but says nothing; I'm to learn from my own mistakes.

We roll and I ask, "What's the toughest thing about directing *Love Streams?*"

"The toughest thing doing this movie is doing a brother-sister relationship. A family that has been decimated, there's nobody there, it's just the brother and sister left, and to find out the nature of these two people and what they are – their own lives, their own screw-ups, their own mysteries. I don't know if that story is going to be a great narrative story, but it's interesting to me to make those discoveries, because my family is gone and I miss them. And Gena's lost members of her family. And family's still to me the most important thing in the world. And *Love Streams,* the whole idea is of going in and out of trying to find a continuity for your life, which can only be found in love."

"Watching you and Gena work together – sometimes I can't tell who's the director because there's so much coming out of you both. Do you feel that way?"

"I don't know how I feel."

I start a follow-up question but he heads me off at the pass: "I don't consider Gena anything on the set except a wonderful actress to work with. It's like that scene where Gena's going out and she meets Ken. She picks this guy up in a bowling alley because she's going to try to be a woman – and here she is, a mature virgin. And the lines are kind of silly, but Gena's a sophisticated woman. She knows exactly what she's doing in the process of flirting. And she does it with great taste. I couldn't help her on that. When she comes home and she kisses the guy and says, 'You're a cute guy' – I mean, we may have a discussion over that line. She'll say, 'I don't want to say he's a *cute* guy. *Wonderful* guy.' I say, 'That's terrible, I don't like that.' So we get into these battles over one word.

"Now, brother and sister are together in the kitchen. She comes in. She knows I've seen her with this guy. Now that's very difficult. Any fool can say, 'I know exactly what to do.' Well, you don't. So the actor walks in, she comes in, she sees me, I don't know what to do. I'm an actor, I'm also the director of the film – I don't know what to do. I see my sister, I've seen her make a fool of herself with this guy, but very happily – I don't know what to think. Somebody might say, 'You're supposed to be jealous' or 'You're supposed to feel *this*' – I really don't feel those things. I feel nothing, or something, or whatever – whatever comes up. She feels nothing or something – whatever comes up. Out of it, we have to follow the lines of that script. You know? And we also have to do it for the camera, it can't just be an accident.

"So, we worked on a very simple scene a whole night. If you were in an ordinary movie someone would say *Pick up the dialogue* or *We need a little pizzazz here,* and all that stuff, and that would be disastrous, I think, for a scene like that. So when it gets out to a movie theater, somebody might say, 'It's dull.' Somebody else might say, 'That's the most devastating scene I've ever seen!' Somebody else might say, 'What was *that* all about?' The way we make pictures is, we make pictures for people who are interested in *specifics.* They're not gonna be interested in everything. They're gonna be interested in *that* scene, 'I love that scene,' someone else says 'I hate that scene' – because it has something to do with their *life.* And in that sense, it's not like a movie. A movie tries to pacify people by keeping it going for them so that it's sheer entertainment. Well, I hate entertainment. There's nothing I despise more than being entertained. And I think if you make a difficult picture like this, then you gotta make it straight. And it all comes out of love."

"You told me you don't know what love is."

"I think anybody's an idiot that thinks they know what love is. You can't know. It's a deep mystery."

He rambles for a few sentences, then says: "I wake up every morning and I begin by hating myself. By four o'clock in the afternoon I've had a couple of drinks, I begin to like people a lot better. Then I get tired and I don't like them again and – the only thing that remains constant is the love of what you're doing."

Later today we interview Seymour Cassel. (Again without slates – the editor, Dan Wetherbee, gently but firmly puts a stop to that after he sees these dailies.) Seymour's son Matt is a *Love Streams* production assistant. Sey tells us, "Matt came home one night about a week ago and told me this guy got fired for this-and-that, and he says, 'It's a Mickey Mouse thing, this picture,' and I said, 'You know, Matt, you don't know what you're saying and you drive me crazy, 'cause of any people that you'll ever work with there's nothing Mickey Mouse about John.' He said, 'No, I don't mean John,' and I said, 'Matt, John *is* what this film is.'"

Eddie Donno, a stocky Italian, looks not at all fetching in a blond wig and red fingernail polish. They're about to film the car crash in Sarah's brief vision at the London phonebook: after her call to Jack she sees herself in a speeding car trying to run him down, the car hits a pole, it almost turns over, a window shatters, the car hits Jack. Sarah gets out, dazed, sees Jack dead beneath a tire, then sees that her daughter has also been hit and is lying bloody and lifeless beneath the fender. On the next set-up, after the crash, Gena will get out of the car.

Eddie's choreographed the stunt. He's rigged the car for safety. He'll drive. He insists he doesn't need crash pads.

He needs crash pads. The crash is more violent than he'd anticipated and he's injured. Not seriously (Eddie insists), but his arm is peppered with broken glass and a tooth has been "dislodged." That's the word used; I take it to mean the tooth is still in his mouth but it no longer sits right. He's stunned. We're all stunned

– for several sickening moments, everybody running toward the car, things looked much worse than they turned out to be. All the color's drained from John's face. "Why the *fuck* didn't I *order* Eddie to use those fucking pads!"

For Gena's scenes there are four set-ups, 19 takes. John re-writes as he shoots. The scene he and Ted wrote for the May 13 shooting script is, as usual, more expansive: Robert says he doesn't want a pet, doesn't want "to be normal," doesn't want her interfering with his life; Sarah echoes this with Mrs. Kiner. Today John cuts those lines, and adds Sarah telling Robert on the phone: "You're going to be the happiest little baby in the world" – a reprise of the Big Sister theme. He doesn't wait to cut that in the editing room; he tells Gena to leave out the line on the next takes.

More dialogue written today will be cut, such as Mrs. Kiner saying and Sarah agreeing that "men love horseshit, they even love women who say horseshit." John continues deleting specific attitudes – anything that takes away from the dream-like quality he's been consciously creating for days now.

THURSDAY, JULY 14 – *Speak, Jumbo, speak!*

Mrs. Kiner introduces Sarah to Jim the dog. The dog is with old crusty Lenny [Leonard P. Geer]. Lenny's drinking a beer and petting Jim. Mrs. Kiner mentions that Jim and Lenny are "inseparable," "the best of friends," so there is a cruelty to the scene because she has no compunction about separating these friends if it will profit her. Sarah is at first frightened of Jim, but Mrs. Kiner demonstrates that this dog is "is so much like a man! And you admire, and you praise, and the dog opens up, and he's a warm, wonderful, and fine human being." After a couple of nervous attempts, at which the dog barks, Sarah gets the hang of it, winning the dog by kneeling, petting, and saying, "You don't wanna scare me, you're so much bigger, you're so strong, and you're very handsome," and the dog suddenly likes her, she likes him, "He's a wonderful dog!" Sarah becomes enthusiastic (manic) and wants to buy not only the dog but other animals. As Mrs. Kiner and Sarah go off to see the animals, the scene cuts on Sarah's exclamation, "Oh, this is terrific!"

At the completion of this (much revised) scene, we're on page 91 of the May 13 shooting script, with 43 pages to go. Those pages follow Ted Allan's play more closely than any other section of the script:

Sarah buys Jim and some other animals. Jim's a fierce intelligent pit-bull who takes an instant dislike to Robert Harmon (as most males do). Their mutual hostility is key to driving the remaining pages, during which Susan and her mother Margarita arrive at Robert Harmon's (at Sarah's invitation) for an evening that is quite an ordeal. The last thing Susan says to Harmon as she and her mother leave is, "The only person you're in love with is your sister!" Then Sarah says she's leaving. Robert wants her to stay. She calls Ken (the guy from the bowling alley). Ken comes to pick her up. There's hostility between Ken and Robert. As Sarah and Ken drive away the dog barks. The End.

But of those 43 pages, only five will be so much as referred to in what John finally decides to shoot. The climactic scene of Ted's play, the dinner with Susan and Margarita, will be discarded. Why? Cassavetes will claim, at least in part, that it's the dog's fault.

On stage the dog was played by Neil Bell, who was uncannily convincing. Neil's compact, muscular body, his thick trim red beard, and his knowing, piercing eyes made for the ideal dog – a dog, that is, as it exists in its master's imagination. Neil is on the set today, and will be for the remainder of the shoot. He mostly hangs out and reads, but he's here because John wants the option of, at any moment, substituting Neil for the dog.

As for the real dog… he doesn't seem nearly as much of a dog as Neil Bell. The dog's name is not Jim but Jumbo, famous as Jennifer Beal's hound in *Flashdance.* A beautiful animal, Jumbo is a pit-bull with jaws capable of exerting 2,000 pounds of pressure per square inch. Jumbo can bark, wag his tail, come and go, jump and sleep on command. He looks meditative and/or sleepy always. And he's no actor. No matter how he tries he looks always sad, never fierce. There is no a gleam of intelligence in his mournful eyes. This dog gives the impression of constantly trying to remember something at the very edge of his awareness. Whatever it is, it would make him so happy to remember it! But he never will. And he seems to know this. And it makes him sad.

This is the beast that, in the shooting script, must terrorize Robert Harmon. Well, Jumbo can't even frighten me and I have a thing about dogs. When I was two years old a pack of dogs ran me down in Saint Mary's Park in the Bronx. It's my first vivid memory and I've been frightened of big dogs ever since. But even I have no fear of Jumbo.

Jumbo has been miscast. But contracts have been signed, money has been paid. He's our dog. In today's scene he must bark at Sarah. That's all. But it takes a while to get him going. His handlers repeat, "Jumbo, speak! Speak, Jumbo!" Finally Jumbo speaks. Alas, his bark suggests no bite. He's wagging his tail! Gena does a marvelous job of looking startled and frightened, but Cassavetes can use only Gena's takes. Jumbo's takes show a sleepy creature who's proud he remembered how to bark.

Is John serious? Will he apply his aesthetic of acting to a pooch? He's said to me, "I don't really have a preconceived vision of the way a performer should perform. Or, quote, the character, unquote. Once the actor's playing the part, *that's* the person. And it's up to the person to go in and do anything he can. If it takes the script this way and that, I let it do it." Yeah, but – is this dumb dog to determine the direction of our film?

(Or maybe he's not dumb. Given how dangerous he can be – he's a pit, remember – he may be doped to the gills. If that's true, will John let a drug-dependent canine dictate the mood of Ted's scenes?)

Cassavetes may be taking the dog seriously but nobody else is. From this day forth "Speak, Jumbo, speak!" will be a joke on the set, directed at anybody who's temporarily incoherent and/or unforthcoming.

Jumbo will be beautifully treated. Everybody loves him. Everybody feels sorry for him. And the dog has the vaguely ashamed expression of one who inspires pity.

During the next week, after watching hundreds of feet of failed Jumbo dailies, Cassavetes, true to his aesthetic, decides he cannot shape Jumbo to the role but must shape the role to Jumbo. Jumbo is a very convincing sleeper. And, when awake, his eyes brim with sympathy. The dog's hostility was to move the narrative and give *Love Streams'* concluding half hour its comedy and, if you'll excuse the expression, its bite. Instead, Cassavetes will use Jumbo only as a presence. He stages scenes *around* this dazed, good-hearted creature.

Is this the same Cassavetes who wasted a full day's work, called a wrap, because Margarita's home wasn't properly decorated? John Cassavetes will stand up to any man for the integrity of his vision, but he expects us to believe that Ted's scenes won't work because Cassavetes miscast a dog?

The thing is… many will believe it. Because John said it.

An exhausting day in this brutal heat, 11 set-ups and umpteen takes, but when yesterday's and today's work are edited the finished scene is 4:10. (And the car crash scene yesterday makes another minute or so of screen-time.)

FRIDAY, JULY 15 – *Limbo*

Only two brief scenes are shot today:

After his fight with Sarah [shot July 12], Robert Harmon goes into his bedroom, sits, lights a cigarette, turns a lamp on and off.

The next morning, Harmon paces in a dining room full of flowers. The phone rings. It's his sister at the animal farm. [Gena's side filmed July 13].

A limbo day. Five set-ups, 12 takes (most of them rehearsal-type takes). Almost no lines but for a few on the phone. And, except to tell the crew what he wants, John's not talking. When the shots are done he heads down to the editing room at Cannon, and doesn't want my company.

Later it will be clear that Cassavetes is in the throes of making a decision. Except for the insertion of a dream to be shot August 10–11, he's got two weeks to finish his picture. Will he follow the script or not? He's given himself the leeway not to in what he's shot so far; but if he jettisons the remaining pages he must conceive, write, perform and direct an entirely different conception.

Maybe now he's mulling how to pull it off – both creatively and, if you will, politically. How to present that decision to his friend Ted Allan (and risk losing the friendship)? How to tell

Diahnne and Margaret Abbott they will have no climactic scene and, without it, their featured roles are cut almost to bit-parts? Or has he already decided how to pull this off and he's simply working himself up to it? He's not talking.

The odd thing is, John doesn't look as ill as he did – and he hasn't looked very ill, not for the last week or so. Perhaps it's the energy of playing those scenes with Gena, combined with the creative excitement of re-visioning his film? Is his health improving? Or has he tapped into a fierce hidden resource of will to finish this thing his way?

What's shot today will be in the final cut.

MONDAY, JULY 18 – *It's like music*

A cab pulls up in Robert Harmon's driveway and in its backseat we see not one but two miniature horses! Sarah is crowded in that seat behind the horses. The cabbie [John Finnegan, a Cassavetes regular since the late '50s] gets out first and has a hard time getting the horses to exit the cab. Sarah gets out, he goes back into the cab for two birdcages, but he can't find the duck. Then he manages to get a goat out of the front seat. The animals' reins become entangled, Sarah and the cabbie disentangle them. This realistic slapstick takes over a full minute of screen time.

Robert Harmon opens the front door quickly, giving the impression that he's been watching from the window and is alarmed. Again he's dressed formally – slate-gray sports coat, black shirt. His expression is deadly serious and it's clear that he cannot believe his eyes.

Sarah proudly leads the horses to him – the cabbie follows, pulling the reluctant goat with one hand while with his other he manages two birdcages.

"I know this looks crazy!" says Sarah, bubbly and happy. "But I just got carried away! I couldn't resist these. These, these are miniature horses! Aren't they small?! I was gonna take only one, but then I figured they'd get lonely, and if you have one you might as well have two… Anyway, the goat, the goat gives milk, so that's not a waste. And the chickens, and the duck will, uh, they'll have eggs, eventually, and we can eat those and, and we'll – we'll all live here at the park!"

Harmon says nothing. She pauses, then says she's going to give them water and then he and she can talk about it – and she proceeds to lead the horses right past him through the front door into the house! As she passes her brother she says, "It's going to be alright, Robert." He stands aside and watches as Sarah, the horses, the cabbie, and the goat go by him. (An in-joke that John will keep in the film: Finnegan the cabbie addresses the goat as "Phedon," "Come on, Phedon, Phedon, come on!" The goat doesn't want to go and Finnegan is using all his strength to pull him.)

Robert just stands there as Sarah and the cabbie lead their menagerie down the hall, through the bar and into the backyard, struggling all the way.

In the backyard, the cabbie helps Sarah get the chickadees out of their cages (the way Finnegan just grabs and tosses them is very funny, though the chicks probably didn't like it), and Sarah gets water for the animals. Then, for several moments, the cabbie and Sarah just stand there. She says to him, "I don't know, I don't know if this is such a hot idea. He didn't seem – too enthusiastic about my park. I'm sure he thinks I'm crazy as a bedbug. What do you think?"

The cabbie turns his head and looks away, stone-faced as Buster Keaton.

Sarah works up some enthusiasm again for showing the horses "the high country," the hill in back of the house, saying to the horses, "You are such darling guys, I hope I'm doing the right thing for you fellas too."

As they run up a steep walkway amidst the foliage she says, "Just run, run free!"

A close-up in profile: Sarah watches the horses with the expression of someone perceiving something inexpressibly lovely.

Our documentary crew comes today to shoot the menagerie scene, including our editor Dan Wetherbee. Dan excuses himself to go pee, returns with a question. "What I want to know is, would you have a painting of your two mothers in the bathroom?"

John and Gena spend most of the morning in their bar hammering out what the scene will be. Helen Caldwell takes notes, Robert Fieldsteel and I look on.

"Here's what we're discussing," John tells Gena, "the attitude, basically, the attitude. The writing will come."

Says Gena, "She's totally bananas if she brings these things in –"

" – and she doesn't know it's a crazy thing to do!" John finishes her sentence. "Leaving her with Finnegan [for a few moments in the backyard], who's replaced my attitude for the moment – when she sees *his* attitude, it will leave you with a situation where you've forgotten the dog and you're only concerned with my *attitude.*"

John starts giving her new lines of dialogue. It's impossible to say how much he's thought of beforehand and how much he makes up as he goes along – when asked, John himself doesn't know. As John recites new lines Gena nods, very receptive, concentrating. Helen writes everything down in shorthand. She'll go off and type it all up as soon as this session is finished.

John says that after the horses go in the backyard Sarah will come back into the house and find Robert standing where she left him, at the front door. She'll tell him a dog is coming in a truck.

John says, "'Is he gonna stay here too,' he'll say, and that's a cut down to the driveway, to the foot of the driveway, to a truck pulling up the driveway. When the truck comes up we're in a different beat." John pauses. "We'll have to do something when we switch beats. 'Robert, I have to say this dog is very dangerous, I know this sounds crazy, but he's not really dangerous if you don't think he's a dog yourself!"

John doubles over laughing at what he's just said. Gena just stares at him. Nobody else laughs.

"I'm sorry," he says, tears of laughter in his eyes, "I don't know why I think that's funny."

Lenny, the geezer from the animal farm, will get out of the truck and bring the dog to the front steps where Sarah and Robert are standing. John floats some lines Lenny might say and Gena breaks in firmly with: "Don't give Lenny too much dialogue, *please.*"

Her voice is very quiet and very like steel. She doesn't want them to waste time creating an inessential scene for a non-actor's walk-on.

"No," John says quickly, "this isn't the writing." At any rate, it "isn't the writing" anymore.

They've outlined the scene now, today's shooting and part of tomorrow's. It's not yet nine o'clock in the morning.

"Let's go over it again now that we have the whole thing and simplify what the beats are," John says. "And then the next beat will be the justification for what we've done, which we have down there [Helen's shorthand], I can't remember exactly what it is, does anybody have that part?"

Helen reads back the lines. John's surprised at them, pleasantly so, pleased at their work. He listens with great concentration. "Let me have that part again."

She reads again the speech about miniature horses that ends, "And we'll all stay at the farm."

"*Park,*" John tells her. "Make 'farm' 'park."

"You like 'park' better than 'farm'?" asks Gena.

"Farm isn't funny. Who'd understand what that means?"

John steps out of the room for a moment. Gena takes a deep breath. Looking past us, speaking to herself, she says softly, "The thing is not to get hysterical."

Suddenly she looks up, startled. "Is it nine o'clock?! Is Antonia here?!" Antonia does the Cassavetes' housework. "Why should I worry about that, she knows what to do better than I do." She goes back to her lines.

John comes back in saying, "Let me ask you this, are you alright on the *first* part? Just the thought thing? Then we can iron the words out. Helen will get it typed, and get the beats, and then we'll work on it. I don't think we'll even start shooting for a couple of hours. It's like music, you set it up and set it up, you set it up and then something happens, BAM!"

"What about you?" Gena asks. "Your character?"

"I don't have anything to say at this point. Because I'm concerned with whether you're up over moonbeams now. I'm concerned about you. I don't care about the animals." John laughs. "It's such a beautiful sight, to see a woman take a horse out, just leading the horses off calmly, and the horses just go, and…" his voice trails off.

Gena looks at Helen: "Have you got that too?"

Helen nods yes.

"But when he comes up, the dog," Gena says, "I'm lost from that point on. We have to find out about that."

"We're surely know more about this by *then*," John says – meaning, I think, by the time they've shot what they've now decided on.

"Yeah, we'll find out," Gena says. "We don't know. Which is nice."

"The intriguing part of this picture," John starts, "is that it's all fantasy but –"

"That's for filmmakers, not for actresses," Gena interrupts. "I'm going to study now. Do you need me anymore?"

"I always need you."

The intriguing part of this picture is that it's all fantasy... It's a dream... The animal scene makes it clear just how dream-like *Love Streams* is. One dream overlapping another. Sarah sees Robert run out of the house whenever she needs him – a classic rejection dream. Robert sees Sarah with a lover and doesn't know what to think – a classic brother-sister dream. Then there's "I Dreamed My House Was Populated With Sexy Girls Whom I Did Not Desire"... "I Dreamed I Met The Sexiest Woman At A Homosexual Bar"... "I Dreamed My Shrink Told Me To Have Sex With Anybody" and/or "I Dreamed I Told My Shrink I Don't Need Sex"... "I Dreamed I Hated Paris"... "I Dreamed My Long-Lost Son Suddenly Showed Up At My Door"... "I Dreamed I Left My Little Boy Alone All Night in Vegas"... "I Dreamed I Fled To My Long-Lost Brother"... "I Dreamed My Long-Lost Sister Suddenly Showed Up And I Ran Away"... "I Dreamed I Danced With My Brother/Sister To 'Where Are You'"... "I Dreamed I Danced With An Old Showgirl And Kissed Her Teeth"... "I Dreamed I Went To A Bowling Alley In Evening Clothes"... one utterly improbable dream-like scene after another, played with meticulous realism. Sequence after sequence of 'inner life,' expressed without interpretation, graceful and 'formal' yet raw.

Now, in this scene, the dreamers meet head-on. Horses, goats, ducks, chickens and a parakeet are in the house! And a dog is on the way! "I Dreamed That My Sister/Brother And I Were Dreaming The Same Dream When The Animals Came And Changed Everything."

When we shoot, Robert/John will stand in stolid disbelief as Sarah/Gena and Finnegan lead the animals into the house. Then while Finnegan pulls Phedon-the-goat through the hallway – saying "Come on, Phedon, come on or I'll make a baseball glove outa ya!" – John, out of the shot now, pushes the goat from behind, then doubles over in laughter, clasping his hands to his mouth so he doesn't ruin the sound.

Just before shooting today's first take John muses that maybe Susan and Margarita will get as far as the front door, in the rain. Maybe Susan will fall on the slippery asphalt, Sarah will ask if Susan's really in love with her brother, Susan and her mother will see they've been invited into a brother-sister weirdness and they'll leave without ever entering the house. "After Susan falls, and Sarah is asking those questions, and Susan has come with such expectations, Susan wouldn't go in – she'd leave."

"So you're cutting the party?" I ask.

"It's not needed anymore." A pause. "I can't be definite, because I don't know what's going to be until it's been done."

Gena calls, "Come on, Cassavetes!"

She's sitting in the back seat of a cab with two miniature horses.

Thirteen set-ups but only 16 takes – all but three takes are printed, and most of those are two-camera shots. Nearly 32 minutes of printed film for 2:47 in the final cut.

TUESDAY, JULY 19 – *Fifteen hours a day isn't enough*

The scene, as edited, continues as follows:

A sharp cut from the close-up of Sarah in the backyard to Robert Harmon, seen from behind, still standing in his front doorway, staring down the driveway.

We hear Sarah speak a soft, serious "Hi." Robert turns to her.

Sarah takes two tentative steps toward him. [Shot today, re-shot July 21.] All her enthusiasm has drained. She was so sure her brother would be "crazy about her" and love her "park." She's crushed that he doesn't.

Then there's the heavy sound of a truck in second gear pulling up the steep driveway. Sarah and Robert stand beside each other on the front steps, watching silently as the truck pulls up, stops.

Lenny and Jim get out. Lenny says bitterly, "Come on, Jim – this is it."

Slowly Lenny leads the dog to them. Robert looks only at the dog. Sarah looks nervously at Robert. It's clear her brother can't handle her sense of life any more than can her family.

Robert says darkly, "Hello, Jim."

She says, "This is Lenny, and this is Jim."

Robert just looks. Then says, as he turns to go into the house, "I need a drink." Sarah, her expression uncertain, watches him go.

Sarah and Lenny stand there briefly, silently. Then she takes Jim's leash. [The Lenny-Jim takes are shot today and re-shot tomorrow.]

Robert rushes down the hall, into the bar, nervously lights a cigarette and pours a drink. He hears the dog bark, and then a kind of thump.

We see Sarah falling on the floor, on her back. [Shot today, re-shot tomorrow.]

Robert freezes a moment, then leaves the drink and runs to Sarah. She's unconscious on the floor. The dog is sitting by her. He tells the dog, "Hey, don't give me any trouble now." The dog meekly walks off-camera.

Robert kneels with the cigarette in his mouth, picks up Sarah and holds her to him. Takes the cigarette out of his mouth. Holds Sarah, looks at her face, kisses her forehead, rocks her in his arms.

Eddie Donno approaches but before Eddie can say a word John tells him, "I know you want to talk about if we're going to use the animals in the next scene – you'll have to be a mind reader, because *I* don't even know what I'm doing in the next scene."

There's an added major distraction. Elmer Bernstein has been Cassavetes' friend since he scored John's late-50s TV hit *Johnny Staccato*. Bernstein is one of Hollywood's most respected film composers, an Oscar®-winner and multiple Oscar®-nominee, with credits ranging from *The Ten Commandments* and *Some Came Running* to *Animal House* and *Airplane!* He's to write the opera sequence that Sarah will dream (to be shot August 10–11). But no music has been written yet, there've been no conceptual meetings, and Bernstein at present is on vacation until August 1. John decides today that Elmer is off the picture.

"It's an embarrassing situation for me," John says. "Music is such an integral part of this fantasy! He gets back August 1, that gives him two weeks, and the singers haven't been hired yet. He says, 'I know what to do!' – and if he knows what's going to be then he's a genius, because *I* don't know yet. But I know we can't have an unspecific opera. It's got to be specific, it's got to be more and more specific. He's still a friend, and he's the right man for the job, but…" His voice trails off.

John turns to Bo Harwood. Besides scoring *Minnie and Moskowitz, A Woman Under the Influence, The Killing of a Chinese*

Bookie, and *Opening Night*, Bo has written many songs with John and gives tender, funny descriptions of how John, tone deaf, hums and croons and beats out the rhythm of what he thinks the melody is until Bo finally hears it through a kind of simpatico. Bo then translates John's ideas into music. Early in pre-production John asked him to do *Love Streams'* score but Bo didn't want to take it on. The newly married Bo (he, Leslie Hope, and Phedon flew to Vegas last weekend, where Bo and Leslie tied the knot) now says, a little wearily, "Anything for John."

John will take every spare moment he can, night and day, to work up the opera with Bo. These musical sessions are the only part of *Love Streams'* creation that Cassavetes won't let me anywhere near. He says he's genuinely embarrassed at how badly he carries a tune, but "don't be afraid of being embarrassed" is one of John's credos; I suspect the real reason is that he and Bo have a very special simpatico that John doesn't want my presence to endanger. After all, Bo's never written an opera.

So today the picture breaks in its third sound-mixer while Bo goes off to his piano, guitar, and synthesizer, working with his partner Bobbi Permanent. He'll compose, score, and record an opera sequence – hiring the singers, all of it – in three weeks' time. The scene is Sarah Lawson's emotional climax, and if it fails… suffice it to say that Bo knows the stakes are high.

Bo tells me about John's beef with Bernstein: "It comes down to involvement. That's what got John. The guy isn't here, he's in New York."

And John will tell me: "If you're not involved 24 hours a day I don't want to hear about it. Fifteen hours a day isn't enough."

"It's uncivilized to shoot so much film," John says, almost mournfully. But he's left the script, he's making it up as he goes, so he needs as many choices in the editing-room – as many angles, as many nuances to choose from – as possible. He's like a novelist writing many drafts of every page. While shooting he will move a given scene in one direction in one take, move it in another direction in the next take, shifting tones from take to take significantly, and printing almost all of it. He must *see* how it plays on-screen in order to choose. The process exhausts everybody on the picture but John. He's tremendously excited.

"I'm crazy about the rest of this picture – I'm *crazy* about it!"

"Good," I say. "Why?"

"Because I be CRAZY!"

And he laughs that devil-laugh.

But he's not laughing when he comes up against the scene where Sarah collapses in the hall and Robert Harmon – following the old script somewhat – fends off the dog to get to her. He still wants a struggle between Harmon and the dog in which Harmon gets bitten and must brave the beast's wrath to tend Sarah. But that was a dog Neil Bell played in Ted Allan's play. Jumbo – somber, tender, handsome, thick-witted, shame-faced Jumbo – is not that dog.

There are long, long takes while Gena lies on the floor as the unconscious Sarah while John and/or the dog's trainers repeat and repeat, "Speak, Jumbo! Speak! Jumbo! Speak! Growl! Bark!" John: "Say *something* goddamnit!" On and on, incessantly, ridiculously. But that poor dog hasn't a mean bone in him (and/or he's too doped up to know what's going on). When Jumbo finally barks he can't help wagging his tail, as though reassuring us that he's really nice. We're all so embarrassed for him – it does break your heart, how you can see in Jumbo's eyes that he knows he's failing.

John jumps up and down in front of the dog, jumps *over* the dog, trying to excite Jumbo so he'll bark when John/Robert comes near – to no avail.

"I'm exhausted already," John laughs, out of breath, convulsed with both the urgency and the comedy of his situation.

All the while Gena lies motionless on the floor, eyes closed, waiting.

Hoping to inspire Jumbo at least to whimper in sympathy for Sarah, John yowls and then weeps for the dog.

Gena opens one eye: "Get this! We've got to have John crying in ONE movie!"

Then they do the scene with Neil the dog-man while Jumbo watches. Now Jumbo's *really* confused. The man's a better dog than he is. Jumbo lies down.

Eddie Donno, for some reason, starts serenading the dog with 'The Star-Spangled Banner'! John *films* Eddie singing 'The Star-Spangled Banner'!

That absurdity makes everybody feel better.

Again they try the scene. Perhaps in filming Eddie and acting so crazy John's vented the tensions and cleared the way for the scene to reveal itself. He is Robert Harmon again, his sister's brought a menagerie into his home, she's collapsed, he's frightened and deeply concerned for her. He goes to her, kneels down, lifts her in his arms. In one take he tries to lift her off the floor but can't, afraid of a hernia – a bit of absurdity again. They laugh. They get serious. In another take he slaps Gena's cheeks lightly to wake her up. Another take. Another. He kneels, holds her, kisses her forehead, rocks her to and fro. We see Robert Harmon's shell breaking. He clutches his sister to him. Cut. (That will be the take on-screen.)

Gena doesn't open her eyes.

"Gena?" John says, really concerned. "Are you all right? Are you?"

She opens her eyes: "Is it over?"

"Yeah."

She punches him in the stomach.

"I'm gonna hit you," she laughs, "I'm gonna wait till you're asleep and *then* I'm gonna hit you!"

They get up off the floor. It's the last shot of the day.

Eddie Donna calls out, "John Cassavetes! I won't hold you to it, but – tell me what's the first set-up in the morning?"

Including five re-takes on the 20th and 21st, today's scenes will have required 21 set-ups, 49 takes, 46 minutes of printed film, for 1:56 of screen-time.

Again Cassavetes cuts all the specificity he can. On screen, when Sarah approaches Robert she merely says "Hi." That is all that remains of a page of dialogue about "the park" composed in their sessions yesterday, including "the dog is dangerous" bit that made John laugh so hard.

WEDNESDAY, JULY 20 – *If it was easy anybody could do it*

Robert Harmon opens his front door to Dr. Williams [Robert Fieldsteel], who carries a black medical bag. Harmon is anxious and incoherent as he leads Dr. Williams through the house.

"Tell me, who's the patient?" asks the doctor.

"Sarah. Sarah had – these two miniature horses and a goat and she didn't know, I mean, that I was going to respond so poorly when Lenny and Jim came over, see, so they couldn't find the duck and the little chicks disappeared, anyway –"

"Excuse me, where is she?"

That stops Harmon and he shows Dr. Williams into a small room where Sarah lies unconscious on a narrow bed. Dr. Williams turns on a lamp beside the bed – it makes a bright cone of light in the dim room. He examines her face, she wakes slightly, he says, "Don't be alarmed. I'm Dr. Williams." With a small flashlight he examines her eyes, asks, "What seems to be the trouble?"

Very softly she says, "I don't know who I am."

Robert pushes the doctor out of the way, leans in close to her, speaks intensely, "Wait a minute, wait a minute, who am I, who am I, hold on just a minute, am I your brother, am I your mother, am I Jim, who am I?"

The doctor tries to break into this, to stop this, but Harmon brushes him aside, tells him, "We don't need you."

Harmon pulls Dr. Williams from the room and is rushing him down the hall. The doctor stops and firmly says, "Can I talk to you for a minute, please? Come here."

Michael Stein, the make-up man, is doing John's face in the kitchen.

"I want to be high-blood-pressure now," Cassavetes tells Stein. "Blotchy. The drinking comes out. It's easier with make-up than with me doing it. I don't think I have any blood left."

Robert Fieldsteel comes in, in costume, intent, prepared to play Dr. Williams.

"What I need to do," John tells him, "is to make it almost impossible for you to play the scene. Then you'll really be responding to something."

"Thanks, John," Fieldsteel says sardonically. "I'm really looking forward to that."

They go into the small first-floor room where the scene will be played. The props are set out. John tells Fieldsteel, "Take the liberty of moving these cups and things wherever you want, anything that makes you feel comfortable. I don't mean *do* that – I mean, if you *want* to do that."

Fieldsteel starts handling the props to get familiar with them.

"No, don't work it out," John tells him. "I don't want you to work it out, just do it, when it's time. You have to be as uncomfortable as possible in this scene. If you're uncomfortable, it's good."

The morning is spent shooting Dr. Williams' scene and some retakes of Lenny and Jim. Then we head into Hollywood to see yesterday's dailies, nearly an hour's worth of film.

The way John and George Villansenor cut the finished scene, yesterday's work will play. But nobody knows that yet – including and especially John and George. All we see today is that Jumbo can't act. John, George, Carole Smith, Helen Caldwell, Al Ruban, Fieldsteel, myself, others – everybody's squirmy through the ordeal of shot after shot of that poor dog just not getting it. When the footage ends, nobody moves. Our silence is

thick, oppressive. After what seems a long time, John speaks:
"Well – if it was easy, anybody could do it."

It's still early afternoon. Everybody heads back to the house. John comes with me. We drive in silence. At the house he says, "It's not the dog's fault. It was forced. It was the only 'force' in the picture. Everything else has worked very easily, the horses, the goat, very easily. If it's not to be, it's not to be. From the front door [where Sarah introduces the dog to Robert] all the dog stuff is forced. She doesn't have to say all that about the dog, all she has to say is that there's a dog coming."

Then he gets a strange look, his eyes alight: "And I *liked* some of that – the scene with Gena on the floor. There was one take I liked. It was very strange. *I* didn't know what I was doing, she didn't, the dog…" His voice trails off. "It was very strange."

No more scenes are scheduled today. It is mid-afternoon and everybody's just hanging around, clots of people in the living room, the kitchen, the yard. A glumness has settled upon John. Some of us are sitting in John's bar. John walks in and says simply: "We have no picture."

Again, more definitely, as though saying it out loud has made it more real to him:

"We have no picture."

"You've never heard a roomful talking so fast!" Helen Caldwell will say later. Everybody starts talking at once, others come in, drawn by the commotion, people walking in and out of the room, in and out of the discussion, if such a cacophony can be called a discussion. "Have you thought of such-and-such an ending," "Hey what about this," "Have you considered this," "Maybe you could try such-and-such…" From John down to the production assistants, ideas, tangents, mostly off-the-wall, all hyper and mostly unremembered, ventings that evaporate as soon as they're said. But the commotion, and that everybody *cares* so much, seems to revive Cassavetes. His own ideas start to form. He's talking, Helen's writing: Robert Harmon will go to Sarah, he'll say, "I know you're not crazy, I know you're not sick, you gotta fight it, you gotta fight it, I fed the dog, I got the horse upstairs, in the bedroom, I gotta get the goat," while it's pouring rain outside. "He's falling in love with her," John says, "and maybe *he* doesn't know it." Then she'll have the dreams about her family, the make-me-laugh dream and the opera-dream (sketched in the shooting script), and she'll wake from the opera-dream, and tell him she's got to leave. And they'll do the leave-taking scene as planned. But Robert Harmon will have decided to care for her, not to run from her – to commit himself. She'll leave, "because she has to," but he'll still have made that commitment. His situation at the end may be more desperate than it was at the beginning, "but it's a higher kind of desperate, a *better* desperate." There's even the implication that Robert's commitment has fed Sarah's spirit, fed her dreams, so that she awakens stronger.

And I remember John saying in Vegas, "It bothers me that he doesn't change. All this happens and he doesn't change." Not anymore. Robert Harmon changes.

Late in the afternoon, John shoots a small scene – for luck, I feel.

The scene: Robert Harmon gets some tea for Sarah, who lies there oblivious, he speaks to her, then she laughs a little in her sleep. It's a little like the scene in the May 13 shooting script that precedes her first dream, but in the script she scrunches up and doesn't laugh as she does today.

Before shooting that scene, Gena learns of the film's new direction.

She makes a vague gesture in the air, part salute, part as though wafting smoke away:

"Well – another adventure."

Dr. Williams' scene requires five set-ups and 20 takes – due mostly to the difficulties of shooting in such tight quarters, the narrow hallway and small room.

The tea scene: three set-ups, one take a-piece, all printed. For all the confusion, what's shot today will fit easily into the final cut.

FAST FORWARD: MONTHS LATER – The best story

So, it's decided. There's to be no Cassavetes-esque embarrassing crazy dinner party. Robert Harmon will not (as he does in Ted Allan's play and the shooting script) suddenly ask Susan to marry him and Susan will not shoot back the insight that the only one he loves is his sister.

Of that decision, John tells me: "It's a performing art. With all its technical things, it's still the performer that leaps at you. The minute I saw that stuff with the dog I knew we were done. We couldn't go on. We were done. When I kiss her – when I saw *him* kiss her [after she collapses and he holds her], there is no place to go after that. I can't *propose* to anyone after that! How can I ask Susan to marry me after looking at Sarah like that?!"

A pause, and he smiles, "I knew we'd discover the story sooner or later."

And, after another pause, "Anyway – nothing changes. Only the script and the shots – and what is that? The actors stay the same." (Whatever *that* means.)

And Gena will say, "It's funny, how one shot, sometimes, can change the whole thing. You see it, and it's *there.* That's what's magical about movies."

*

"People always believe the best story." So wrote Zelda Fitzgerald.

A miscast dog, plus one revealing take of one shot of one scene, has changed the course of John Cassavetes' film... a very 'Cassavetes' story.

And it's partly true – except for the part that's not quite true, not true at all really.

Months after *Love Streams* wraps and not long before its final edit, I receive what I thought was a copy of John's editing-script. An editing-script is the script as finally shot and edited. On facing pages the script-as-shot appears on the right; on the left are scene numbers, take numbers, how many takes, from what angles, what takes were printed, their precise lengths, and so on. In a ringed binder this editing-script is on white paper, followed by the May 13 shooting script on yellow paper.

For our documentary, editor Dan Wetherbee needs a copy of John's editing script to order *Love Streams* footage from the lab; he will require, say, Scene 203E, Take 5; we'll then insert that footage into our doc. I need the editing-script too, to confirm my notes, so when I write I can be exact about what was changed from the shooting script, how many set-ups and takes, the dates, and so forth.

In John's editing room are the original editing-script and a copy. John hands me one of the two. I assume it's the copy, I don't look at it, I give it to Dan. Later still, as I'm writing, I realize that mine isn't the copy, it's the original – or so I conclude when I discover three stapled pages folded in the binder's flap. Their blank sides faced out and they shared the flap with several inconsequential papers (order forms, etc.), so I'd not noticed them before. These three pages, dictated by John and typed by Helen Caldwell, are titled "LOVE STREAMS NOTES 6/20/83."

What happened on June 20? I go to my notes. On June 20 John blew up at Priscilla, Cannon's publicity person. That was the Monday after we got back from Vegas, where John had been so tired, looked so ill, and spoke (for the only time in my hearing) of feeling tired and ill. So on June 20, the first working day after Vegas, dangerously short of temper, John dictated these notes (I've marked the significant passages in ***bold italics***).

The notes are divided into two sections. The first section deals with Robert Harmon's encounter with Albie, Albie's stepfather, ex-wife Agnes, Robert dancing with Sarah by the jukebox, then Robert's visit with Margarita and Susan returning with her date. This concludes with: ***"The party, the rain sequence inclusion, etc., will be determined at that time,"*** i.e. when Casasvetes sees how these scenes have played.

The second section reads:

"The dog –

"If the Albie sequences work as we have planned, ***and if Susan's introduction to Sarah is brought forward,*** I think it frees her [Sarah] to reconsider her own problems and to take action such as in the bowling alley, and her first sexual encounters following the Psychiatrist's suggestion for sex.

"When Sarah returns from her outing with Ken and inquires about what creativity is, she must be totally at ease with herself, relaxed, happy for the first time. But what is really taking place is a transference of needs. The need of Jack and Debbie versus the needs of Robert, a sharing.

"The four-way phone conversation [Sarah-Debbie-Jack-Robert] interrupts this and brings back to reality all of Robert's failures as seen through Sarah's eyes. It's making up for these failures which the picture uses as its structure and so the getting of the animals and the consequent introduction to Robert is an offering by Sarah, much like the offer of visiting sick people (for her, herself, to stay out of the way, and to offer interesting alternatives to the needful, therefore Robert).

"His inability to accept substitutes – goats, dogs, miniature horses – is a major rejection for Sarah, ***and, in my opinion, can not be complicated by the dog biting. His attitude alone is gun enough to shoot her down,*** and the stimulation needed for her to return to her own obsession, which is her own family, which then prompts her dream sequences / insights into how to cure her own problems with her husband and daughter – making them laugh in the middle of the day and finally creating an opera that, even in her own mind, does not work as a solution.

"If we can fit this in, Robert must keep trying as Sarah begins to exceed [*accede*?] to the reality that her husband and daughter in no way love her, but only need her. This reality is in terms of romance, the most elusive thing for a man Robert's age."

First: ***The party, the rain sequence inclusion, etc., will be determined at that time...*** As of June 20, Cassavetes hadn't "determined" the final party scene. The meaning is unclear. Perhaps he hasn't decided on the scene's final elements; perhaps he's wondering whether to film the scene at all.

Second: ***and if Susan's introduction to Sarah is brought forward...*** Cassavetes is considering that Sarah and Susan might meet, or speak more extensively on the phone, or Sarah and Robert will speak more extensively about Susan, before Ted Allan's dinner party. According to these notes, that encounter 'frees' Sarah to do her thing – go out on the town and attend Robert. Cassavetes would ultimately reject this notion, finding no need for Sarah and Susan to meet in any way because the relationship between Robert and Sarah is rich enough not to require outside stimulus. (John won't finally decide until he *sees* the richness of their relationship, which he can only do after shooting Sarah and Robert alone together.) So the notes again indicate that a month before the supposed Dramatic Day of Decision, which is supposedly Jumbo's fault, John may have been searching for a way to make Ted Allan's conclusion unnecessary.

Third: ***and, in my opinion, can not be complicated by the dog biting. His attitude alone is gun enough to shoot her down...*** Jumbo is not a failure. Jumbo is exactly the dog John wanted: a creature that would not bite and would only occasionally bark. If the dog isn't hostile to Robert Harmon when they first meet, there's no logic to its hostility later. Without that hostility, the last 40 pages of the Cassavetes-Allan script lose a great deal of motivation and a prime source of verve.

John's June 20 memorandum argues that the *Love Streams'* conclusion he finally decided upon was a long time in the works and not the succumbing-to-circumstances that he made it appear. While I've observed it to be true that Cassavetes discovers his scenes moment by moment, and that each scene organically changes the next, those are what may be called his *tactics*. I've also observed that John has an overall vision or *strategy*. It evolves, but it's consistent. The notes indicate that as of June 20, Cassavetes was considering cutting Ted's ending, but he never stated this in my hearing until July 18, when it kind of slipped out. When I asked, "So you're cutting the party?" he answered, "It's not needed anymore," then quickly qualified that with, "I can't be definite." He played his cards very close to the vest, because even Helen Caldwell, who typed the notes, was genuinely surprised at the decision's finality.

I conclude that, for reasons of his own, John part-concocted and part-improvised an elaborate real-life 'play' to convince all concerned that his ultimate changes were the result of circumstances beyond his control. He made it appear that he didn't *decide* to cut the ending, but that the cut was required by the exigencies of performance – especially the dog's performance. But the memo proves that mid-way through shooting he had serious doubts about the ending.

Why pretend that cutting Ted's ending was a necessity rather than his choice? Well, it would be hard to tell Ted Allan that *Love Streams* as filmed would be nothing like his play. Hard, too, to tell Diahnne and Margaret Abbott that their featured roles had been cut down to character-parts. Hard enough to tell them if he could convince them that it couldn't be helped, but harder still to admit to them that now he had another film in mind altogether and the ending as written had no place in it. So John, in effect, staged reasons for the changes. He made a big deal of the dog's passivity when that passivity is what he really wanted. Did he do this to minimize the hurt of those most impacted by his changes? Or perhaps he didn't want to deal with their reactions while creating the film he really wanted, especially when he didn't quite know what that film would be?

I do know that it's not like Cassavetes to let anything – certainly not a dog's performance – get in the way of making *his* picture. In the scene of Sarah's collapse, by the tenth take the dog had almost no part in it at all, and that's the take John used, the take that supposedly changed the picture. I believe now that Cassavetes was working toward that take all along, and finding justification for it through all those takes that proved the 'failure' of the dog – because John wanted people to think he had no choice but to change the film.

It was on June 9 that John said, "If I die, this is a sweet last film." That's when he was becoming aware of the seriousness of his condition. In Vegas, just a few days before June 20, he felt a still greater urgency. I believe that's when he decided to make a film that could serve as a final statement – and, to do that, he could not shoot Ted's vision but must express something all his own. After June 20, John kept all his options open; that is, what he filmed after June 20 could flow into Ted's ending or could serve as the basis for another. Hence the cutting of so much specificity as he re-wrote and shot.

Ted's play, and the shooting script, are nothing like a dream. But after June 20 – starting on June 27, to be exact – John continually said, "It's a dream, it's a dream."

So, finally, in what might turn out to be his last great gamble, Cassavetes decided to throw out the last 40 pages and 'discover' (one of his favorite words) how to express the dynamics of his inner state. Understandably, he didn't want to explain the real reasons for his changes to all those who would require, and were perhaps owed, an explanation. Instead he gave them "the best story" – the most entertaining story he could concoct and enact.

Knowing Cassavetes, this would not have been a *plan*. He'd play with possibilities, making decisions as he went along. But these notes indicate, at the very least, that John's dramatic decision of July 20 wasn't sudden; that by June 20 he was seriously considering cutting the ending; and that he'd decided against the hostile dog (therefore the ending, if not cut, would be seriously changed). He kept these considerations to himself, telling only those who most needed to know – Helen, who was part of his writing process, and almost certainly Gena and Al Ruban. I know he didn't discuss much of this with Ted Allan because I sat beside Ted when we viewed the first full-length 'assembly.' As the lights went up I saw Ted's shock. He said to me, "Did you see my play on that screen? I didn't see my play on that screen."

*

By the time I discover the June 20 memo I've been on the project nearly a year. By now I've learned for certain that John is dying – or, at any rate, that doctors have not given him long to live. I can't bring myself to ask about the memo. Oh, he'd probably repeat yet again, "I *never* know what I'm going to do, that would be *boring,* the way we make pictures anything can happen," – but that's not why I don't ask. I don't ask because I don't know how. I can't bring myself to show up at his house with questions that mean, underneath it all, "John, is this how you prepared to die? Did you *mean* the final shot to be your very last scene of all?" So what I've written now must remain speculation. All that is certain is the memo, dictated at a key juncture in the film and in John's life.

Because *Love Streams* does turn out to be John's last film, some will conclude that Robert Harmon is how John felt at the end. No one who's spent significant time with John would agree. The entire film – its intentionally dream-like quality, its 'formality,' its stripping-down of all pretense, Gena's role as much as John's, and how, as John says, "They never give up" – the entire film expresses his inner life at the point of discovering that he may soon die. These notes indicate that June 20 was when Cassavetes began opening *Love Streams* to the possibility of that final expression.

THURSDAY, JULY 21 – *Hating okra*

Dr. Williams leads Robert Harmon into the kitchen. They stand far apart, at either side of the room.

"Mr. Harmon, I think Sarah is in trouble. Her eyes are not responding the way I'd like them to, and her neck is stiff. Now, you can do what you want, but I'd like you to get her to see somebody if it's not me. Ok?"

"She's fine. Thank you."

"You're very welcome. I'll see myself out."

Cut to Harmon running down the narrow hall, very agitated, saying to himself, "Ok, now, now, what, what, yeah, oh yeah, got that, got that."

In the small room the dog lies awake beside the sleeping Sarah. Robert Harmon leans over Sarah tenderly, but very excited. "Ok, Sarah, Sarah, you're one of the greatest people that I've met in my life. I've fed the horses. I've fed the goat." A pause. Quietly and intently: "Sarah. You've gotta get well. You're not sick. I have chicken soup on, and I put okra in it, and (he smiles, really smiles) I know you hate okra. You're the best. You've gotta fight it. You're the BEST."

The dog lifts its head. Harmon strokes its chin.

Yesterday afternoon John Cassavetes walked into his bar saying, "We have no picture." This afternoon Robert Harmon hurries out of the same bar talking to himself, excited, dashing breathlessly into the room where his sister lies unconscious, uttering a version of the dialogue he sketched yesterday: his scattered statement of faith.

Before the shots John says, "As long as I get these thoughts in my head they'll come out in some reasonable manner."

He shoots 10 takes of the hallway scene, all of them different, and what Robert Harmon says makes no sense every time. That's how he wants it.

There are two takes of the bedroom scene. They cut quickly on the first take because the soundman can hear Phedon and John's son Nick playing backgammon in the kitchen. On the second (and final) take John goes through the speech a little differently several times. The "okra" line won't be spoken until his last run-through. A deft touch. Robert knows Sarah hates okra so he puts it in the chicken soup, as though to remind her who she is – for she'd told the doctor, "I don't know who I am." It makes the moment distinctly Robert Harmon's. Even when he expresses love enthusiastically he must do it in some fashion that challenges, even grates. This keeps Robert Harmon's shift of stance, from disengagement to engagement, in character.

After all John's preparation, can the okra line be called a Cassavetes improvisation? The likeliest explanation is: Robert Harmon said it.

In addition to these scenes, Cassavetes will re-shoot those moments after Sarah's backyard scene with the cabbie and the animals: she quietly comes to Robert and tells him a dog is about to arrive. Today's work will be in the final cut.

FRIDAY, JULY 22 – *Every line in your life*

Robert Harmon brings the sleeping Sarah a cup of tea, saying, "Ok, nice hot cup of tea. Come on there, try this now, come on – come on, nice hot cup of tea, smell it, smell it, mmmmm."

She opens her eyes, closes her eyes, laughs a strange little laugh.

Lovingly, smiling, Robert says, "You're crazy as a bedbug." [Shot July 20]

There are strange sounds and music, and Sarah's little laugh, and a sharp cut to:

Jack Lawson's mansion, enclosed by a high fence. Sarah stands beside the pool. On a small lawn-table are mechanical 'joke' devices – a ring and a flower that (as we shall see) squirt water, a pen that will shoot foam, plastic ketchup and mustard containers that emit red and yellow strings respectively, chattering 'false teeth,' et cetera.

Glum and angry, Jack and Debbie step from the house. Sarah's called Debbie from school and Jack from work – to make them laugh. Debbie says,"You're not gonna make me laugh, I don't have a sense of humor." Jack calls the idea "ridiculous." Spiteful Debbie says, "You're pitiful!" Yet they've come, and they don't leave, which demonstrates Sarah's hold on them.

Sarah's giddy, jumpy with manic energy, and she serves them beverages and tells them she's going to give herself 30 seconds to make them laugh. She sets a timer on the table. "In 30 seconds you are going to be laughing helplessly – ok? You don't believe me, huh? You wanna bet, whata you bet?"

Jack, listlessly: "A dollar."

"Oh, cheapskate, eh? Hey, I'm the high roller, I'm gonna bet, I'm gonna bet – love! I'm gonna bet the ultimate."

She makes a 'fox-face' at Debbie, then asks the kid to imagine "a spider – with breasts!" Not surprisingly, that doesn't make Debbie laugh, perhaps because her mother is behaving at the moment not unlike a-spider-with-breasts.

Sarah springs the phony ketchup on Jack ("Some people think that's my best joke, most people laugh just at the word 'ketchup.'"). She squirts him with a phony flower, sprays pen-foam on him, spills stringed popcorn on him. He just looks at her (it's one of Seymour Cassel's finest moments) – just looks at her, his face expressive of disgust, concern, hopelessness. Debbie is a study in passive-aggressive adolescent fury. Sarah, undaunted, still giddy, laughs almost demonically with strange gestures and sudden contortions. She doesn't give up, says "You guys, you guys are a couple of 'em, you truly are, two of a pair!"

Finally her time runs out and Sarah runs onto the diving board, throws off her shoes, does a back-flip into the pool. The camera holds on the calm surface of the water for some time. Sarah does not emerge.

Last night John said to me: "Every line in your life is eaten up by the movies that you do."

The make-me-laugh game is a benign example. It's a regular event in the Cassavetes family. Just the other day, when John shot the arrival of Sarah's menagerie, I witnessed it at lunch.

When we shoot at his house the caterers set up their dining and food tables in John's backyard. I was eating with our documentary crew. Giddy Porath sat across from me, his hand-held 16mm camera beside him. Looking past me he said, "Michael, do you want that?"

John was playing make-me-laugh with his daughter Zoe. Oh yeah I want that. Giddy leapt up with the camera, Peter Tullo grabbed his sound stuff, and they shot that scene as though John and Zoe rehearsed it for them, Giddy flawlessly zooming in on their expressions at precisely the right moments.

On one side of the table was John, in his Robert Harmon clothing and make-up. Beside him was tall, always-smiling, dependable Dermot Stoker, one of the grips. On the other side of the table, Zoe Cassavetes (who's about the age of the girl in the film) and *Love Streams'* costumer Jennifer Ashley-Smith. John and Dermot are trying to make Zoe laugh by playing with their food and everybody's taking bets.

John grabs something off his plate, says, "Dermot, put one in your nose," and as they stick food-stuffs up their noses Zoe busts out laughing. She determines not to laugh at their next antic – Jennifer saying, "You can do it, Zoe!" Money's bet all around. John and Dermot carry on, Dermot spraying milk all over and John licking his plate and cackling while Zoe holds out, she does, she holds out until Dermot sprays milk on John and Jennifer shouts, "John! Your wardrobe!" That's too much for Zoe, she cracks up as people repeat, "John, your wardrobe!" Victorious, pocketing the money, with milk-spots in his hair, John walks off while most of us are still laughing. (Spookily, in our doc you can see him becoming Robert Harmon again about three strides from the table.)

Gena will tell me, "We play that make-me-laugh game with the girls all the time – it goes on for hours! And John played it with me even before we had children. I remember when we were just married and I'd be going for an interview, a reading – and I'd be so tense, as young people usually are. And he'd say, 'I can make you laugh.' I'd say, 'Don't. Don't do anything. I have to be thinking of Ophelia.' And he'd say, 'No, it's better for you, I can make you laugh.' And I'd say, 'God couldn't make me laugh today, John.' But he always could. And I can never decide if it's gaiety, you know, or just cosmic sense of humor. I don't know what it is."

So Gena also plays the game with the family, but John introduced it. Today John will direct Gena 'doing' John, but Gena is Sarah Lawson, and Sarah Lawson is Sarah-Lawson-in-a-dream, and in the scene she makes no one laugh.

Perhaps someone with degrees in psychology, literary theory, film criticism, and quantum physics can analyze that. It's beyond my powers, except to say that this is precisely what John means when he says he's making a film that portrays, embodies – but will not footnote or attempt answers about – "inner life."

In the May 13 shooting script the scene is simple: about a page and a half in length, if shot it would run perhaps a minute, perhaps less. There are few lines, and they're short. That's what Gena's prepared for: "I had learned the scene he had in the script. I thought it was just going to be a couple of small things we do with our own children." She's not ready for the scene John springs on her this morning.

We shoot at a mansion in the very rich Hancock Park section of Los Angeles. It's the hottest day of the summer.

"Does anybody know what this scene is?" Al Ruban asks as they set up. "All I know is she has 30 seconds to make her daughter laugh."

People think (thankfully in this heat) that it'll be another light day. Shoot the short scene in the script, then shoot Debbie's and Jack's end of the three telephone conversations: Sarah calling Jack from London, Sarah calling Jack from Robert Harmon's, and Debbie calling Sarah (the call that turns into a four-way free-for-all between Jack, Debbie, Sarah and Robert).

John has other plans: a long, crazy, many-nuanced, mostly improvised scene.

Gena will tell me, "The first time I heard about it was when you were hearing it. This is a scene I didn't know about till we got there – because I wouldn't have slept for several nights had I known what was in store."

Our documentary crew is shooting John setting up the shot, and we film Gena taking him aside and saying, her voice tense, "Listen, have you got a minute?"

We don't get on film what she tells him. She tells me later: "I said, 'John, I'm not going to do it. I'm just not going to do it. I haven't rehearsed that.' I went into a sort of panic. And I said that at least we should have a complete rehearsal on it. But he said no."

Giddy, Peter, and I stay away from them while they argue. Then they seem to be rehearsing. We edge up closer and roll. Helen Caldwell is standing nearby, but she thinks they're still talking privately so she doesn't have her notebook. John, after all, hasn't told anybody but Gena that they're rehearsing – and they haven't budged from where they were having their discussion, so nobody knows. (Me and the crew, we're just guessing.)

John says, "'I'll bet our love.'"

"I'll bet what?" Gena asks, her voice frail.

"Our love. 'I'll bet our love that I can make you laugh.'" John turns fiercely on Helen, "Now you gotta write this down, sweetheart, you can't stand around listening."

Helen dashes off for the notebook.

Eddie Donno walks up. "John, just look at this for me, tell me if this will work for you so I'll know."

"No! I'm right in the middle of a *rehearsal*, babe!"

Eddie retreats with, "Oh, I didn't know you were rehearsing," as John says, "Christ! I can't..."

He bends all the way over, trying to regain his concentration.

Gena prompts him: "'I'll bet our love I can make you laugh.'"

But his concentration has been shot. He looks around for Seymour and Rita (Debbie). Gena says, "They were right here." (Were they? We didn't see them.) John mutters something about finding them, and then they'll go through some lines, but he stops, says to Gena, "I tell you what, go relax, and..." his voice trails off.

"You wanna walk?" Gena asks.

They walk off, arms around each other's shoulders, talking quietly.

The shoot is brutal and takes hours as this hot day gets hotter. All they decide in advance is: Sarah tells Debbie and Jack what she's going to do, she bets their love, she tries to make them laugh with the gadgets, when they don't laugh she heads for the driving board and back-flips into the pool (a stunt-double does the actual dive). Those are what John calls "the beats." They work out a few lines. Risa and Seymour work on them while Fieldsteel reads Sarah's part. Risa – a friend of the Cassavetes family – tells me, "John and I used to play make-me-laugh." Then, in front of Gena, John does make-me-laugh with Risa and Seymour, using the props. Then: "Ok, you guys, split, get dressed, get ready."

Through the punishing hours Gena and Seymour, with Risa following their lead, develop a many-layered portrayal of the unbridgeable gap between Sarah and her family.

"I hate ad-libbing," Gena tells Seymour between takes. "I'm bad at it."

"*Hey*, Gena – this is Seymour. Don't tell *me* that."

He turns to me: "She's great at it. And she loves it."

She ignores us both, between takes, for the rest of the day.

She plays the scene this way, plays it that way, John tells her it's almost there, John tells her it's drifted off. After one take Gena says the sun is so bright that she can hardly see the props on the tablecloth. On Seymour's close-up John directs, "Sey, as soon as your daughter comes just look at Gena completely cold."

More takes. The sun is terrible. Again Gena plays the scene this way, that way, then John tells her, "I want it really crazy this time, Gena. Just the way you did it on the take when I told you it was wrong."

She does it really crazy. That's the footage John will mostly use. At the end of that take – it's a long take, the entire scene, and it's the last take – we all applaud, John's crew, my crew, everybody. Gena shakes her head, exhausted, relieved it's over, says, "Joan Rivers on a bad day."

Later Gena makes a revealing statement, belying how Cassavetes presents himself. She says, "I think John had it very well planned out – as he always does."

Seven set-ups, 19 takes (many of them printed, 11 of them shot by two cameras) – more than 55 minutes of printed film for 4:20 in the final cut. John jump-cuts the action at the beginning of the scene such that Debbie and Sarah appear suddenly, then suddenly are beside the table. Also: at odd spots in the scene he inserts black footage, the screen goes dark for a moment now and again.

Asked what the black is for, Cassavetes merely smiles: "I put it there."

MONDAY, JULY 25 – *That's very dangerous*

Jack and Debbie Lawson's participation in three phone calls.

In the morning I park down the street from the mansion in Hancock Park.

"Hey, kiddo!"

It's John's voice but I look up and down the block and don't see him. He calls again. He's in his car across the street. I go to him, he tells me to get in.

Bo Harwood has given him a cassette 'draft' of the opera. John's very proud of Bo. "He came through like a champ." John turns up the volume on his car's tape player. What Bo's written for John in the past has been folk-ish, a kind of jug-band vaudeville sound. Nothing like this. Bo has composed something solemn but unpretentious, self-contained, darkly dream-like, as though Bo has taken his cue from *The Threepenny Opera.* John tells me the words as I listen to the music: "In love/ I'm not sure of/ I'm not sure/ Of me..." "I love that face," Gena will sing to Seymour. (In *Minnie and Moskowitz,* when Gena's classy Minnie struggles against falling in love with Seymour's funky Moskowitz, she tells him: "Let me see that face again. It's not the right face, it's not the face I'm in love with.") "I love you both," their daughter will sing at the opera's end.

John is exultant. His gamble paid off. It is only a week since he replaced Elmer Bernstein with Bo.

In the car John talks a meandering ramble of his thinking about the film, less to tell me than to test his thoughts on his own ears.

"The film has to be formal because it's about a brother and a sister – it's *got* to be formal." The elegance of the photography, the very clothing Robert and Sarah wear (always formal), are how Cassavetes is trying to embody the emotional density, the barriers, and the traditions – both familial and societal – that enmesh brothers and sisters. In *Love Streams* we're looking at *family feeling itself,* in visual terms.

"And I love it being reduced to that tiny room" – the room where Sarah lies unconscious and/or sleeping, where Robert brings her soup and declares his faith – "this tiny room, after being so open. It's all reduced to this. Now, they're all alone." Very intently: *"And when two people are all alone, that's very dangerous, because they don't know what to do."*

Cassavetes speaks of love, the give and take of it, and what he and Gena have learned. "When it's her turn, she does for me. When it's my turn, I do for her. That's how we've been able to stay together all these years. You have to take the *time* to love, and you have to do for each other. Otherwise love is just moments, bullshit.

"When we *can't* do for each other – childrens' problems, crises – then we can't stand each other. Because those things have nothing to do with love. They're just what happens. They have nothing to do with two people."

He's playing with the idea that Sarah perhaps lacks the courage to love. "She loves love. She'll do anything for it. Anything. She's trying to get with her brother what she couldn't get with her husband, and that's not possible. And now he's trying to get something that's not possible from her. And *he* hasn't the courage for love either." John laughs: "I always like to do the same story."

Parallelism: as different as their reactions are, Robert's and

Sarah's *situations* are the same, and by their reactions we're exposed to their 'inner life.'

This is different from John's idea of Sarah earlier in the picture, before Gena started acting, when he said, "A woman like this, who can love so totally but stay individual, independent – one in a million. They [Jack, Debbie] want her to change, but they don't know – a woman like this changes, you lose her, that's it, she never comes back." Gena's performance and his own have evolved the character (so John believes this morning) so that Sarah just "loves love," which is very different from loving people.

"The audience doesn't want her to go back to Seymour," John says. "They want her to stay with me, even though I'm her brother. They see love, and they want that to go on. If they get love from someone, anyone, they want it, they want to accept it, they don't care, they don't care what terms. Now I may not agree with *that,* that's not the way I feel, but a lot of people do."

Maybe Sarah is keeping some sort of secret and that's why she's cut off from others, he's not sure. "Because when you have a secret, that part of you is dead to the other person. And if it's a sexual secret, a physical secret, *that* part of you is closed to them. But that's…" his voice trails off, his expression is as though he's finishing the sentence to himself rather than to me. Then: "And to tell the truth can kill love, too.

"The only thing that remains is love and change and going through time together."

John and Helen Caldwell sit in director's chairs at the edge of the mansion's tennis court. John wants to hear the dialogue for one of the phone conversations.

Giddy, Peter and I are four or five yards away, our camera set on a tripod. We're rolling.

"So," John says. His legs are crossed, he's looking at her, cigarette in hand.

"So here's what we've got." Helen reads Jack's line: "'I'm just saying it's hard to take care of a kid and that's what you should be doing.'"

"And she says..."

"'Well, I'm almost not crazy.'"

"Ok, well don't do that," John says. She crosses out the "crazy" line. (I'm thinking I should never have told him how much I like that line, never should have told him that maybe I'll use it as the title of the book and the documentary. He's cut it ruthlessly ever since.)

John: "And he says, 'I know we're divorced but –' Silence. His lips move slightly, as though he's speaking to himself. Picking up Jack's line he continues: " –'the house seems very empty without you.'" A long pause. "And then she says?"

"'I love you, you dumbohead.'"

"Right, ok. He says – what's our next – what's the speech that follows that?"

"'We're divorced, that part of our life is over, I'm just saying it's hard to take care of a kid and that's what you should be doing.'"

Silence. Cigarette ash falls on his shirt, he wipes it off. Again his lips move as though he's speaking to himself. Several times. Finally he tells her his rewritten line, "'I know it doesn't make any sense but that's what you should be doing.'"

In our documentary, what with John's long silences, that sequences runs 2:22, one minute and 40 seconds of it an unbroken shot: John thinking of one line. Inserting this passage in our film, Dan Wetherbee and I determine to fight for keeping it no matter what. That choice is the only time I really feel like a director: filmed proof of the attention John gives even to the most minor-sounding line.

(When I'm figuring where to place the scene in the film I say something high-sounding about our 'intentions' and Dan says firmly though kindly, "Our intentions don't mean shit – if it doesn't work it doesn't work."

This time it works.)

When they shoot the conversation, after a take John tells Seymour: "Perfect! Perfect means – it stinks."

*

That night, in a large screening room at the Burbank Studios, we watch the first 'assembly' of all of *Love Streams* to date, from the beginning through the make-me-laugh dream. It will be a 'workprint,' that is: the negative has been developed in black-and-white, not expensive color. This cut is "for narrative, not for character," John cautions me. Before he concocts and films his new conception of the ending, he wants to see how he's gotten to where he is. This cut will emphasize the flow of the movie, without the fine-honed placement of shots that will emphasize the nuances of individual characters.

The Burbank Studios are actually the old Warner Bros. lot. Driving through its gates at night one is again in the presence of what most people mean when they say "Hollywood." These days TV's *Dukes of Hazard* is filmed on this lot, on a set that's been standing for decades and which you've seen in many guises in hundreds of films and television shows. Around the corner from that set is the 'downtown' where the Warners gangsters of the '30s lived and died, Bogart and Cagney and Edward G. Robinson. The New York set built not long ago for *Annie* is still up, used mostly for commercials. There are blocks of huge, hanger-like sound stages. In the dark we can't see the Hollywood Hills, but in daylight their outline is familiar to millions as the Korean hills that helicopters fly over in the opening credits of TV's *M.A.S.H.* Studio executives, stars, and hundreds of technicians go through these gates every day. The lot houses the offices of Columbia, Warners, Ladd, Orion, Raystar, and dozens of studio-connected producers. An interesting site for Cassavetes' first, all-but-the-ending screening of a working draft of *Love Streams,* a picture as un-Hollywood as could be.

Interesting, but not so out-of-place as it may seem. Contrary to Cassavetes' reputation, he loves classic Hollywood. "I mean," he'll tell me, "you've got guys like [Frank] Capra, who are really gigantic people who have a sense of beauty in them for people. It's always a pleasure to watch [Capra's] *Mr. Smith Goes to Washington* or *Mr. Deeds Goes to Town* or *Meet John Doe.* They become, in a sense, extremely political pictures because he says, 'Okay, rich people are all screwed up. They're lonely. They have nobody. They've made the money. They're successful. And they have nothing to live for. And it's the poor people who should be understanding of rich people because the poor are still alive and rich people are dead, and you gotta be kind to dead people.'

"And I like the *Casablancas* [shot within a couple of hundred yards from where we see *Love Streams* tonight]. But when I see an action picture I want an *action* picture, raw, no bullshit." Like *The Dirty Dozen,* John's best Hollywood-movie performance.

After all, Cassavetes, like everyone else of his generation, learned to love movies from Hollywood. There was no television when he was growing up, no foreign films distributed regularly even in New York until the late '50s. Hollywood films taught John to *see,* cinematically – pictures you would hardly associate with Cassavetes, like George Stevens' *A Place in the Sun* (adopted from Theodore Dreiser's novel *An American Tragedy*).

"I was in the Army, and I went to see a movie directed by George Stevens with Montgomery Clift and Liz Taylor and a lot of very good people. I went to see this long, drawn-out picture. It made me very angry. I walked out, I said, 'That's the worst picture I've ever seen in my life. What kind of a piece of crap is this? I mean, how dare they! What is this! Some guy goes, walks into a house, you know, of a rich man, and he's all uptight about it. What is that?' And then I went to see the picture again, the following night. And I saw it 11 times or 12 times, 20 times, I don't know. I just kept going back. And every time I saw it I said, 'This is the worst picture I've ever seen in my entire life.' And then some guy said, 'Why do you go to see it so many times?' – very angry, very straight, no kidding around. About three times later, I realized I liked the picture enormously, and it had something to do with something.

"But movies – you go with the expectancy as an audience to see something that's going to knock you off your feet, and you settle for a nice movie. You know? And you think, 'I don't *want* to see something different! I don't want to! I hate it! I hate it! I want it in my form, I want action.' And then when you do see something that's different, you can't get it out of your mind. You're still angry with the son-of-a-gun and you think, 'Oh, I hated that picture, I hated it, I hated it.' But then, you know, 10 years later you remember it. You think, 'Hmmm, I saw something that's interesting.'"

But ask John who influenced him as a filmmaker and he doesn't speak of Hollywood. He says, "I think I watched my mother. And my father. And their friends. And my friends. I think I was always guided by the enormous love, primarily, my mother had for people, and the wonderful intellectual charm that my father had – tremendous. When I was a kid I was like any other kid, I wanted to run away as soon as possible, get out of their influence, and go anywhere. But they were always enormously courageous about life and very positive, with enormous love and loyalty to their friends and their family. I'm making this picture for my mother. I made *Husbands* for my brother [who died in 1957.] *Woman* for my father – and for Gena.

"But you're talking about movies, and when you talk about movies – I don't particularly like movies. I'm not really fascinated by them. They're usually a double-cross. I think you like 'em when you're a kid. You like the adventure of it. And you like when it doesn't get mushy, and you like it when it's tough and hard. And it's an expression. But I don't usually like movies because movies are made for people to go in and see them and make money on them. I don't know – somehow I got hooked. I got hooked on it being an expression. A substitute for living. And a good one."

"A substitute?" I ask.

"Uh-huh. *I* don't know how to live. I don't know how to dress or – get on with people. I don't even understand all that stuff. It drives me crazy.

"And if somebody says an *art* picture, I don't want to go either! They usually mean it's beautifully shot, or they used certain techniques, or it's about loneliness, an empty room with beautiful lighting. And somebody walks through and you hear eerie music. Very few things come out of the people themselves, or their own frustrations. And when you see something *really* frustrating, people say, 'No, no, we don't want that because it looks frustrating!' But as a filmmaker you *pray* you can get a script and a feeling where you can have somebody become frustrated truly."

On another day he says, "If you find something you like to do, you think that's a beautiful thing. I like to act in films, I like to direct 'em, I like to be around them, I like the feel of it, and it's something I respect. A lot. It doesn't make any difference to me whether it's a crappy film or a good film. Anybody who can make a film, I already love – but I feel sorry for them if they didn't put any *thoughts* in it. 'Cause then they missed the boat.

"You should never do any project that you wouldn't *die* to do."

John brings a bottle to the screening. It's passed around. Here are Phedon, Ted Allan, Bo Harwood, Helen Caldwell, Robert Fieldsteel, Jennifer Smith the costumer, Al Ruban and his wife, George Villasenor and his wife, Seymour and his son, others. Out of the dark, midway through the screening, John calls out, "Smith! Where's the bottle!"

"Fieldsteel has it!"

Scurrying and shuffling as the bottle gets passed from one to another over empty rows to John – we are scattered about a huge, theater-size screening room. We are watching something exciting, unformed, something that never will be seen again. Such moments are not part of the legend of filmmaking, but are the marrow of its craft and its art – this viewing of a tentative notion of what a picture may one day look like, viewed by the people to whom it means most. Thousands of choices are yet to be made. What we see tonight may seem terrible, but may one day be a great picture; or tonight it may be moving, but ruined later by too much fussing. All that we know is that what we see tonight must change. Months of editing are to follow. We are the only people who ever will see this particular *Love Streams* that exists only tonight. By tomorrow afternoon, Cassavetes and Villasenior will have already made changes.

After attending dailies nearly every day, viewing nearly every version of every scene, it's a shock to see chunks of dialogue, favorite lines, whole scenes absent, edited out forever or for the time being, we don't know. And it is lovely to see the story live on its own, on a screen, apart from the endless daily hassles and apart from John's intense conceptualizing. The work of our summer passes before our eyes as though with intents of its own, demands of its own, a sense of purpose all its own. What happens to Sarah and Robert lifts off slowly, like a Saturn V rocket, from what happens on the set. With this assembly, the 'shoot' and the film begin to part company. The furious flurries of 50-plus people fade and will become more and more unreal, displaced by the film itself as it becomes more and more itself and, finally, takes its place, a finished work in a world that may or may not be ready for it.

What's shot today will be in the final cut.

TUESDAY AFTERNOON TO SATURDAY DAWN, JULY 26–30 – *Double sixes*

Tuesday's afternoon until Saturday's dawn will pass, for us, as one very long day that happens mostly at night.

During these four-days-that-are-one, John Cassavetes will create Love Streams' conclusion. Somehow this ill man, for the last time (he'll tell me that he knows it's the last time), will draw fully upon that passionate crazy-sane will that has served him all his life – the will to create what he never calls "a work of art" but rather "an expression." He'll exhaust and out-distance the rest of us, and keep going for as long as he must to get what he wants for this picture. He'll seem flat-out crazy to most of us for most of these four days – we won't know what he's doing because little is shot in sequence. In the final cut of the picture's conclusion a scene shot this Tuesday is followed by a scene shot Wednesday, then in succession are scenes shot Tuesday, Wednesday, Friday, Thursday, Friday, next Monday, next Tuesday, this Tuesday, next Monday, this Tuesday, next Monday, this Friday – with an insert of a dream to be shot in two weeks. And those are only the scenes he'll use. Others, shot with great care, are never used (some not even in 'assemblies'). He'll write pages, shoot them, then two days later write and shoot something to be inserted into those pages, then something to go just before, just after, mixed in with inspirations he has while performing. He shoots a lot to give himself many choices for the editing room. It's all in his head, all the time, but it doesn't stay put in there, it moves around, changes – changes because of new inspiration and/or because what he's just shot teaches him that what he shot two days ago needs another nuance. Always, or almost always, in or out of the shot, there's a cigarette in his hand or dangling from his lips. Always his eyes blaze. The words he speaks most often are "fuck" and "fucking." Always he's in motion, even when sitting – his hands gesture, his feet tap, smoke constantly flows from his nostrils and mouth. Cassavetes is burning.

Best, then, to relate now the conclusion of Love Streams as we'll see it on the screen, so that a narration of the eight super-charged shooting days will make some sense. Here is what John will use of the footage shot July 26–30, August 1–2, and August 10–11:

After her collapse, Sarah dreams of trying to make her husband and daughter laugh. When she can't, Sarah jumps into the pool. We watch the surface of the water for some time. She does not emerge. [Shot Friday, July 22]

From bright sun on blue water, with the only sound the quiet hum of traffic, we cut to the interior of Robert Harmon's house, a narrow hallway. Sounds of a thunderstorm outside. Harmon, in a rain-shiny black raincoat and a soaked wide-brimmed straw hat, struggles to pull the two miniature ponies inside the house – he's also holding birdcages. He coaxes the horses in, the birds in the cages chirp, he guides the horses down the hall, goads them to trot up the stairs, and follows with the birds. [Shot Tuesday, July 26]

In "the tiny room" (as John always calls it) downstairs, flashes of lightning wake Sarah. She's disoriented, and looks out at the storm. [Shot Wednesday, July 27]

Robert runs downstairs, goes into the tiny room, sees Sarah is awake and turns on a wall-lamp. It glares one harsh circle of light on the reddish wall while the rest of the room is in almost total darkness. Sarah sits on the bed, and we see her in stark dark profile. Robert stands and his image is vague, often blending with the darkness of the room.

Breathlessly Robert says, "I got the horses in! And I couldn't get the goat, I mean, the goat is impossible. You know, there are secrets – a young girl, you know, when she comes up to you, she's infatuated with you, you know, she always wants to tell you her secrets, she volunteers them, you know, 'I've done some nude modeling,' you know, so the delicate balance of that relationship won't break. But, uh, if you're in love with someone, and the woman keeps a secret, and she doesn't give it to you, doesn't offer it to you, then that part of her goes dead to you." He pauses. "That's..." He can't go on with it. Breathless again, "I'm gonna get that goat. You alright? Good. You look wonderful, you do, really." He hastens out of the room. [Shot Tuesday, July 26]

Sarah sits a moment, lightning flashes through the window, she lies down – a motion that places her face in the cone of the lamp's bright light. Her expression: solemn, pained, yearning. Suddenly there's operatic music; she closes her eyes. [Shot Wednesday, July 27]

She dreams an opera. Backlit by a tight spotlight she is alone on a stage in a flowing gown, her face cupped by lace ruffles that glow blue in the light. The entire scene is lit in such stark contrasts of light and dark that, though we are aware of the stage and the orchestra pit, we never really see the theater or even its walls. From shot to shot the lighting changes such that there seem to be bright passageways in a black space that is otherwise indecipherable. The dream is often shot from angles that obscure the action, with sweeping long camera-moves that engage rather than reveal. The colors are Degas-gone-noir.

We see Sarah from a distance, standing on the stage, then we come nearer as a strong baritone (Jack, dubbed) sings: "You promised me that I would be the only one/ You promised me/ The only one/ You promised me/ You promised me." Sarah backs out of the spotlight, looking ghostly, and we hear her daughter's voice sing, then we see her daughter, also in opera-garb, wearing a princess tiara but lit so that she might be hovering in darkness. She sings, "How I missed you/ How I missed you/ Honey!/(More softly) Mama."

Close-up of Sarah as she sings: "In love/ I'm not sure of/ I'm not sure of/ I'm not sure/ Of me/ In fact/ I'm not sure of/ I'm not sure/ Of you/ I'm not sure of love/ Sure of love/ I'm not sure of me/ Of you."

A long shot of Debbie, now in a white ballerina tutu. A half dozen girls her age or a little younger, also in tutus, toe-step to Debbie, their arms (attempt to) gracefully wave up and down. They surround Debbie.

(Another Cassavetes parallel: at the film's beginning his house is occupied by beautiful young women of loose morals; at its end, in Sarah's dream, are beautiful little girls in white, looking the essence of purity.)

As Debbie sings the word "Mama" over and over again, she and the girls toe-step across the stage toward Sarah. Then Seymour's voice, as Jack, shouts over the music: "Debbie, no! No Debbie don't go! Come back, baby, I love you. She's a KILLER. You KNOW she'll kill you."

Jack's words stop the little dancers in their poses. Jack, in a tux, with a long white scarf that flows about him as he moves, runs across the stage, scoops Debbie up in his arms and runs away with her, whirling as he runs and as she sings "Mama" over and over.

On Sarah, singing quietly: "I love that face/ And I will be the only one/ To love that face/ The only one/ The only one," and Jack chimes in, "You promised me," and they both sing "You promised me/ The only one/ You promised me," and now the movement is hard to decipher, shot from far off, we realize slowly that the dancers and Jack have moved to Sarah. Jack sings, "I love that face/ I love that face/ You promised me/ You promised me." Then we are on Jack and Sarah, Debbie in the middle, the arms of the little dancers swaying Swan Lake-like in and out of the shot (we don't see the dancers full on). Debbie faces the camera, Jack is in profile, Sarah's face is concealed by her hair. Debbie sings, "I love you/ both," then she kisses Sarah's cheek, then Jack's nose. They kiss her. [Shot August 10–11]

Lightning flashes through the window as Sarah awakes smiling in the tiny room, the dog Jim licking her face. She pets him, says, "I had the most wonderful dream," and asks the dog, "Where's Robert?" The dog goes off to find him.

As the dog moves through the narrow hall a gust of wind slams open a door to the backyard and shatters the door's window, spraying glass. The dog bolts back. Sarah gets up and finds something with which to prop the door closed – her action is obscure because it's so dark and we're seeing her in a long shot from down the hall. Then she steps carefully over the glass and walks down the hall toward the camera. She goes through the rooms calling for Robert.

Robert is outside in the howling storm struggling with the goat. With great effort he manages to get the goat inside. Sarah looks at him with a strange excited smile. [Shot Friday, July 29]

"Robert," Sarah says, "I've come to the most fantastic new understanding with Jack. I've made it up with him. And, and, and with Debbie too."

Robert is suddenly all business: "You talked to him on the telephone or you dreamt this?"

Her reply is that strange smile, excited with epiphany.

Robert isn't having any. Wearing a wide-brimmed straw-hat made comical by the rain, its front brim turned up clown-like, he says very seriously, "Look, I'm not kidding around. I do not want you to go to some guy who doesn't love you. I love you and I want you to stay here, and I want you to stay here forever. I'm taking care of the animals, I'm taking care of EVERYTHING." He glares at her. He really isn't kidding. He's found something to live for.

But so has she. She says, softly, while storm-sound rages outside, "I'm gonna get a plane tonight."

"No! Hey, listen." He pauses, looks at her long and hard. "NO."

Softly she tells him, "I have to." A pause. "I have to."

She turns away, walks down the hall.

A long medium close-up of Robert: with no hint of self-pity, he takes it in. [Shot Thursday, July 28, and re-shot Friday, July 29; takes from both days are used in the final cut.]

She opens the door to the upstairs bedroom – there's a pony. She smiles. She packs. We see also a parrot, a cage full of chirping chicks, a duck, and the other pony. [Shot Monday, August 1]

Robert sits in his living room, smoking and sipping from a goblet. The storm rages outside. Headlights suddenly shine through the rain. He says, "Who the hell is that?"

Then he looks intently, bugged-eyed in amazement, at something across the room, something we can't see. He laughs a wild crazy laugh that is nevertheless a laugh of amazed delight. He puts down his glass.

Now we see, sitting in the chair across the room, a naked man [Neil Bell] with thick red mane-like hair, moustache, and beard. The man carefully smoothes his moustache, then looks seriously at Robert as we hear Robert exclaim, not with hostility but surprise, "Who the fuck are YOU!?"

On Robert, leaning forward, his face scrunched up in an expression of – fun! As though this is the funniest thing that's ever happened. "Who the fuck ARE you?"

On the man: the camera closes slowly in from mid-shot to tight close-up as the man looks at Robert with compassion and understanding.

Slowly, slightly, seriously, the man smiles.

Then suddenly we're looking at the dog – whom Robert, we realize, just saw as a man.

The doorbell rings. The dog turns toward the sound. Robert slowly rises to answer the door. Four flute-ish notes play the melody of "You promised me." [Shot Tuesday, August 2]

Robert runs to the door with the dog. Robert's holding the wet straw hat.

He opens the door to see a tall man in a blue rain-parka.

"Who are you?" Robert asks.

"I'm Ken." It's the man Sarah picked up in the bowling alley, last night? Two nights ago? Time behaves in this film as in a dream. Apparently she's called him to take her away. [Shot Tuesday, July 26]

As Sarah struggles to carry luggage down the stairs [shot Monday, August 1], we hear Robert and Ken, Ken saying, "Hello, doggie. You Robert?" [Shot Tuesday, July 26].

In the hallway Sarah struggles with luggage as Ken and Robert approach, Robert offering and Ken declining a drink. Ken says to Jim, "That's a good dog." Sarah greets Ken, thanking him for coming out on such a terrible night, "but I've got all this stuff and I don't know what to do with it." Ken and Sarah go upstairs. [Shot Tuesday, July 26, and Monday, August 1; takes from both nights are used in the final cut.]

Alone with the dog in the hallway downstairs, Robert, a drink in one hand and a cigarette dangling from his mouth, tries to sic the dog on Ken: "Jim, come on! Kill the big man!" The dog barks but won't cooperate. Robert sighs a disgusted, "Chickenshit." Then: "Wanna listen to music? Hm? Wanna listen to music? That-a boy, come on." [Shot Tuesday, July 26]

In the living room, with the jukebox lit, Robert stands with a cigarette. Jim gets into a chair. [Shot Monday, August 1]

Ken comes down the stairs loaded with luggage, Sarah comes down with more luggage. As Ken goes up for still more luggage he gives her a quick peck on the cheek. [Shot Tuesday, July 26]

Sarah and Robert are in the living room, embracing, a tight shoulder-and-head shot, while mysteriously one bar of a song – with two sung words, "an invitation" – plays then stops.

Robert says, "I don't want you go. I love you. You're the ONLY one

I love."

"Oh, shush."

"Now don't shush me, who the hell do you think you are to shush me?"

"Come on."

"I don't want you to go. Where you gonna go out in all this rain?"

Her plans have changed. Coyly she says, "I'm gonna stay the night with Ken. Ok?"

He kisses her cheeks and they embrace. She gives him one last look and whirls off, running outside in the rain. [Shot Monday, August 1]

Ken follows, catches up with her. He gets her into the car and continues loading the luggage. There's a shot of her through the window, looking in sorrow back at the house.

Ken tells her, "The trunk won't fit."

"Oh leave it, just leave it."

"Leave it?"

And Ken leaves it.

Music. A fragment of a mid-tempo Beatles-esque tune: "And I didn't know what to do/ But I'll leave it up to you/ An invitation/ To the house that I knew so well/ An invitation/ And I thought that it started well… And I didn't know what to do/ Oh yeah/ But I'll leave it up to you."

The song plays through the shot from outside the house, in the rain: Robert Harmon in the living room, smoking, looking at the hat, putting it on, coming to the window, taking it off, moving dazedly to the music, turning to reach for a goblet of booze, turning back to face us, standing there with the goblet in one hand and the hat in the other, then waving goodbye, his expression solemn and calm, waving with the straw hat, slowly waving goodbye.

He stops waving, looks out the window a moment more, walks out of frame as the tune stops suddenly on the words "an observation." [Shot early Saturday, July 30]

The word LOVE and the word STREAMS come from opposite ends of the screen and credits roll to the 1940s tune that ends, "Where is my happy ending? Where are you?"

In the Cassavetes kitchen, on a large page of white paper fastened with magnets to the refrigerator door, in neat large-looped script:

> "IF THIS REFRIGERATOR-FREEZER IS TURNED OFF FOR SOUND OR WHATEVER IT MUST BE TURNED BACK ON AFTER SHOOTING. IT WAS OFF ALL DAY THURSDAY, THURSDAY NIGHT, AND FRIDAY, AND BY THE TIME I FOUND IT FRIDAY NIGHT IT WAS REALLY HORRIBLE SO PLEASE DON'T FORGET."

A drawing of a skull-and-crossbones, then the signature: GENA.

Between set-ups John talks a great deal, usually about anything but the work at hand. He raves against Socrates, muses about Gena, discusses the dangers of President Reagan's bellicosity and the cruelty of his policies – and tells me, in a quiet moment, that every night he prays for Reagan. It is the only time in my hearing that John mentions what he otherwise, in conversation or in his films, never alludes to: that he prays, every night, and has some sort of faith in some sort of God.

During these four-days-that-are-like-one, old friends drop in and hang around the house as though this is a wild on-going party and not a job of work. John hugs them, is glad to see them, takes them into the bar for a drink, talks with them for a half hour while the set-up waits to be shot and the crew grouses. One friend is Richard Dreyfuss. (He and John starred together in *Whose Life Is It Anyway?*) Dreyfuss tells a chilling story. He was invited to the White House – Ronald Reagan, a Hollywood guy from way back, often invites movie-people for visits. They had a pleasant conversation, Reagan was quite engaging. Just when Dreyfuss was getting antsy about taking so much of the President's time, Reagan offered to show him around the White House. The President gave him a personal tour from top to bottom, including the bowling alley. Dreyfuss thought it stranger and stranger that President Reagan had so much time on his hands and could spare Dreyfuss his attentions. It was as though he was glad Dreyfuss was there, so he'd have something to do.

Their time together went uninterrupted. Later, back at his hotel, Dreyfuss turned on the TV. He was horrified to see that this day United States Marines invaded Grenada – while President Reagan was not in the Situation Room and not in contact with anyone but Richard Dreyfuss.

I laugh. John shoots me a really dirty look. This is not for laughing.

Meanwhile the crew is waiting for John to show up for the next shot.

Night and day, whenever he can squeeze it in, between set-ups and sometimes even between takes, John plays backgammon with Phedon. (Phedon, Gena tells me, is "a master player, all finesse.") They slam down the backgammon pieces with relish, curse each other's luck, exult in their own. They could be two Greeks playing at a sidewalk café in Athens, for during their games they seem utterly unaware of the 50-plus people in every corner of the house.

Late one afternoon, on their second round of vodkas, our documentary captures a dialogue over backgammon that goes like this:

Phedon quotes Socrates and John says decisively, "Socrates – was a jerk."

"Don't talk to me about Socrates," Phedon says, "you know nothing about Socrates."

"Socrates? If you believe in atomic bombs, you believe in Socrates."

"That's not a way to talk about Socrates!"

"That's the way *I* speak."

Phedon looks at John as though John has gone mad: "Socrates had nothing to *do* with the atomic bomb!"

"No, he's just a jerk."

"To you."

"Yeah."

"*Read* about him!" Phedon pleads.

"Totally unemotional man! He's a jerk!"

"You might be able to gain something if you read about him."

"Anybody who has no emotion is dead," John argues over Phedon's sentence, "and he's dead anyway, so you can't dispute that."

And they go back and forth with sentence-fragments I can't follow about "freedom," "democracy," Phedon to John, "You, an American, don't believe in democracy?" and John shooting back with, "That's what Socrates said, that's the kind of stupid thinking –"

"Socrates didn't say that, that's why I told you to read about him –"

"He did say it."

" – 'cause you know nothing about him."

Phedon tries to add something and John runs him over with, "'Make an assumption,' that's Socrates' thinking, you can make any assumption you want, and every damn lawyer in the world has made that assumption forever: whatever you do is right, as long as you can get off!"

"Really? Who said that?"

"That's Socrates."

"Socrates said that?"

"Yeah."

"Well, you see, you are ignorant."

"I am ignorant –"

"Too bad –"

" – but I have feelings."

"No one said you don't."

"I'm not a dead man, like all the rest of the people that believe that everything that benefits them is right."

All Cassavetes-Papamichael backgammon games this week, at three in the afternoon or three in the morning, are accompanied by similar dialogue – Socrates, Aristophanes, Sophocles, baseball, is Anthony Quinn (Phedon's close friend) losing his mind, more baseball.

And all the while I'm certain that, while playing, John is figuring the ending of his movie – because it's not unusual for John to leave the game with a new idea for a scene, cancel his previous instructions for a set-up, call for a new set-up, or retreat upstairs with Helen Caldwell to dictate notes or dialogue.

During these backgammon games Cassavetes' luck with the dice borders on the supernatural. Correction: it *is* supernatural. If he needs *three consecutive five-and-threes,* he gets them. I swear it. Again and again John has no right to win and wins anyway, wins handily, mightily, crushingly. Doubles are a great advantage in backgammon. Cassavetes throws doubles with incredible frequency. Double-sixes are the greatest advantage. Cross-my-heart-and-spit, I witness him throw seven double-sixes in a row.

At which Phedon goes insane. No kidding. Phedon – as wide-eyed as though he's seen the Devil – explodes in a volcano of Greek-accented "motherfuckers" while John laughs like Mephistopheles until it seems the very glee of it might well burst his soul from his body.

Fieldsteel tells me that the picture "is less free for John, at this stage" – that John has focused the film at a very special pitch of intensity now and his choices within that narrow spectrum have to be perfect or the ending will fizzle out. He sounds like he's quoting John. "It has to do," Fieldsteel says, "with the character of Robert Harmon focusing so deeply on Sarah now. The picture is all John's, Gena's, and Bo's now."

And Bo Harwood tells me, "John says that usually, in a picture, you want to tie it up at the end. But the continuity of this picture is so strange! Every scene you have no idea what's gonna happen next. And that's true, because people don't *play* what's gonna happen next."

He, too, sounds like he's quoting John.

We're all quoting, *doing* John. You see exchanges between crew members, arguments or jokes, that are mini-John moments. We're catching John like some strange kind of virus. He's upped the stakes of intensity such that we're feeling it as though it's coming out of us.

Helen Caldwell approaches me with a secretive air: "John is a madman impersonating a sane man. Somebody said that to me tonight, and I'm not telling you whom."

You have to wonder about a gal who thinks John is even remotely impersonating someone sane. But I respect anyone with the grammatical grace to employ "whom" correctly in a madhouse.

John is explaining, clearly and meticulously, a camera-move in the tiny room. Al Ruban likes it, they agree on it. The crew sets it up. They're about to shoot. Suddenly no one can recall what the movement is supposed to be.

"I remember," John says vaguely, "we wanted a little movement – here."

Al turns to one of his grips: "Dermot – do you remember what was said here?"

"I can't remember –" Dermot makes a gesture with his arm " – a slight move here."

"A slight movement – that sounds right," John says. "That sounds *right* – but I don't know what it means!"

Only Gena seems completely calm. She tells me, "All I'm thinking of now is the script, and where will Zoe go to school in the fall?"

For some reason about six of us sit idly in her bedroom while she applies make-up for a scene, a make-up person assisting her. As though nothing could be more natural when you're a guest in another's home – a guest, in fact, in their bedroom – someone idly opens a closet door just to see what's inside.

In the closet are many, many, many shoes.

Gena, unfazed, glances at me: "That's one thing I never throw away, any shoes I've worn in a movie."

We're waiting for chickens. Chickadees, to be precise.

They're to shoot the scene where Robert Harmon brings the

horses and fowl inside the house, but there are no chickadees present.

"He cancelled the chickens while we were standing there," Eddie Donno tells Al Ruban.

"That's right," a crew guy says, "I was there."

"And we asked him," Eddie says, "'You need the chickens?' And he says, 'No, we don't need the fuckin' chickens!'"

The chickens left Cassavetes' conception one moment and entered it again an hour or so later. The thing about filmmaking is – a writer can want a chicken in the scene, type it in, decide it's not right, cross it out, change his mind, type it in again, but a filmmaker can't do that. For a filmmaker, the *concept* of a chicken is also a *chicken*.

You need a chicken to film a chicken. A chickadee, that is. Several. If the chickadees temporarily leave your imagination and then return, somebody with some other job must stop doing that job, commandeer a vehicle, drive 30 miles to a farm and 30 miles back in the middle of the night to fetch the chickadees – while 56 people wait and bitch.

Film scholars take note: The chickadees are no mere whim. John needs his chickadees. Their perky tinny chirping creates important (albeit "subliminal") atmosphere in several scenes. Quoth Cassavetes, when this conjunction of chickadees and cinema scholarship is brought to his attention: "Some pimply-assed Ph.D. will footnote my chickens. Fuck 'im."

The chickadees arrive. Lots of us are in the backyard with John and the camera-crew and everybody is giddy except the animal-wranglers. They seem concerned to have landed in the midst of such an atmosphere. Will their animals be safe running about (essentially unsupervised) in John's house?

We're about to shoot the scene where John drags the horses into the house while carrying a birdcage filled with chicks, parrots and a duck. John wants all the birds in one cage. This worries the wranglers, but they submit. Then John is surprised that the cage is heavy. "What the hell is in this thing?"

Fowl are not concepts. Fowl weigh.

"Alright," he says, "lets go guys, come on, roll this thing, wet us down, wet the horses, they gotta be drippin', kid, they gotta be really wet."

The miniature horses are so nervous they defecate frequently. One gets panicky, almost stomps the birdcage. John loves it.

"Nice kitty cat," he says to the horse, "nice kitty, look at the eyes, he's gettin' a little crazier every minute."

The horse is one of us now.

"That's it, wet 'em all, they gotta be really good – now he's gonna *piss* and shit."

They're ready for the shot, John is leading the animals through the narrow laundry room, we're all laughing, and he turns to us, focused and furious:

"Quiet! SHUT UP everybody!"

If a writer wants a storm all he needs are the words. If a filmmaker wants a storm, with thunder and lightning, he needs an entire extra crew, with two huge Ritter wind-fans, and hoses, and piping, and 50 yellow raincoats and 50 pairs of galoshes for his people. Plus there's the danger of electrical equipment getting wet and shorting out, and the likelihood of your set (in this case, your home) becoming dangerously water-damaged, water leaking from the roof through the second floor to the first floor, leaking even through light fixtures – which makes everyone, excepting John, nervous.

Somehow (double-sixes?) nothing shorts out, nothing bursts into flame.

They've set up a master-shot of the house in the storm. The wind-machines will blow and water – an amazing amount water – will pour, while the lightning-machine flashes and thunder rolls.

John, in yellow rainwear, will operate the camera. Dermot will pull the dolly.

"What I wanna do," John tells Dermot, "is I wanna go real fast. Think you can?"

"Sure I can, but you're up so high –" Dermot gestures the

camera swaying back and forth. He doesn't want John to fall.

"Don't worry about it."

Don't worry about the ailing director who's had the odd drink or two – but never, ever appears affected by it. Don't worry about him falling from that perch as you drag the dolly. Don't worry about being the guy who takes him down.

They do the shot several times at several speeds.

Our documentary crew shoots them shooting the shot – a shot that will not be used in the film, but makes for pretty footage in our doc.

Between shots I ask an electrician, casually, "How's it going?"

"How's it going?" he shoots back, darkly. "After the first *take,* I know what he wants. But don't write that, I don't want to ruin his reputation. Interesting how he talks nice to the guys on the wind machine and so bad to us. They are here two days, and we…" His voice trails off.

"And you're mad."

"Of course."

John has told me, "This is one of the greatest crews I've ever seen, because they're all individual. And none of them, not one person on the crew, is a kiss-ass. They all have their opinions. If they like something, they like it. If they don't like it, they wouldn't give you a nickel for it. And I think that's a very healthy way to approach a picture.

"An electrician has to stand there until some dumb fool says, 'Turn on those lights.' And when he does it, he knows the light is in the wrong place, he has an *opinion* about it. So if people stay individual and keep thinking, then the movie isn't made by one person, the movie's made by a lot of people.

"So our irritations mount, our happinesses escalate at times, we joke around, we try not to be *too* serious about the film, but underneath we really *suffer* over trying to make a film, whether it's good or bad we don't any of us know.

"I mean, I can get the crew irritated – you know? After a while they don't get irritated because they know it's all bullshit. But we still have conflicts, everybody has conflicts every day, some days you're thrilled because everything is totally creative, and some days it's – horror. Because nothing is working. But in the form of the *way* we're working, you just don't know what's going to happen."

It's after 'lunch' – they call it lunch, but it's a very late dinner. People are finishing their coffee and cigarettes, getting back to work, setting up the next shot. John's pacing with arms folded, having a moment with himself at the edge of the yard, where the hillside rises steeply. He calls out, "Anybody got a cigarette?"

As I'm nearest John, about 10 yards away, a crew-guy throws me his pack from the next table over. I take out a cigarette, throw the pack back, bring the cigarette to John. He starts to say "Got a light?" but I take from my shirt pocket the matches I've made a habit of carrying since being so embarrassed at not lighting Gena's cigarettes during our interview. Anyway there's always someone saying "Got a light?" on this shoot.

He lights his cigarette, pockets my matches.

"This is it, kiddo."

"What's it?"

I reach for the notebook in my back pocket, as I always do, but he shakes his head no. I wouldn't have written this down anyway. Not because it's a secret but because you don't take notes while a man's telling you that this is his last time out, the last time he'll be able to push himself this hard, give this much energy, get this crazy with belief in something.

John bumps into me, literally, in the hall. He's seeing something in his mind, not what's ahead of him. And he says, with no build-up or cue, "All artists should work with distrust. They should not trust anyone." He cackles. "*I* don't trust *anybody.* I'm the only one I can trust to do *any*thing for the movie. Because I'll do anything. Humiliate myself. Anything."

*

Late that night Menahem Golan, that bear of a man, visits the set. It's not a surprise, John knows he's coming. John tells me, "He wants to be in your doc. Wants a shot of me and him together."

"He told you that?"

John just laughs. "Trust me."

So when he comes Giddy, Peter, and I set up in the bar. Golan leans at one end of the bar, Cassavetes leans at the other. But something is weird. This is not a Cassavetes I've seen. He's looking at Golan sweetly, a little slyly, at times almost adoringly – he's playing the kid brother! The mischievous kid brother. Golan is eating it up. He says, "So will we be doing *Husbands II*?"

John says, smiling like a little boy, "I'm very proud of this picture – and very proud of you too. 'Cause no one else would have made it." Though that last sentence is true, John doesn't quite keep a straight face.

"You're laughing," Older Brother observes, with a touch of admonishment.

John does not want Golan looking over his shoulder as he shoots, he keeps stalling, avoiding doing the next shot. They've been sitting around the bar for about a half hour and Golan, who's paying for this half hour and all the other half-hours, gets a little concerned: "By the way – are you shooting tonight?"

"Yeah."

"When?"

"They're lighting."

"It's one of these days," meaning "one of *those* days."

Older Brother says, "I have to show a cut to Frank Yablans [head of MGM/UA, with whom Golan has a distribution deal], as soon as possible."

"To Frank?"

"Yes."

"You want me to tell you what to tell him?" John laughs slyly. Golan smiles patiently, with complicity – what new quirky cuteness will Little Brother concoct?

"No," John says, "he can see it."

"When do you think we can show it to him?"

"Whenever he wants to see it." John's being so nice-nice I may have to leave the room not to laugh.

"I want him to see a full assembly," Older Brother says with authority.

"Show it to him, but nobody else, he can't bring anybody with him."

"No, just him alone."

"Yeah."

"Okay."

"'Cause that would be okay. And then, he has to go to dinner afterwards. You tell him, he has to take me to dinner, and you to dinner, to sit, and suffer, even if he doesn't like it."

Both men laugh now. Or rather, both men are actors now, acting a laugh and seeming to enjoy the act.

"He thinks I'm crazy anyway, Frank," Little Brother says.

"And you think you're *not* crazy?" Older Brother tells it like it is.

"I *know* I'm crazy. But I'm trying to fool 'em."

"We're all crazy," Menahem affirms, "one big crazy family."

Then we shoot an interview with Golan for the doc, for which he's also paying.

Golan's admiration for Cassavetes is sincere. He speaks of Swedish director Ingmar Bergman and says, "It's about time that America recognizes they have their *own* Bergman, John Cassavetes." He says, "I understood that I'm going to do a John Cassavetes film, and once I accepted this fact I had to give John Cassavetes the *full* freedom to create his film."

This he has done, and this he will continue to do, right through to the final cut. He even extends this courtesy to me. Dan Wetherbee, his assistant Seth Gavin, and I, will edit our documentary for nearly two months without so much as an inquiry from Golan or his people. Golan won't even ask to see our film before we strike the final print. Then he'll screen it once, by himself, and tell somebody to tell me he likes it.

John walks into our interview, says to Golan, "Wanna check this shot? I want you to check this shot."

Golan watches one set-up. The informality of John's set seems to make him antsy and after a couple of takes he bids goodnight gracefully.

They're about to shoot again in the tiny room. John tells me, "It's hard to film a dream."

During the scene John says his speech a little differently each time. Here's the take he'll finally use:

"I got the horses in! And I couldn't get the goat, I mean, the goat is impossible. You know, there are secrets – a young girl, you know, when she comes up to you, she's infatuated with you, you know, she always wants to tell you her secrets, she volunteers them, you know, 'I've done some nude modeling,' you know, so the delicate balance of that relationship won't break. But, uh, if you're in love with someone, and the woman keeps a secret, and she doesn't give it to you, doesn't offer it to you, then that part of her goes dead to you. I'm gonna get that goat. You alright? Good. You look wonderful, you do, really."

But almost until he locks the picture in mid-December he'll use another, not as breathless:

"I took the horses in out of the rain. I found the duck and the little chicks – and – I couldn't get the goat in. There are secrets, you know, that young girls have – and I – once a young girl came to me and she said, 'Look, I did some nude modeling.' I thought, well, she's just trying to protect herself because the relationship is so frail and she wanted it to last, you know, until the infatuation was over. But you're a beautiful woman and beautiful women should not keep secrets, because a secret to someone you love precludes them from ever having that part of you, because you have to protect it so hard. Let me just feed the goat, all right."

In both speeches it's clear Robert Harmon is now relating to his sister as a woman rather than simply a sister, telling her what he told women earlier in the film. The first speech flows better and is crazier. The second is more specific. Again and again, as John cuts his film, he'll go for flow and crazy over specific, involving us in a dream rather than telling us what's going on.

Watching John and Gena shoot these scenes can be disorienting. They go so seamlessly from being John and Gena to being Robert and Sarah that often you don't catch the moment of shift and you get embarrassed – as though you're listening to John-and-Gena's private conversation, hearing things you don't want to know and are not supposed to know. Then Casssavetes calls "Cut" and they're John and Gena, without so much as a blink in between – and they behave differently, completely. And the experience, in the room, is very like *you're* having a dream, a dream in which identity is bafflingly flexible.

Meanwhile the goat is shitting in the living room.

That seems so normal to us by now.

It's 3:30 in the morning, Saturday morning. They're preparing to shoot the film's last scenes. In the kitchen I'm making tea, Gena's making instant coffee.

"I just can't believe we're shooting this scene," she says quietly. "You start the picture, and its end seems so far away. And then it's here. And another part of your life is over."

She has no lines in the next scene – running from the house through the rain and getting into the car while John Roselius as Ken struggles with luggage. However, she's been wired for sound just in case. The wind machines will be blowing, lightning will be flashing, rain will be pouring, and there is some doubt as to whether Roselius will be able to get all Gena's luggage in the car and the trunk. Rather than have the scene go on endlessly, if he can't do it Gena is supposed to tell him, "Just leave it. Let's go."

"Think what we're doing to those poor people in film schools!" Fieldsteel laughs. "Tomes are going to be written on that line!"

I watch the shot from the safety and dryness of the living room. The wind-fans roar, water falls thickly in sheets, and John Cassavetes stands outside in the middle of it all, no parka, soaking wet, oblivious: "Come on, guys, let's go!"

Three complete set-ups, one take per set-up, each set-up shot with two cameras. And after each Gena goes upstairs to take off the wet clothes, dry her hair, dry the clothes, drink a cup of coffee, and do it again.

They're shooting a version (there are several, on different nights) of Robert and Sarah's last words to each other. Giddy, Peter, and I shoot them shooting it. It's not going well. They pitch the tone of the dialogue up, they pitch it down, John isn't satisfied, neither is Gena. John glares at us. "Guys, that's getting on my nerves, can we cool it?"

We cool it. We stop shooting, but we're ready. Giddy keeps the 16mm in hand. Peter holds his sound boom, and the heavy portable recording equipment remains slung over his shoulder. In between takes Giddy suggests we get shots of the house, and we roam a little. In the hallway the still photographer, Francois, is attempting shots too. He and Giddy are waving their light-meters around.

Giddy asks, "Francois, what are you reading?"

"Nothing. In this movie there is no light."

We go back to stand out of the way and watch the next take – the next several takes. It's still not going well. Gena and John, in place for the shot, discuss in whispers. They don't look like they're arguing, they look like they're searching for something. After the next take John calls a cut and he and Gena retreat down the hall – to speak privately, I assume. Without needing to be told, Giddy whips the 16's eyepiece to his eye, Peter follows him, I follow them, we're shooting John and Gena going down the hall, John whirls around, "Hey, guys, FUCK OFF with the camera!"

John and Gena disappear into their dark bar and everybody leaves them alone.

"You got that, Giddy?" I ask.

"I got that."

"Great."

It makes my third-favorite moment of our film. (My first is

John's long thoughtful consideration of one line; my second is Gena saying, "No matter how much you are into a character, you can just see an actor's *soul* on film.")

Finally John and Gena do a take that they like.

It's maybe a quarter to five in the morning. I'm in the kitchen again making tea. John comes in to make coffee. He looks at me, I look at him, I smile, he smiles and shrugs, and, with his head tilted down, glances through his eyebrows at the ceiling.

"Every picture should start at the ending," John said to me the night before. "That's where it really starts."

Soon it will be dawn. Finally, they prepare for the last shot of the night, the last shot of the story.

I watch out of camera-range from the hallway. The camera looks into the living room from outdoors, through windows streaked with wind-blown rain: Robert Harmon stands by his jukebox, moving awkwardly and sadly to the music, looking much like a little boy but also like an old man. He wears his raincoat and his drenched shapeless hat, then takes off the hat and, as though in a daze, waves out the window, an odd wet lonely man with a goblet of whiskey in one hand slowly waving that ridiculous hat, waving at Sarah departing, at the audience watching, at a part of his life that is over.

He walks out of frame.

John calls "Cut" – then turns to me and says quietly, "That was fun."

For these four days the editing-script records 27 set-ups, 72 takes, and well over an hour of printed film for about 11 minutes of the final cut. But that doesn't tell the whole story. The editing-script records the set-ups that were finally used or were in consideration for use at that stage of editing. Many set-ups never made it to the editing room. Others were discarded by the time the editing script reached the late stage of my copy. There's no way to know how much work was actually done, but my educated guess would be about a third more than the editing-script notes.

I don't get to bed until about 10 o'clock Saturday morning. Except for the opera-dream, there's nothing more to shoot. The plan is to watch dailies Monday and maybe re-shoot some of this week's interior shots Monday night if necessary. Emotionally, it feels like we're done, and I hate it being done. I hate that these four days are done. Only the likes of John Cassavetes get days like these more than once in a lifetime.

MONDAY, AUGUST 1 – *The fuckin' end of the world*

John has said to me, "There's something alive about film that says, 'I resist you.' The film itself resists. And it says to you, 'Aha! You think you're gonna do this, but I'm gonna do something else! And I'm not telling you want I'm gonna do!"

The plan is that maybe John shoots a little tonight, maybe even some pick-up shots tomorrow, the opera dream on the 10th and 11th – and then, as they say, "That's a wrap." So we thought, until watching the dailies from Thursday and Friday.

John is furious. "It looks like the fuckin' end of the world!"

Not only does the storm come across like a hurricane, but "it's lousy how the electrician manipulated the lightning." While shooting, nobody noticed that the lightning comes at regular intervals: a flash, a beat, two flashes, a beat, a flash, a beat, two flashes, a beat – take after take. "Looks fake," John says. And if you say you're not so sure it looks fake, or maybe he can edit around it, you receive an incoherent blast of Cassavetes' rhetoric. We need "the rain" (its crew and their apparatus) again. Need to re-shoot John's last scene at the window, Gena's in the car. Can we get "the rain" for tonight? Calls are made. Tomorrow night. "Can we get the friggin' animals tonight?" Calls are made. We can get the friggin' animals.

An extraordinary phenomenon will rise from this 'mistake': an inspiration that gives John's ending an entirely new twist. And when that inspiration is filmed, won't it be wonderful how the footage that today seems so terrible will, on re-consideration, be just right and included in the final cut?

So maybe "the rain" wasn't so bad after all. Maybe there was no mistake with the lightning that couldn't be gotten around. Maybe John needs to shoot some more because he feels something brewing, he's on the edge of an idea. Or maybe John knows what that idea is, or what it might be, and needs "the rain" again to perform and discover it – but maybe he doesn't want to look like a schmuck in Menahem Golan's eyes, saying he's done with rain and animals one day and the next day needing more cash for both. Maybe this temper-tantrum is an act. Maybe it's not. Maybe it's half an act. Maybe, too, "the film itself" has "resisted," it has something new in mind, and it won't tell John what it is until he shoots – maybe he has a sense of that. Maybe, maybe, maybe.

As Gena has said, "You never know with John.... John's very mysterious... you just *really* never know."

Eddie Donno has the parakeet on his shoulder and he's taught it to say "Cut!"

It's like a party tonight, lots of us hanging out between takes in Cassavetes' bar. Diahnne Abbott is here, dressed to the nines, gorgeous, nervous, unable to hide her disappointment that her big climactic scene was cut. She's written a new scene to give her character, Susan, closure. Is John going to shoot it? She asks more than once.

"Yes, yes, yes, I'm gonna shoot it. Be here in the morning."

He told me about her scene earlier and I, too, asked if he'd shoot it.

"Sure. Who am I not to shoot her scene? She cared enough to come up with that – and it's sweet, it's good. I'll shoot it and we'll see if we can get it in."

*

Neil Bell, the dog-man, has continued to come to the set, awaiting a time when John might want to shoot him as Jim the dog. Now and again John has used him, sometimes playfully, sometimes half-heartedly. In spite of Bell's uncanny imitation of dog-ness, the footage hasn't worked. But tonight John films the real dog, poor Jumbo, in a chair in the living room, just sitting; then he films the dog standing still beside the chair. And then he films Neil in the same chair, just sitting, naked from the waist up (which is all the camera sees) – a medium shot that zooms slowly into a close-up as Neil looks at Robert Harmon and half smiles, very seriously, knowledgeably.

John tells me, "It's taken me all this time to realize Neil can't be a dog, he has to be a man. Just sit there. Otherwise, it's a joke."

We'll see in the dailies tomorrow that Neil's shot has a rare strange power.

Tonight, with little fuss, John shoots the scene of Sarah packing in the room with the animals; some Ken-and-Sarah luggage confusion; the dog's two shots; Neil's shot; and Harmon standing in the living room beside the lit jukebox lighting a cigarette while the dog gets into the chair. It will all be in the final cut.

TUESDAY, AUGUST 2 – *I didn't make it for you anyway*

Diahnne Abbott's scene, as directed by Peter Bogdanovich and edited by John Cassavetes:

Susan pulls into Robert Harmon's driveway. She's hesitant. She picks a flower from his garden. She knocks on the door. Robert opens it. He's not glad to see her.

"Hi, Robert," she says, "how are you? How've you been?"

"What are you doing here?" He says it tough. She's hurt, but she sticks.

"Well, I happened to be in the neighborhood and – actually, I hadn't heard from you and I wondered how you were. Actually, my mother was worried about you. I think she misses you."

"Everybody's always worried about me! Actually, I'm fine, you can see that. And I can't let you in."

"That's ok. I don't want to come in. I guess you have company."

"You're right there."

"Well, I've gotta go to work. I wanted to ask you something. Do you think we should see each other again or what?"

He just looks at her.

She braves on. "I'd like for us to be friends, if you want a friend?"

He kisses her hard on the cheek and just looks at her, a half-smile on his face.

"Take care of yourself, Robert. Keep in touch, ok?"

He sort of winks.

"'Bye," she says.

He says nothing, watches her leave, raises his eyebrows, and 'waves goodbye' by wagging one forefinger.

Peter Bogdanovich and John Cassavetes are friends. Cassavetes ran dailies for *Opening Night* at Bogdanovich's home in Bel Air. When John fell behind schedule on that picture Peter shot some second-unit scenes to help out. They have something rare in common: both have used Ben Gazzarra as an alter-ego in their films – John in *The Killing of a Chinese Bookie* and *Opening Night,* Bogdanovich in *Saint Jack* and *They All Laughed.* The choice of an alter-ego is no casual act. As different as they appear, and as different as are their films, John and Peter have simpatico.

John has invited Peter to his home this morning. Peter shakes my hand: "Hi, Michael, how are you?" We met a year before when I'd interviewed him for my newspaper and before that at the stage play of *Love Streams.*

Peter and John chat about this and that until John asks suddenly, "Do you want to shoot this scene?"

The question flummoxes Bogdanovich. He says John doesn't need anybody to shoot his scenes. John coaxes, goads, brings Peter outside to look at the set-up, introduces him to Diahnne, wants to know if there's anything Peter would like to change. Peter looks at me, shrugs, says, "I guess I'm directing."

To no one in particular he says, "This will be the first scene I've directed in two years. I'm a retired director."

Bogdanovich was badly shaken by the murder of Dorothy Stratten after she starred in his last film. He's laid low since, devoting most of his time to writing a book about her.

It is remarkable how quickly Bogdanovich *is* today's director. Wasting no time he says to John and Diahnne, "You wanna read the scene?"

"You *do* that?!" John laughs. "I never do that."

The three look from one to the other. John shrugs, "Sure, let's read the scene."

We go inside to the bar with typescripts of the scene.

Peter asks John, "How important is this to your character, in terms of the story? You're just trying to get her out of there? Do you care?"

"I care very much," John says (though he won't play it that way), "I like her very much."

"So it's not easy for you?"

"No."

"Okay."

John and Diahnne read through the scene once. Peter listens intently.

Diahnne is a little vague about the action at the doorway.

"Do you have a knocker or a bell?" she asks John.

"There's a knocker and a bell," Peter says quickly. I'm impressed with his eye. When we were outside he looked at the doorway *as a director* and took in everything. He adds, "But I think somebody should paint the bell a darker color because it's hard to see."

I'm more impressed.

Bogdanovich speaks with relaxed authority. His attitude seems to be:

One does not do these things lightly, ever – not if one is really a director.

"Now what would happen," Peter says, and lets those words hang in the air while he fishes for his thought. "It's the same scene, but you don't wait for each other to finish. Because the whole scene is getting out of an embarrassing moment. I think it would be kind of nice. Try it, see what happens."

What Bogdanovich explores in the relaxation of the rehearsal atmosphere, Cassavetes would explore with the tension of cameras rolling. What Bogdanovich verbalizes precisely, Cassavetes would hint at vaguely, instigating instead of defining.

They do the scene as Peter suggests. John has given Peter the power to direct and is obedient to Peter's direction.

"That's good," Peter says, "the only thing you left out…" He reads a passage from the text that he doesn't want them to skip again. "Some of it's painful," he thinks aloud. "When he doesn't let you in it's obvious…" His voice trails off. "Why don't you run it again, John, run it again and let me make a call. I'll be right back."

They do what he says.

Peter returns, saying, "I can stay a little later – if you still want me to stay."

"I *do* want you to stay!" John says.

"So you won't have to feel pressured," Peter says. Then: "I thought it would be good if we played the whole scene like this –" and he makes a gesture that shows he would film only John's face – "but her whole. And then cut to you watching her go, so you can show whatever you want to show. Then we can jump the walk and be on her in the car."

Outside, Bogdanovich gives his instructions to the crew. His quiet clarity couldn't be more different from Cassavetes' style. This experienced crew adjusts instantly – and I mean *instantly* – to Peter's orderly temperament. The atmosphere couldn't be more different: calm, formal, polite. (I think of John's contention that a director creates an atmosphere and "the atmosphere directs the picture.")

Peter watches a take, pacing up and down. He says quietly, "Cut it. Print it."

Then: "Diahnne, you get out [of the car] and look – you might look around a little. Then notice the flowers. Take one. You might go up to the stairs a little bit faster."

Picking the flower is Peter's idea, to give Diahnne something to hold and focus upon at the doorway, when she doesn't want to look at John. But in the last take she was too quick, for his eye, to go toward the flowers, then walked too slowly to the door – because "the character" (Peter's expression) would consider for a moment before picking a flower, but the picking of the flower would make her more decisive in her movement to the door.

Peter's directions are exact. He gives reasons. The crew relaxes, waits for instructions, leaves it to him.

The constant tension of these last two months is suddenly absent. Things seem fairly sane, except for the fact that suddenly somebody else is the director.

John watches from a perch atop one of the huge Ritter wind-fans, dangling his legs like Huck Finn on a Mississippi River dock. He's attentive and amused, looking at Bogdanovich with the bright eyes of an admirer. I stand near him, watching Peter shoot Diahnne's approach to the door.

Bogdanovich calls a cut and remains silent a few moments looking at the door, his hand on his forehead, puffing his cigar.

"The lonely life of a director," says Cassavetes softly.

Tonight Cassavetes tells the rain crew, "Okay, guys – get the wind machines in the right place, put the rain in there, and let's do it like we did it."

What did he just say? "Do it like we did it"?

So, after all, nothing was wrong with the storm. John missed something about Robert Harmon, something was "off" about his ending for *Love Streams,* some quality was absent. He's searching for how Robert Harmon has been changed by these events – he's found some of it, but he hasn't found all of it. Whatever it is, if it's to be discovered it must be discovered tonight.

Tonight is the last time John Cassavetes will be Robert Harmon. The bitterness, isolation, and yearnings of that lonely man, Robert Harmon, the range of his psyche – there's something about Harmon that John hasn't expressed yet, or we wouldn't be doing this. Some of us whisper about what this 'something' might be.

We whisper – because John is more intent, more absorbed, than I've yet seen him. Tonight he's someone whom one does not approach and near whom one whispers. He's not joking, he's not talking. While they're setting up outside John – in Robert Harmon's raincoat, holding the soaked straw hat – paces up and down alone in his living room, lit only by the neon glow of the jukebox. Phedon comes in, all excited, a ballplayer they admire just hit a home run – normally this would interest John very much for a quick moment. John doesn't react but to wave Phedon away. Jennifer Ashley-Smith comes to examine his costume. She pins back his raincoat's flap. Usually they're easy with each other, joking, conversing – he respects Jennifer, has emphasized that he considers her wardrobe work a significant contribution. Tonight he stares right through her. She takes the cue and says not a word.

Whatever it is about Robert Harmon that John is searching for, it has something to do with Neil Bell and the damn dog. Months ago on the phone, during our first conversation about *Love Streams*, John laughed and said, "It's the dog's picture." He's had Neil Bell hanging around for weeks without really knowing why. Last night he shot Bell in that chair and this afternoon at dailies he saw the power of the shot. John had been so relaxed with Bogdanovich, and afterward; he'd enjoyed the morning immensely. But after watching that Neil Bell shot John clammed up and began to build to this hour's intensity. Since the crew started working tonight, Bell has been the only one with whom John seems himself.

John decides to re-shoot the very last shot of the picture: Robert Harmon staring out the window and waving goodbye to his departing sister. He wants Neil in the shot.

Neil in the shot? Nobody questions why, but we all – Al and Eddie especially – share a general feeling of shock. Nobody voices it, everyone obeys quickly, quietly, as though there's an unspoken agreement of "Let's get this craziness over with."

John places himself by the jukebox. He has Bell stand near the chair. From outside, through the rain-blown windows, the camera will pick up Harmon, stay with him a few beats, then move to reveal Neil Bell, who's naked from the torso up, naked as far as the camera is concerned.

They cue the song that plays through the last scene: "And I didn't know what to do/ But I'll leave it up to you..." The rain pours, the fans blow, lightning flashes, thunder, the storm-sound overwhelms everything but that strange song. The camera picks up Robert Harmon swaying to the music in his raincoat, wearing his soaked straw hat. Then the camera picks up The Man, The Spirit, The Dog, whatever Neil Bell signifies.

I'm standing by the wall just inside the living room, directly in John's line of sight as he turns and looks at Neil – and I'm stunned by the raw energy bright in John's eyes. 'Incandescent' is not too strong a word. From only a few steps away it's even a little scary.

Then… Robert Harmon steps toward The Man, puts his arm around him, dances with him! Harmon is smiling an enormous bright spot-light of a smile.

There is a bellow of "Cut!" from outside. The rain stops, the wind-machines slowly die down.

Cassavetes is baffled.

"Why'd we cut?"

An assistant yells out the front door, "Why the cut?"

Eddie Donno comes in, more baffled. "I thought when you started dancing…"

"I don't wanna cut. I mean, *Eddie*…"

Eddie doesn't know what to say, he just stands there, kind of wide-eyed. Clearly Eddie can't believe that John wants to film what John wants to film. John tells him to get the camera in position, we're doing the shot again. Eddie, usually demonstrative, doesn't even shake his head as he leaves but quickly does what he's told.

"I like it," John tells Neil. "I like it as well as I like anything in the film. Maybe it's a little strange, but I don't know, I'm an actor, like you, I'm trying to get behind it. I just don't want the audience thinking, 'She's going back to her husband, oh, what's he gonna do,' I'm gonna have my *own* life, I'm gonna have MY OWN LIFE, maybe it'll be miserable, but, you know?"

"If you do that again," Bell says, "I should stay in character as the dog, right?"

"Yeah, but sophisticated."

"I can't laugh then," Neil says. He'd laughed on the take.

"*No,* you *can* laugh, but – whatever you feel to do will be okay. It's – I can't explain."

"I know – I know what it is," Neil says. Neil was the dog in the stage-play, he's worked intensely with John; if he hadn't learned to understand John's signals, coherent or not, Neil wouldn't be here.

John smiles. "Good. Now, if we can not anticipate, and think of something else."

They do the take again. It's freer this time, they dance around in a circle, then look out the window with linked arms. Again there is that look of John's – incandescent, indecipherable.

John turns to me after he cuts. "I don't know what happens, all I know is – I had a good time. I had a great time in that scene." He pauses, then: "I don't know. When people go to movies and look for an answer – I've never seen an answer."

He looks out the window at the crew as they're getting ready to do the shot again.

"They're mad at us!" He laughs and laughs. "They're mad! They've been working all this time, they're thinking, 'All this time on this picture for *this?!*'"

He cracks up with laughter, wheezing, bending over, he's trying to speak but he can't for laughing.

When his laughter exhausts itself he says to me, eyes full of glee, "Imagine doing this shot on the first day?!"

Last night John shot the Man-Dog in the chair, looking at Robert Harmon. In that shot we don't see the front window, we see only a smaller window over Neil Bell's shoulder, on the back wall. Through it we see rain pouring through bright light, an effect that was easily done with a spotlight and a garden hose. (They'll mix in storm-sounds later.) John didn't shoot Robert Harmon's reaction to the vision of the Man-Dog until tonight because he wants a shot that includes the front window and the full storm. Also, until he saw last night's footage he didn't know whether he'd use it and couldn't anticipate its strange quality; and only when he saw that could he begin to discover Robert Harmon's reaction.

If Cassavetes decides to use the Man-Dog vision and whatever Harmon's reaction will be, this will be the first time he depicts a man journeying as far off the beaten trail as Gena's characters in *A Woman Under the Influence*, *Opening Night*, and this picture.

Especially since he discarded *Love Streams'* original ending, John has been using performance as a mode of thought, driving everybody mercilessly and sometimes needlessly for the pleasure he gets in exhaustion – the "edge" that unrelenting fatigue brings out in people. He likes being surrounded by a crew driven beyond their usual limits, where they have no manners, no false faces. With *this* edgy audience surrounding him, he can reach the level of performance he needs for his discovery. He doesn't care how pissed, crazy, intimidated, anxious, giddy we may get – he wants us that way, he wants the atmosphere of all those emotions churning together. "The director creates an atmosphere, and it's the atmosphere that directs the picture." He's gambling that this atmosphere *will direct him.*

He's to shoot Robert Harmon's reaction to the Man-Dog. The camera is set up in the living room to see Harmon seated in a chair and past him out the front window into the storm. The chair in which the Man-Dog sits is out of the frame. The shot belongs to John Cassavetes, Robert Harmon, and the storm.

The sequence in the final cut will be:

Sarah has told Robert she's leaving. He's tried to convince her not to, futilely. He sits drinking from a goblet, smoking a cigarette. He is lingering in those anxious and oddly sweet moments when one tastes a loneliness coming before one is actually alone. Headlights shine through the rain. He looks toward them. "Who the hell is that?"

Then he catches something out of the corner of his eye, turns his head, his eyes widen, he can't believe it and he does believe it at the same time, he's amazed, he's delighted, his laughter builds from wheezing gasps to body-racking guffaws. In the picture we don't yet know what he's laughing at as he says, "Who the fuck are you?!"

And he laughs more.

Then (on screen) we see The Man (we don't yet know this is a Man-Dog): that slow zoom into his expression, the kindly serious eyes, the slight, knowledgeable smile.

Then there's a mid-shot of Harmon from The Man's point of view, laughing, delighted, "WHO the fuck ARE you?!" [This will be shot in a half hour or so.] Then, for a few seconds, from Harmon's point of view we see the dog. [Shot last night.]

But tonight nobody knows this yet. They've set up the camera to film John in the chair, smoking and drinking, then the reveal of the headlights outside in the storm, then – whatever John comes up with. He hasn't said, and he may not know.

I'm standing in the living room maybe three yards away from him and a few steps away from the camera. John registers the headlights and says, "Who the hell is that?" Then John looks at the chair – at me, actually, in his line of sight. His eyes bug out, he's amazed and delighted and crazy, and he laughs a laugh such as I have never heard. From the expressions of the crew, they've also never heard such laughter. They look at one another uneasily and with alarm. John calls a cut.

"What the fuck am I doing? Am I crazy?" He says this more or less calmly, to himself, though he's looking at me. Then: "Print it."

He springs out of the chair swiftly toward me, grabs my shoulders, very excited, his face close to mine, "This picture, THIS picture –I don't give a FUCK what anybody says. If you don't have time to see it, don't. If you don't like it, don't. If it doesn't give you an answer, FUCK you. I didn't make it for you anyway."

Toward whomever this "you" may be, Cassavetes is implacable.

He goes right back to the chair, does the shot again, laughing (I wouldn't have thought this possible) more madly. Again he's shocked at himself, paces up and down with hard thudding steps rubbing his face. Again he does the shot, not letting up one bit till he calls the cut, springs up again, again grabs me by the shoulders, smiling wildly, "I'm crazy but I love this fuckin' movie! They hate it, but I love their faces! This is when we should begin the movie. This is the *beginning*! Now she goes home, and the movie begins. FUCK 'em if they want answers! *Fuck* 'em."

Diahnne Abbott's scene: all-but-forgotten until editing is almost done, when John inserts it into the final cut, after Sarah's arrival, to finish off Susan's character. The scene passes too quickly for most people to register that Robert Harmon's face is noticeably thinner than it was in mid-June, when the scenes just before and after Diahnne's were shot.

Robert Harmon's dance with The Man: Cassavetes never considers using it. These takes served to fully acquaint John with his/Harmon's feelings about the Man-Dog, literally looking into the vision's eyes, dancing with it. John wouldn't do that in the friendly confines of a rehearsal; to get what's deep down he ups the stakes, no matter what it costs or what anybody thinks, cameras rolling, lightning flashing.

"Who the fuck are you?": this scene is central to the ending. The final effect of the film is unthinkable without it.

No one knows for sure tonight, but John certainly suspects: this wild scene will be John Cassavetes' last performance.

WEDNESDAY-THURSDAY, AUGUST 10–11 – *That is a wrap*

"Took Gena out to dinner last night for the first time since the picture started. Hamburger Hamlet."

We're at the Pasadena Civic Auditorium to shoot Sarah's opera-dream. John is gaunt. Colorless. Exhausted. During those days when he'd cast away *Love Streams'* ending and composed the last 20 minutes of his film moment by moment, he stayed awake longer and worked harder than the youngest and strongest of us. That energy has left him. During the week since his "Who the fuck are you?" scene, he's constantly edited, handled business at Cannon Films, and attended preparations for this opera; it all seems to have drained his reserves. Nothing but will keeps him standing.

But his picture isn't done. *Love Streams* is a dream, and the opera is the dreamiest moment of that dream. If the opera doesn't work, his daring ending doesn't work.

John's never shot a musical. Neither has Al Ruban. So John won't know when or if he's made a mistake until he sees the footage. By then it'll be too late for re-takes. Therefore he's got to shoot enough film to give himself and George Villasenor a plausible way to put this scene together, no matter how many mistakes are made. In these two days he'll shoot 30 set-ups that make it to the editing room and at least 10 more that don't. Those

30 set-ups will total 73 takes. The 10 or so discarded set-ups are at least another 25 takes. Well over an hour of printed film to create a four and a half minute scene.

Nor is his conception of the scene easy. He wants its lyrics, actions, and emotions, to be very specific, but visually he wants something correspondingly abstract – unlike anything he's ever shot. It's an opera, on a stage, there's a lit orchestra pit, an orchestra, but that's all he wants the viewer to see. "The theater has got to be invisible." Pitch black, no detail, no seats, ceilings, walls, or curtains. Stark contrasts of light and dark. Also, he wants camera angles and movements that give the viewer no firm point of view from which to judge the scene. He's conceived a space that can only exist in dreams, but he's shooting it in a space as real as any. The dream must be made in the camera.

He knows what it's going to take before he starts. He looks as though the very thought of it exhausts him.

I've witnessed that, no matter how tired, John's energy replenishes when he works. Not this time. Oh, he cuts up for our documentary crew – sitting in a spotlight and clowning with a violin – and there are some laughs, there are always some laughs. But he's more short-tempered than I've seen him and the set of his face is grim.

He shoots and re-shoots the white-tutu'd girl ballerinas. "I know you're tired," he tells them, "but you can't be more tired than me."

He tries over and over for a low-angled dolly-shot of the dancers. "Cut. Once more right away, first places, let's get it back to playback right now, no movement, no make-up, stay out, leave us alone, let's go, right now!"

That take disgusts him too. "Cut, cut, bullshit. Horseshit."

The girls have tried so hard. They look stricken. He attempts to make up for his outburst. "Ok, good, good horseshit, alright."

He shoots fog sequences with dry ice. A beautiful white cloud hovers just above the stage at about knee-height. Little-girl tumblers in white tutus somersault through it. Seymour strides through it to his daughter. John walks through it just for fun. It makes for pretty footage in our documentary, but John will use none of it in *Love Streams*.

On the very last shot he speaks harshly even to Gena – and does so in front of 50 people. In my experience, that's a first.

In that shot, which ends the dream, the camera moves swiftly from far off as it approaches the actors and dancers, then stops and holds a tight shot of Gena, Risa Blewitt, and Seymour standing together while dancers toe-step around them. The girl is to kiss her parents and they're to kiss her. As they rehearse the kisses, Gena's head keeps going where John doesn't want it to go.

"Gena, you're a genius – Gena, I don't know where you're hiding –"

"I'm trying to get out of the way of this ornament, John. Look it, honey, look it – try to look at this just a second."

"You want me to shoot it?"

"Sweetheart –"

"*No*, I *don't wanna hear it*! You kiss her over here on her cheek on this side."

She gives him a look, furious.

They shoot that shot with a long fast dolly-movement, John manning the camera, he falls off the dolly, motions for them to keep going as Sam Gart – a camera assistant – jumps on the dolly and keeps shooting while John somehow catches up, climbs on and trades place with Sam as the dolly is in motion.

The shot's done, John climbs off the camera and calls out, "Where's Sammy?" Sam appears and John gives him a flurry of fast high-fives, except they're low-fives, the way they did them on New York streets when he was young.

Quietly John says to Eddie Donno: "Ok, that's it."

Eddie booms out, "Gentlemen, that is a wrap!"

The *Love Streams* shoot is over.

Everybody's milling about shaking hands and congratulating each other, John moves toward Gena, Seymour intercepts him to give and get a hug but John slips past him. Gena's to get the first hug. She looks away as he nears her and she smacks her lips, looks at him, not pleased, purses her lips, he kisses her on each cheek, her expression is tight, her pursed lips kiss air. He yelled at her in front of us not five minutes ago and it'll take longer than five minutes to forgive him. Ten minutes maybe. But not five.

John turns and plants a smooch on Seymour's nose.

In just three days, on Sunday, John flies to New York to direct a play by his friend Meade Roberts, with Ben Gazzarra, Patti LuPone, and Carol Kane – a plan he made before his illness progressed and was diagnosed. Of course, John won't change the plan. He edits Love Streams *in a New York hotel room with George Villasenor through the fall while working on the play, then finishes editing in Los Angeles in November and the first week of December. There are many versions of the picture. The early assemblies are in the style of John's earlier films; long, long takes and every scene a climax. Then he works like a sculptor, cutting, paring, with great precision, and by the time he's finished he has a different edit from any film he's ever shot – the dream he so often spoke of.*

Most films conclude with the words 'The End.' This film concludes with a title that can also be read as a sentence: 'Love Streams.'

I'M GONNA HAVE MY OWN LIFE

Ceberus

Some years after John's death, Gena recalled a conversation we had about *Love Streams*' last scene: 'That shot where John waves goodbye with that strange hat on, that's a killer. You were the first one who pointed it out to me, Michael – because I couldn't even look at it again. You said, 'You know, Gena, when John waves out the window? I think he was saying goodbye to us.' And I thought, 'Oh my God.'

John Casssavetes spoke in his fragmented way, and at the slightest instigation, of Socrates and Aristophanes and the roots of Greek philosophy. He knew very well what creature guards Hades' gate: Ceberus, the many-headed dog with a mane and with a tail of snakes. John's dog – *Who the fuck are you?* – had two bodies, two heads, and the hair of its man-head was mane-like. This Ceberus smiled at Cassavetes, not unkindly, with the absolute certainty that is Death's.

On screen, where for him it counted most, Cassavetes' response was wild delight at the absurdity of it all.

John did not exactly welcome this new visitor to his home but he recognized him, responding in his art from the depths of his soul, expressed in the renewal of Gena's character as well as the epiphany of John's. That response took two months for John to decipher and express, but once he understood it he gave it everything he had – a worthy way to treat so distinguished and inevitable a visitor.

As John intuited from the first, "It's the dog's picture."

You're gonna close your eyes

Sometime in the last months of 1983 John's doctors gave him a year to live. In 1984 he wrote and directed another play in Los Angeles, *Lady of Mystery,* with Gena and Carol Kane. Peter Falk's picture *Big Trouble* got into big trouble, the director was fired and Peter asked John to finish the shoot. John managed it sitting in a chair, his midsection much huger by then. He told me, "I directed a picture sitting down. I *never* thought I'd direct a picture sitting down!"

Those were the last manifestations of any energy that could take John Cassavetes much beyond his home on Woodrow Wilson Drive in the Hollywood Hills, where he'd shot so many films. But he never stopped writing, right to the end, dictating to his son Nick, Helen Caldwell, and finally to Carole Smith. One night in the-day-that-took-four-days he'd said he wouldn't have the energy to direct another picture, but he didn't abide that notion long. In his last years he tried to get at least two directorial projects going that I knew about.

We had a conversation while he was directing *Lady of Mystery.*

"Michael, you're gonna be in my next picture. You're gonna play a wop." *Wop* is a derogatory word for Italians, not much in use anymore; my ancestry is Sicilian, as John knew. "This wop is a gangster, but he's too sensitive to be a gangster. When you shoot people, you're gonna close your eyes."

Gena will be the wife of a gangster. To keep her happy her husband produces a stand-up-comedy act that she performs all across the country. In her act she intentionally reveals secrets of the Mob, making fun of them. The other 'families' are incensed. They call a big sit-down. They tell her husband that "we gotta whack her." Very calmly, as though he's reading a list of chores, her husband ("Benny's the husband") tells them that if they whack his wife he'll kill their wives, their children, their dogs, their plants, and then he'll kill them.

At which John and I said on the same beat, and with the same inflection:

"That's fair."

Come for coffee

Soon after that my life went into free-fall – what I call now "a walking nervous breakdown," beginning about a year after *Love Streams* and continuing for the better part of a decade. John was bedridden by the late '80s. In my free-fall I rarely had it together enough to visit, and then only when I felt I had something to offer. When I wrote a picture called *Echo Park* I brought a tape to show him. Ted Allan was there. We watched in John's bedroom, a room I'd first seen when Robert Harmon slept in his clothing with two young women. Now John, in a robe, sat up bed, under the covers, I sat at the edge of the bed, Ted sat in a low chair by the window. Fifteen minutes into the picture I wanted to crawl under the bed. The mood in the room was: patience. They watched, patiently. So patiently. And then they were so polite about my little movie. It was "nice." That's how much they hated it. Bedridden or not, politeness was the kiss of death in Cassavetes' world.

In October of 1988, more than five years after *Love Streams* wrapped, John summoned me.

We visited in his bedroom. But for his now-enormous midsection, he was skeletal. A strange luminescence emanated from his skin. His face, stretched flesh on bone, was startlingly beautiful. Radiant. And all the life that was left in him was concentrated in his eyes.

Not at first. At first his eyes were lifeless – a shocking sight to anyone who's known him. Then soon, as we spoke, they filled with, well, with *John*. From that moment, though his voice was weak and sometimes faltered, it was like talking to John at anytime.

He spoke of losing the ability to distinguish between the living and the dead – his dead mother, father and brother seemed as present, even more present sometimes, as Gena and his children. He spoke of seeing all his works side by side on the horizon, far off, each neither better nor worse than the others. His pictures were "soldiers without weapons, my tin soldiers, marching over the horizon." He said his films represent "the sum of myself, good and bad."

He spoke of the ancient Greeks. "How can you *live* without the *Iliad*, the *Odyssey*, Plato? How can you live without art?"

When you're alive, he said, "it's all about your body." But as you sicken "nobody wants your *body*, it's not good for anything." There was, in his voice, no self-pity. He'd simply stated a fact.

He asked about my life and I told him my six-year marriage was on the rocks, I didn't know what my wife and I were going to do. He gave me the kindest of looks and regretted that many marriages, even when they last, "degenerate into affection and respect." As I'd witnessed, this wasn't true of his marriage. So there was John, in bed, in pain, nearing death, trying to make *me* feel better.

He didn't like to see many visitors anymore. "I don't *do* chit-chat, I hate chit-chat."

He thought he had strength in him for one more screenplay, an adaptation of *Lady of Mystery.* Gena thought that was beyond his powers and that he should write *Gloria II.* But: "Mike, it's not my dream."

Then he spoke of *Love Streams.* "They put it out in VHS, didn't they? No one will tell me, but I think I overheard that they cut it." I told him yeah, they'd cut 20 minutes on the VHS.

"I taped *your* picture when it played on Z Channel, fuck their VHS."

"How can they be so silly? People who hate me won't buy it anyway, and people who like me want to see it *all*, if they hear it's cut *they* won't buy it either. So *nobody* buys it. Stupidity."

He said everybody knows he's dying. Everybody wants "last words." And there's some academic guy who wrote a book about him and who's been bugging him. He couldn't remember his name. He just rolled his eyes, "That *other* guy, that professor, *that* guy."

The presidential election was in two weeks. He thought the Democratic candidate, Michael Dukakis, was "throwing" it. "Somebody's got something on him. A photograph. Something."

He gave me some pages of a script to read aloud. I did the best I could. "That's Sean's part." Sean Penn. "That cocksucker. Fuck him, fuck his lawyer, fuck *chickenshit indecision.*" When John still might have had strength to direct a movie they'd stalled and stalled and now it was too late.

"Maybe I can direct pictures Up There, Down There, wherever." He pointed in both directions.

For movies, I told him, Down There would be better. A devil can act rings around an angel. He chuckled a quiet echo of that old devil-laugh. I said, "So will I still get to kill guys with my eyes closed in those pictures?"

"Always."

He smiled so beautifully, I can't describe it.

Then he told me why he'd summoned me. What was then called the United States Film Festival (and is now called the Sundance Festival) was planning a retrospective of his films in January. He wanted me to curate it. Select the pictures, write the booklet, "anything you want." I had it all in my head the moment he asked me: early films he'd acted in, everything he'd directed, and later acting like *The Dirty Dozen, Mikey and Nicky, Tempest.* He mentioned a comic short he'd performed in, *The Haircut,* and I said I'd find it. "Tell them to find it. Order them around. They said they'd do anything, make them do anything."

"Everything you've done," I said, "but – not *Big Trouble,* right?"

John rolled his eyes again, shook his head no to *Big Trouble.* He wouldn't even say the title.

Gena brought him a tray of vegetables and rice. She seemed exhausted and didn't stay to speak. He doused his food with Tabasco sauce and pepper. "Can't taste," he explained.

"The doctors gave me one month to live five years ago. I don't do anything they say to do and I'm *here.*" Then, looking up through his eyebrows at the ceiling: "I don't know what He's waiting for. I'm not gonna do it for Him."

He spoke about being ill, then shrugged. "Is life about horror – or is it about those few seconds you have?"

That question still runs around in my head. John, as usual, did not attempt or want an answer.

January, 1989: the hour I returned from Sundance I called John.

He asked how I was. I told him that aside from a bad toothache I was well enough.

I asked how he was – and bit my tongue, saying immediately, "Christ, John, I'm sorry. Forget the question."

But John was laughing, that spooky laugh, more phlegm-soaked and wheezier than it had been in October, but still: the laugh. "No," he said, "it's a *good* question – 'cause the answer's so *easy.*"

Then: "Finally, a question with an *answer*!"

At that, we both laughed.

I told him of the festival, that every screening of his films was packed, people who couldn't find seats sat in the aisles, and I overheard many discussions and arguments about his pictures in theater lobbies and bars. He'd love the new prints. They were sparkling. And with these new technologies, *Shadow's* sound was better than he'd ever heard it. They should make a VHS for him, he wouldn't believe it.

I told him that when I'd seen *Husbands* many years before, I hadn't been married. Now that I'm a husband, with my marriage in the shape that it was in, I *got* that picture, or it got me.

Gently John said, "I love men. We're so stupid."

Then: "Come for coffee tomorrow."

Tomorrow was Tuesday. I needed a dentist tomorrow. I'd come Wednesday.

But Wednesday John was in the hospital. Friday he died.